SKI JUMPING IN
Washington State
A NORDIC TRADITION

Terry:
    Thanks for the great
pictures from Leavenworth 1960.
They illustrate how ski jumping
was a spectator sport

JOHN W. LUNDIN

Foreword by Eric Nelson

John W. Lundin

THE
History
PRESS

Published by The History Press
Charleston, SC
www.historypress.com

First published 2021

Manufactured in the United States

ISBN 9781467147828

Library of Congress Control Number: 2020945775

Notice: The information in this book is true and complete to the best of our knowledge. It is offered without guarantee on the part of the author or The History Press. The author and The History Press disclaim all liability in connection with the use of this book.

Contents

Contents

Foreword

When Norwegian, Swedish and Finnish immigrants arrived in the Pacific Northwest, the topographical features and climate conditions of the region were not wholly unfamiliar to them. As you will read, the varied, rugged terrain and heavy, moist snow ensured the continuity of a Nordic tradition spanning millennia. In the middle of the nineteenth century, postal carriers and preachers strapped on pairs of serviceable slender runners and introduced cross-country skiing to the United States. In the 1860s, pioneers realized the recreational potential of skis in California's Sierra Nevada range, the first U.S. site of a downhill race. From the 1910s through the 1940s, the Northwest became a center of winter sports activity. There, intrepid Norwegian Americans leaped into ski jumping.

Ski jumping originated in the latter half of the nineteenth century in Morgedal, in Norway's Telemark region. Members of the Norwegian middle class had started to look beyond skiing's practical function to its potential as a leisure activity. In time, the sport's connection to Norwegian culture strengthened, and it attracted male and female enthusiasts of all social ranks. Interestingly, the modernization of the sport occurred during a moment of mass immigration. Between 1836 and 1915, at least 750,000 Norwegians made their way to North America. The immigrant community's cultural emphasis on the outdoors and its healthful effects persisted even in new environments. Norwegian *friluftsliv*—a term that gained currency in the nineteenth century—led to the exploration of the Northwest's mountain ranges. Thus, the history of ski jumping in the

United States—and in Idaho, Oregon and Washington more precisely—is the history of Nordic America.

This publication accompanies an exhibit devoted to the golden age of ski jumping in the Pacific Northwest. Titled "Sublime Sights: Ski Jumping and Nordic America," this exhibit has been co-organized by the National Nordic Museum and the Washington State Ski & Snowboard Museum for display in 2021. Seattle attorney and historian John W. Lundin and the team at the Washington State Ski & Snowboard Museum shed light on objects in the collection of the National Nordic Museum, which stewards a treasure-trove of ski equipment, photography and oral histories, such as that of expert ski jumper Gus Raaum (1926–2014). The exhibit examines an important chapter in the history of ski jumping and comes at a transformative time for the two institutions. The Washington State Ski & Snowboard Museum opened with a state-of-the-art exhibit on Snoqualmie Pass in 2015, and the National Nordic Museum relocated to a new permanent, purpose-built facility in 2018. The National Nordic Museum has widened its storytelling scope beyond Nordic Americans in the Pacific Northwest to include twelve thousand years of history in what is present-day Denmark, Finland, Iceland, Norway and Sweden. The topic of skiing—a winter sport with deep roots in the Nordic countries—fits naturally into the National Nordic Museum's broad purview, and we are thrilled to host this remarkable show.

—ERIC NELSON
Chief Executive Officer, National Nordic Museum

Acknowledgements

This book was written in conjunction with a joint exhibit on ski jumping between the National Nordic Museum and Washington State Ski & Snowboard Museum that the author helped organize.

John W. Lundin is a founder and board member of the Washington State Ski & Snowboard Museum, a high-tech "story-telling" facility with interactive exhibits using the latest technology. The museum features artifacts showing the history of snow sports in Washington, including an operating rope tow. There are displays about the state's nine Alpine ski areas; six Community ski areas; twenty-four Nordic Ski Centers; one helicopter and snowboarding center; eighteen "Lost Ski Areas"; Washington Manufacturers; Ski Mountaineering; and Alpine and Nordic Traditions. The featured exhibit shows the thirty-nine Washington Olympians (fifteen of them medalists) who participated in sixteen Winter Olympic Games since 1936.

Although ski jumping has largely faded from public consciousness, several books capture the sport's history: *Jumping Through Time: A History of Ski Jumping in the United States and Southwest Canada*, by Harold "Cork" Anson; *Fifty Years of Flight: Ski Jumping in California, 1900–1950*, by Ingrid P. Wicken; and *The Ski Race*, by Sam Wormington. The history of the Spokane Ski Club is discussed in *Spokane's History of Skiing, 1913 to 2018*, by Chris M. Currie, and *Wandermere*, by Ty A. Brown. Lowell Skoog's website, alpenglow. org, contains a treasure-trove of information about mountaineering and backcountry skiing.

Special thanks go to several people. Ingrid P. Wicken provided guidance and pictures and from her California Ski Library (www.skilibrary.com). The library has an extensive collection of ski books, magazines, photographs and paper memorabilia related to all facets and disciplines of skiing. Brian Praye located and identified Leavenworth pictures and provided information about the area's history. Ty A. Brown provided materials about the Spokane Ski Club. The Cecelia Maybo family provided Cle Elum Ski Club materials.

Materials for this book were obtained from the following sources, whose cooperation is greatly appreciated: the Cecelia Maybo family and the Archives and Special Collections of the James E. Brooks Library, Central Washington University; Alan Engen and the Special Collections, Marriott Library, University of Utah; the Matt V. Broze family; Chris Raaum; Lowell Skoog; the Museum of History and Industry (MOHAI); the Milwaukee Road Historical Association; the *Seattle Times* historical archives; Kirby Gilbert; the Center for Regional History, The Community Library, Ketchum, Idaho; the Hollyburn Heritage Society; the Revelstoke Museum; the Tacoma Public Library; the University of Washington, Special Collections; the National Nordic Museum; the Washington State Historical Society and Washington State Archives; the Greater Leavenworth Ski Museum; Leavenworth Ski Heritage Foundation; the Bakke-Gehring family; Walt and Bill Doan; the Wes Sauer family; Stan Harrison; and Terry Love.

This book is a sequel to John's first publication, *Early Skiing on Snoqualmie Pass* (The History Press, 2017), which traces the history of skiing in Washington State. In 2018, the book received a Skade Award as outstanding regional history book from the International Ski History Association.

Introduction

Ski jumping originated in Norway, according to Harold Anson's *Jumping Through Time*, where it was just a part of normal skiing, and children learned it at a young age—"[g]etting from one farm to another in Norway in winter often involves a climb on skis up one side of a hill, and ski jumping developed as a means of clearing obstacles when skiing down the other side." Alf Engen and his brothers Sverre and Corey lived in a house in Norway that was on a steep hill. In Sverre's *Skiing a Way of Life*, he noted they skied "down to school in the mornings. And it didn't take long for us to get there. We built small snow takeoffs above the fences so we could just jump over them and not have to stop and crawl under. Then we got cross-country training, walking and climbing home after school." Their father, an excellent ski jumper, put them on skis as soon as they could walk. He took them into the woods and then hid behind trees to see how fast they could ski home. He always wanted them to ski hard. He showed them how to build takeoffs and how to prepare the underhill, and they took part in small tournaments both in jumping and cross-country while they were quite young.[1]

In 1792, the Norwegian government introduced prizes for ski jumping and cross-country skiing for its rural population. The first measured jump (9.5 meters) was reportedly made in 1809 by Norwegian lieutenant Olaf Rye. In 1860, Sondre Auverson Nordheim jumped 30 meters, "without sticks and upright," providing the impetus for the sport's development. The Christiania (later Oslo) Ski Club was founded in 1877, and in 1879, it held its first ski jumping event, attracting several thousand spectators. The jump was a snow-covered hill called the "Huseby-Bakken," which had the basic shape of ski jumps built later.[2]

Olav Ulland, a famous ski jumper from Kongsberg, Norway, coached skiers in Washington after his arrrival in December 1937. Olav described the development of skiing in Norway and the competition for the longest jump in his article published by the *Seattle Times* on April 6, 1941, "Jumper's Version: Olav Ulland Gives His Views, Slalom Old Stuff." Ulland noted that "modern" ski jumping started at Telemarken in southern Norway, where it was combined with slalom, and slalom contests were held as early as AD 1000. Slalom racing "was regular Sunday entertainment in the narrow Norwegian valleys around the year 1850." The first tournament was held in Kongsberg, "which later became famous as the paradise for ski-jumpers," a combination of slalom and jumping. Skiers followed a course down mountains, using trees as natural obstacles, with a jump set in the middle.

Ulland was amazed at the development of ski jumping since his early days. "A 75- to 100-foot jump was considered something really big. As late as in my childhood we hardly believed it when we heard about a 130-foot jump. But when 14 years old I had jumped 175 feet myself." Norwegians thought the distance limit was reached when Sigmund Ruud jumped 230 feet in 1927, but he jumped 280 feet two years later. When Birger Ruud jumped 312 feet in Planica, Jugoslavia, in 1934, jumpers realized that a 100-meter jump (330 feet) was possible. Reidar Andersen jumped 98 meters (324 feet), but on the same day, Olav jumped 103.5 meters (339 feet) in Ponte di Legno, Italy, the first to break the "100 meter barrier."

The Planica jump was enlarged, against the advice of the International Ski Association, and its hill was soon twice as large as any other hill. In 1936, Ulland and Birger Ruud were sent by the Norwegian Ski Association to compete in Planica. When the ski association learned of the hill's size, it refused to give them permission to jump more than 275 feet. Olav jumped once with reduced speed, went 250 feet and landed "way up on the knoll and had a downhill race down the landing-hill." Ruud jumped 270 feet and "took a terrific spill. Then we quit." Joseph Beadl of Austria jumped 101 meters (333 feet) on the hill and, two years later, jumped 107 meters (361 feet), the unofficial world distance record in 1941. The competition to set new distance records played out in Washington tournaments.

The Holmenkollbakken ski hill, at Holmenkollen on the outskirts of Olso, is the world's most iconic ski jump. Competitions have been held there since 1892; it has been rebuilt nineteen times and has a capacity for seventy thousand people. Norway's national championship tournament

The Holmenkollbakken ski hill in Holmenkollen, Norway, is the world's most iconic ski jump. Norway's national championship tournament, held at Holmenkollen, is regarded as the "gold crown of ski jumping" and the country's "World Series," with the winner being awarded the King's Cup. *Author's postcard.*

held at Holmenkollen is regarded as the "gold crown of ski jumping" and the country's "world series," with the winner being awarded the King's Cup. The current record is 144 meters, set by Norway's Robert Johansson in 2019.[3]

Norwegians dominated ski jumping for decades, winning the first six Olympic gold medals from 1924 to 1952. The time between 1928 and 1948 was known as the "Kongsberg Era," as jumpers from the little mining town fifty miles from Oslo dominated the sport. In the 1920s, Sigmund Ruud developed the "Kongsberg Technique," where the jumper's upper body is bent at the hips and he has a wide forward lean, with arms extended at the front and skis parallel to each other.[4]

Birger and Sigmund Ruud from Kongsberg dominated ski jumping during the 1930s, winning medals at Olympic Games and FIS World Ski Championships and setting distance records. Birger described the secret of Kongsberg where "most great ski jumpers are born." They learned to jump at a young age. Each afternoon, the village gathered around the ski jump. "The boys, who are training there each day, have many harsh and professional instructors and spectators." In Kongsberg, ski jumping was a way to avoid hard manual labor. Birger's father asked him, "What do you want to become? Mine worker or ski jumper?" Kongsberg was the center of Norway's silver mining industry and home to the Royal Norwegian Mint. Birger said, "Those who cannot learn to be a good jumper, must go to work. That is the law of Kongsberg."[5]

Showing the town's influence, seven of the sixteen jumpers in the Class A section of the Seattle Ski Club's 1938 tournament were from Kongsberg: Birger and Sigmund Ruud; Olav and Sigurd Ulland; Rolf Syverrtsen; Tom Mobraaten; and Hjalmar Hvam. When Petter Hugsted won the Olympic gold medal in 1948, he said that winning in the Olympics was easier than winning the Holmenkollen tournament. "In the Olympics you jump against four Norwegians, in the Holmenkollen you face fifty."[6]

Harold Anson described the development of ski jumping in this country in *Jumping Through Time: A History of Ski Jumping in the United States and Southwest Canada*. Ski jumping began in the Midwest in Minnesota, Michigan and Wisconsin, becoming the "thrill sport of winter." Jumps were built on small hills with enough vertical drop to provide good landings. "Through the influence of Scandinavians, ski clubs sprouted up all over the northern United States." By the end of the 1890s, Michigan had more than thirty ski clubs.

The Scandinavian Ski Club of St. Paul, Minnesota, was organized in 1885, followed by the Aurora Ski Club of Red Wing, Minnesota, in 1886; the Norden Ski Club of Ishpeming, Michigan, in 1887 (becoming the Ishpeming Ski Club in 1891); and the Dovre Ski Club of Eau Claire, Wisconsin, in 1888. Norwegian brothers Torjus and Mikkel Hemmestvedt (who dominated the King's Cup competition between 1883 and 1888), moved in the late 1880s to Minnesota, where they promoted ski jumping. The first recognized meet was held by the Aurora Ski Club in January 1887, staged by Mikkel Hemmestvedt. The Dovre Ski Club's first meet was in January 1888. The Norden Ski Club's first tournament on February 25, 1888, is claimed by some to be the first in the country.[7]

Anson noted that a trend developed during this period that was inconsistent with the Norwegian principle of *idræt*, the philosophy that an individual develops strength and manliness through exercise. A person jumps because of the love of the sport, not for reward. However, a trend started of giving cash prizes to winning jumpers or for the longest jumps. The size of jumping hills was increased to set new distance records, "compromising the grace and beauty of well controlled flight," and clubs offered top jumpers employment to get them to join.

In 1891, the Central Ski Association was formed to organize tournaments in Minnesota, Michigan and Wisconsin. In 1891, the Ispheming Ski Club proposed forming a national ski association, with the "goal of reducing the emphasis on distance and hill records, and return to the Norwegian goal of stylish flight." In 1905, the National Ski Association (NSA) was formed in Ishpeming to promote skiing, standardize rules governing competition, establish standards of amateurism and bring uniformity in ski jump designs. In 1906, the NSA decided there should be no cash prizes, believing that money made ski jumping less of a sport, although it took ten years for cash awards to disappear. Conflicts arose later between jumpers insisting on receiving on cash awards, who started a professional tour, and amateurs who competed for pride. The NSA published rules for judging ski jumps and flight characteristics designed to maintain Norwegian standards for the sport. Jumpers were judged on both distance and form. Up to twenty style points could be awarded, with each part of the jump assessed for point reductions, including the inrun, flight, balance, landing and finish. There were point reductions for falling or touching a hand to the snow.

The National Ski Association declared the Fourteenth Annual Ishpeming Tournament, held in 1904, to be the first National Ski Jumping Championship tournament. Twenty-eight jumpers from eight clubs in Michigan and Minnesota participated, jumping off a 40-foot tower erected at the top of the hill, watched by eight thousand spectators. In 1907, the American distance record was set at Duluth, Minnesota, of 117 feet (35 meters). In 1911, Anders Haugen from Telemark, Norway, set a new American record of 153 feet (45.5 meters). In 1926, the Ishpeming Ski Club created its famous 90-meter "Suicide Hill," with a 140-foot man-made scaffold for takeoffs, towering over the tops of trees. Ishpeming is the site of the U.S. National Ski Hall of Fame and Museum.[8]

Ski jumping is typically seen as adventurous, dangerous and exciting, more so than Alpine skiing. ABC's portrayal of ski jumping on its *Wide World of Sports* program shown from 1961 to 1998 colored the country's view of the sport. "Spanning the globe to bring you the constant variety of sport...the thrill of victory...and the agony of defeat...the human drama of athletic competition." "The agony of defeat" scene showed Slovenian ski jumper Vinko Bogataj falling and sliding horribly out of control off the end of the large ski jump.

For most, it is terrifying to consider climbing a high scaffold and then sliding down it at a high speed, soaring into the air and flying for several hundred feet. Ski jumping has been described as "the breath-taking pastime of risking life and limbs on skis....To the uninitiated, a ski-jump is close to a death-defying act." Filmmaker Warren Miller said that "[j]umping takes great courage, or a low IQ....The agony of climbing, the shakiness of the scaffolds built out of scrounged lumber, and the lack of safety bindings kept most people from ever becoming ski jumpers. They were smart."[9]

The casual attitude of ski jumpers was expressed by Torbjörn Yggeseth, a Norwegian exchange student at the University of Washington, who competed for Norway at the 1960 Squaw Valley Olympics. Torbjörn learned to jump at age six on a mound of snow his father made, jumped competitively at age eleven and "sailed" 432 feet at Flying Week at Oberstorg, Germany, in what he called "snow-flying." He scoffed at the idea of being afraid while flying the length of a football field over frozen terrain. "It's not really as dangerous as downhill skiing....You're only going about 60 miles an hour at top speed. As you follow the curve of the hill, you're never more than 20 feet high. And there are no trees to wrap yourself around. You land at 40 miles an hour. Some skiers land so gently they don't even leave a mark in the snow."[10]

Norwegian champion Reidar Andersen made similar comments. Andersen was a Nordic-combined skier, a three-time winner of the King's Cup at the Holmenkollen who won the bronze medal in the 1936 Olympics. He toured America in 1939, winning every jumping tournament he entered, and secured the amateur downhill title at the 1939 Sun Valley Harriman Cup. In a featured interview in the *Seattle Times* of April 6, 1939, Andersen said, "This downhill racing business is getting crazy....Look at Mount Hood. Look at Sun Valley. High speed courses, both of them. You might break your neck. I'll tell you the right competitions—jumping and slalom racing. Slalom gives you balance. Jumping gives you the true thrill of skiing."

Alpine skiing started to become popular in the 1930s, eventually surpassing ski jumping. In the 1930s and 1940s, many of the best skiers were Four-Way athletes (who competed in downhill, slalom, cross-country and jumping), and college ski teams typically competed in all four disciplines. The transition to Alpine skiing was led by men such as Portland's Hjalmar Hvam, Sun Valley's Alf Engen, the Ruud brothers and Reidar Andersen, who were outstanding Nordic and Alpine competitors. According to ski historian Ingrid P. Wicken, ski jumping was the king of winter sports in California in the 1930s and "was a key force in the awakening of winter sports possibilities throughout the state." In 1936, U.S. Olympic jumping team member Roy Mikkelsen said, "When slalom and downhill competitions came into being, the enthusiasts predicted that these would overshadow ski jumping and possibly obliterate it.

The last few seasons of ski competition have brought out that ski jumpers... make by far the best downhill runners."[11]

The Northwest has long attracted Scandinavian immigrants because of its climate, geography and employment possibilities. By 1910 in Washington, Scandinavians were the largest immigrant group, making up 20 percent of the foreign-born population, and one out of every twenty Seattle residents was born in Norway or the child of Norwegian-born parents. By 1930, 1 million people in the United States were born in Norway or had Norwegian parents, and 47 percent lived in New York, Chicago, Minneapolis or Seattle. Anson, in *Jumping Through Time*, described the influx of Norwegian skiers into the Northwest, many of whom had outstanding ski jumping records in the old country. "Washington state was the most active of the Pacific Northwest states in promoting ski jumping clubs," which were influenced by competitive clubs in British Columbia from Rossland and Revelstoke that started in the early 1900s:

> *The Norwegians brought to their new country a passion for skiing....They organized ski competitions to strengthen their ethnic ties, showcase their abilities, and generate a new sense of belonging to their new country....It has been said that wherever two or three Norwegians gathered together, they constructed a jump and held competitions. This was never so true than in the Pacific Northwest, as a wave of new clubs showed up along the coastal mountain ranges.[12]*

The history of ski jumping in the Northwest reflects the passion of Scandinavians and particularly Norwegians, a heritage brought from their home country, where a number of individuals played significant roles. These include Reidar Gjolme (competitor, event organizer and president of Seattle Ski Club), Peter Hostmark (designer of ski jumps, president of the Pacific Northwestern Ski Association and jumping judge), Hermod and Magnus Bakke (longtime supporters of Leavenworth Winter Sports Club), Olav Ulland (jumping star, instructor and retailer), Gustav Raaum (competitor and tournament official) and many others. Gustav Raaum's unpublished essay, "Scandinavians' Influence in the History of Ski Jumping in the Northwest," lists the many Scandinavians who competed in the Northwest, including fifty-six exchange students on the ski teams at Northwest schools after World War II, forty-one in Washington alone.

Our ski jumping story also includes the many international stars who competed in Washington. These include athletes such as Nels Nelsen (five-time

Canadian national champion and holder of the world distance record until 1930) and his brother Ivind Nilson (1922 Boys' World Champion; he never anglicized the spelling of his name), from Revelstoke, British Columbia; Tom Mobraaten, Nordal Kaldahl and Henry Solvedt, the "Three Musketeers" from Vancouver, British Columbia; John Elvrum and Hjalmar Hvam from Portland's Cascade Ski Club; Sigurd Ulland (1938 national champion from Lake Tahoe and Olav's brother); Sigmund and Birger Ruud (champion ski jumpers from Kongsberg, Norway); Reidar Andersen (Norway's national champion); Alf Engen (winner of national championships in ski jumping and Four-Way competitions); Torger Tokle (ski star for the Norway Ski Club of New York); and many others.

A jumping hill does not require a lot of vertical elevation, unlike those for Alpine skiing. Ski jumps were built along the northern tier of the United States, in New England, throughout the Rocky Mountains and in California. In Washington, ski jumping tournaments took place at Mount Rainier, Cle Elum, Beaver Lake at Snoqualmie Pass, Leavenworth, Mount Spokane, Mount Baker, Ellensburg, White Pass and Mission Ridge. In Oregon, tournaments were held at Government Camp, Multorpor on Mount Hood, Bend, Sprout Springs and elsewhere. Ski jumping sites in Washington were part of a network of areas throughout this country and Canada.[13]

Newspapers were major promoters of skiing in the sport's early days, providing extensive coverage of local, national and international tournaments. Writers such as Ken Binns of the *Seattle Times* provided insightful commentary and analysis during the 1930s. This book tells the story of ski jumping in Washington based on reports about important tournaments from the *Seattle Times* and other sources, preserving the colorful descriptions used that made the sport exciting. Newspaper reports about jumping tournaments were the main way most people followed the sport, and they capture the evolution of ski jumping from local events to regional ones and, finally, to national and international contests attracting the world's best competitors.

More information about Washington ski history can be found in essays by John W. Lundin published at historylink.org, the online encyclopedia of Washington history. Longer versions of his essays are available at Works by Local Authors on the Central Washington University Website (https://digitalcommons.cwu.edu/local_authors).

Chapter 1

1913–1924

Early Days of Ski Jumping

In British Columbia, our neighbor to the north, formal ski jumping events began at Rossland in 1898 and Revelstoke in 1915. In Washington, ski jumping events started in the 1910s on both sides of the Cascade Mountains. Canadian and U.S. jumpers regularly competed in the other country's tournaments.

Washington's earliest formal skiing event took place near Spokane in January 1913. It was organized by Norwegian-born Olaus Jeldness, who made his fortune in the gold fields around Rossland, British Columbia; helped create Rossland Winter Carnivals in 1898; and was known "as the father of competitive skiing in Canada." He moved in 1899 to Spokane, where he promoted skiing.

In 1913, Jeldness organized Spokane's first "skee" jumping and "running" exhibition on what is now Browne's Mountain, close enough to town that it could be reached by inter-urban. Ole Larsen (who set the American distance record of 131 feet in 1909) and Engwald Engen (former Canadian national champion) both jumped over 100 feet, watched by one hundred spectators. Larsen won the inaugural 1915 Inland Empire Ski Jumping Championships (with a long jump of 109 feet) and also the 1915 Rossland Carnival. Skiing remained popular at Brown Mountain through the 1920s.[14]

The first formal ski jumping event west of the Cascades occurred in February 1916 on Seattle's Queen Anne Hill after the heaviest snowfall in two decades. Snowfall began on January 31 and continued for twenty-seven hours, and in three days, thirty-eight inches of heavy wet snow

Olaus Jeldness organized Spokane's first "skee" and "running" tournament in 1913.

blanketed the city—"Whole Northwest Paralyzed by Heavy Snow," noted the *Seattle Times* of February 1, 1916.

Seattle's Norwegian businessmen believed that "skiing is one of the most thrilling sports in existence both from the skier's and the spectator's standpoint" and for years attempted to create interest in ski jumping, though without success. Seattle's snow emergency gave them an opportunity. John Sagdahl, L. Arvuld and John Olsen decided to hold a jumping exhibition on Queen Anne Hill to demonstrate the sport they brought from their home country. On February 6, 1916, the *Seattle Times* noted that "Men from North Jump with Skiis":

> *Ski jumping and speed skiing today will be introduced to the Seattle Public on the steepest slope of Queen Anne Hill from the summit to the level near the Fremont bridge on fourth avenue. A party of expert ski men this afternoon will provide Seattle with all the thrills that accompany an exhibition of the popular Scandinavian sport.*

Queen Anne Hill's Fourth Avenue North was made into "an ideal sliding incline" for the "exciting Scandinavian pastime." A three-block slide with a forty-five-

SKI JUMPERS GIVE EXHIBITION

GIL DOBIE WILL COME BACK FOR ONE MORE YEAR

Famous Football Coach, After Conference With President and Dean at Varsity, Consents to Work Again.

By ED R. HUGHES.

GILMOUR DOBIE will coach the University of Washington football team for the season of 1916, and thus fill out the unexpired term of his contract.

He made this decision today following a conference with President Suzzallo and Dean Priest of the University of Washington.

Ever since Dobie arrived in Seattle last week tremendous pressure has been brought to bear upon him to reconsider his resignation, and today he consented.

He will simply fill out his contract and will work for the same money he got last season.

Dobie resigned after the game last Thanksgiving Day because he felt that he was going stale and he wanted a rest and a change. He was given the greatest send-off any coach ever got in this section of the country; he was banqueted until he nearly had the gout; the students gave him a gold watch and the alumni used up all the adjectives in the language telling how much they thought of him.

Joy Storm Impending.

All this warmed the cockles of old Dobie's heart and when he came back here last week and some of the biggest men in the city began to put the pressure on him to coach just one more year at Washington, he found it mighty hard to resist. He decided today to take another fling at it and when the students hear about it they will let out a whoop of joy that can be heard down town.

Dobie quit because he found interest in football waning at Washington, due no doubt to the fact that Washington had won every game it played in the eight years he coached there. Since Dobie quit the Washington students have realized what a big man he is, and when he goes back there he will get an ovation.

Dobie had no intention of coaching at Washington again when he came to Seattle last week, but beginning last Saturday and continuing all day Sunday and this morning, influences were brought to bear upon him that caused him to withdraw his resignation.

It was because there was a chance to get Dobie back that no action was taken by the board of control last Saturday. Manager Younger was all ready to recommend a coach, but when

SEATTLE FOLK ENJOYING SCANDINAVIAN PASTIME.

Thawing weather conditions and a light fall of rain yesterday afternoon failed to keep ten masters of the skiing art from giving a scheduled exhibition of ski jumping on the north slope of Queen Anne Hill at Fourth Avenue North.

R. Gjolme, Pacific Coast general agent for the Norwegian American Line, with offices in Seattle, proved to be the best jumper of the day, his longest leap measuring 42 feet. L. Orvald was second with a jump of 25 feet, and J. Sather, O. Peterson and A. Flakstad tied for third place with jumps of 34 feet.

The high temperature made the snow soft and adhesive and would not permit the wooden runners to gain a maximum speed.

Yesterday's skiing exhibition was arranged by John Sagdahl, L. Orvald and John Olsen. A "take-off" was built at the bottom of a four-block slide. The exhibition lasted nearly an hour and a half.

The upper left picture shows Flakstad making a jump of 34 feet. The right hand picture is of Gjolme jumping 43 feet and the lower view of Orvald leaving the takeoff.

OREGON RIVERS RAISED BY THAW TO FLOOD STAGE

Swollen Streams Pour Torrents Into Willamette and Columbia and Portland Prepares for High Water.

PORTLAND, Monday, Feb. 7.—Out of the foothills and the Cascade Mountains, swollen streams are pouring their flood waters into the Willamette and Columbia Rivers today and threatening to bring further damage in the wake of last week's snow and sleet storm. Salem and other Willamette Valley towns report small streams out of their banks.

Merchants in buildings near the banks of the Willamette in Portland are moving their goods from basements. Within twenty-four hours ending this morning the Willamette had risen 7.9 feet at Eugene. In Portland there was a rise of 1.5 feet, but the crest is not expected here until Thursday, when a flood stage of 16.5 feet is predicted by the weather bureau. This will inundate the lower floors of practically every dock in the upper harbor and water will seep into the basements on Front Street.

Last night 1.55 inches of rain fell at Eugene and 1.02 in Portland. Today spring weather prevailed here, the sun shining bright and the temperature rising to 51 degrees. Traffic was restored almost to normal.

BOY SNOW SHOVELER KILLED BY LONG FALL

VANCOUVER, B. C., Monday, Feb. 7.—The first Vancouver casualty as a result of the snow storm occurred this morning. Sidney Mills, 12 years old, was shoveling the snow off the roof of his father's home when he slipped and fell forty feet through the skylight. He died on his way to the hospital.

According to the official figures compiled today by Mr. Shearman, the weather observer, more snow has fallen already in February than in all of January. The January fall was 24.49 inches; that of February up to 10 o'clock this morning was 21.25 inches.

SNOW WRECKS ROOF OF EDGEWICK LUMBER CO.

NORTH BEND, Monday, Feb. 7.—Roofs of the dry sheds of the North Bend Lumber Co. at Edgewick have been crushed in by the weight of the snow, causing a considerable loss. The dancing pavilion at Taylor Park has

For Seattle's first ski jumping exhibition in 1916, local Norwegians transformed Queen Anne Hill "into an ideal sliding incline." *From the* Seattle Times, *February 7, 1916.*

degree incline allowed skiers to reach jumping speed. "Reaching the bottom of the hill the jumpers will hurl themselves in the air landing many feet beyond.... Soft snow as a landing area was planted beneath the jump." More than a dozen "crack jumpers" entered, and a "ladies skiing event" entertained the crowd.

Threatening weather and a light rain "failed to keep ten masters of the skiing art from giving an exhibition." Reidar Gjolme had the longest jump at forty-five feet. L. Orvald was second with a jump of thirty-nine feet, and J. Sather, O. Peterson and A. Flakstad tied for third with jumps of thirty-eight feet. Gjolme, who won the Dr. Holms trophy at Norway's 1902 Holmenkollen tournament, immigrated to Seattle in 1903 and helped popularize ski jumping.[15]

This event was so successful that it inspired Reidar Gjolme and his Norwegian friends to organize a jumping tournament in the winter of 1917 at Scenic Hot Springs, at the west end of Great Northern Railroad's tunnel through the Cascades, ninety miles and four hours from Seattle. The area received between three and five feet of snow per year and was a popular winter sports destination. Skis, bobsleds and toboggans were available to use on long sloping hillsides and specially constructed ski and toboggan runs.

A jumping tournament was held at Scenic on February 4, 1917—"the only one of its kind ever attempted in the Northwest"—sponsored by the Norwegian newspaper owned by Reidar Gjolme. Expert ski jumpers from Norway, the Canadian Northwest, Minnesota and Washington entered, "many with championship records." Local businesses donated many valuable prizes, according to the *Seattle Times* on February 5, 1917.

The tournament was marred by rain that softened the snow and the incline was in poor condition for the nineteen entrants, but "the jumps were unusually good." Reidar Gjolme won, although he was so tired that he was unable to stand afterward. Tacoma's Birger Normann was second and O. P. Sather third. The tournament was viewed by 150 people from Seattle and a large crowd from Everett, "who cheered the contestants and laughed at the antics of those struggling in the snow." "Moving picture men took advantage of the snow scene and turned out to take pictures for the news weeklies," noted the *Seattle Times* on February 5, 1917.

Olga Bolstad, a twenty-year-old woman recently arrived from Norway, borrowed skis and created a sensation at the Scenic tournament by competing head to head with the men. "The feature of the tournament was the performance of Olga Bolstad, a small woman who cleaned up the prizes in the women's events and was awarded honorable mention in the men's events with an average of thirty-six feet."[16]

Adverse weather and the low elevation of Scenic Hot Springs caused the next jumping event to be moved to the Paradise Inn on Mount Rainier. At an elevation of 5,400 feet, Paradise Valley had snow well into July. A midsummer ski tournament, an event unprecedented in America, was organized for July 1917. Paradise Inn opened in 1917, built by the Rainier Park National Company (RPNC), a private company that had a lease to operate commercial facilities in Mount Rainier National Park (created by Congress in 1899). The RPNC later built Paradise Lodge in 1928 to develop winter business. Paradise became the primary destination for Tacoma skiers and, until World War II, was one of the state's main skiing centers.

Ski Jumping Tournaments on Mount Rainier, 1917–24

Midsummer tournaments were held from 1917 to 1924 at Paradise Valley on Mount Rainier, generally over the Fourth of July holiday. "Norwegian ski tourney planned....Experts declare that Mount Tacoma has ideal places for such contests." Mount Rainier was "the second place in the world [after Finse, Norway] where the finest skiing may be obtained during the summer months." It was not easy to reach Paradise. The road was open to Narada Falls, where heavy walking shoes and other equipment could be rented. The two-mile trip to Paradise Valley was made by sledge, horse or on foot. A temporary ski jump was built near Paradise Lodge on the eastern slope of Alta Vista, on a long incline halfway down the slope on "a natural ledge that permits a long leap to the sweep below." Just 50 spectators attended the first tournament, but the number had grown to 1,500 by 1923. A cross-country race was added in 1922.[17]

Olga Bolstad, the "girl ski jumper" who starred at the Scenic tournament, competed against the men on Rainier. "Sensational Girl Ski-Jumper to Take Part in Tourney on Mountain," the headline read. Olga was called "champion of the Pacific coast on skis" and "walked away with the first prize over a field of men contestants. She is one of the cleverest skiers in this country, and has performed feats in Norway that rank her high among Scandinavian manipulators of the ski."[18]

On June 27, 1918, the *Seattle Times* announced "Olga Bolstad Is Attraction at Northwest Championships on Rainier...[and] stands high among the ski runners of the Northwest." Olga did not fare as well in

TOURNAMENT TO BE HELD IN VALLEY

Motorists who enjoy snow sports in midsummer are in Paradise Valley today to witness the ski tournament arranged for the first time as a feature of the July season in the valley. Last week more than 300 motorists were in the valley, according to M. S. Brigham, and the delay in opening the road has apparently made no difference in the interest and enthusiasm. Until the opening of the road tourists are being carried in to the valley from Narada Falls by sledges.

Left: The first midsummer ski jumping tournament was held on Mount Rainier in 1917, where "Scandinavian manipulators of the ski" competed. *From the* Seattle Times, *July 29, 1917.*

Below: A skier goes off a jump created for a midsummer ski jumping tournament on Mount Rainier. *Wicken, California Ski Library.*

1918—"Man Defeats Woman in Ski Tournament." She was beaten by experienced Norwegian jumpers who had excelled in the old country. The tournament was won by Sigurd Johnson of Tacoma (holder of several prizes in Norway); A. Flagstad of Seattle was second and Hilmar Nelsen of Tacoma third. Olga placed fourth but was the "favorite with the spectators, but she is a young woman of slight build and was therefore considerable

"Girl ski jumper" Olga Bolstad competed against the men and was called "champion of the Pacific coast on skis." *Washington State Historical Society.*

handicapped against a field of skilled men jumpers. For nerve and grace and general expertness, however, no other contestant, it was generally conceded, deserved greater laurels than she."[19]

The 1919 tournament, called "the most important ski meet ever held in the Pacific Northwest," included a dance at Paradise Inn and attracted five hundred spectators. Olga competed against the "best ski-running talent in

Olga Bolstad, wearing clothing from "her beloved Norway," holds a silver loving cup, first prize from the 1917 tournament on Mount Rainier. *National Nordic Museum.*

the Northwest." Sigurd Johnson won the tournament for the second year in a row, with a 100-foot jump. Tacoma's Hilmar Nelson was second. Seattle's Jack Moen had the longest jump of the day, 116 feet, and finished third. "Miss Olga Bolstad of Seattle, the only woman entrant, is to be given a special cup for her work, which included a perfect jump, with perfect landing, at a distance of 64 feet." "Two moving picture outfits were present and took pictures of the jumpers in action."[20]

The 1922 tournament was a three-day affair. Professionals were invited from Colorado, the Midwest and British Columbia. The Rainier National Park Ski Club was formed to host the event, with Reidar Gjolme as a director. There were two days of exhibition jumping and a third day for an international ski jumping contest. Canada's Revelstoke Ski Club sent five of its best, who had jumped between 125 and 200 feet, including Nels Nelsen, who held the world's amateur record of 201 feet, and his brother Ivind Nilson. There was a gliding contest featuring twenty-five Norwegian women and girls, a five-mile cross-country race and a ski ball attended by one hundred couples. Reidar Gjolme, tourney chairman and judge, supervised construction of the jumping hill that would "enable the jumpers to make as high as 200 or more feet….The jump will send the jumpers through the air at a distance of seventy-five feet above the snow at the highest point." Centralia's Chris Bakken set a new world's record in the cross-country race, and Ivind Nilson won the jumping contest.[21]

The 1923 tournament, attended by 1,500 spectators, had a ski ball and girl's ski jumping event, with "two girls who are rapidly coming to the front as daring jumpers. Isabel Coursier, 16-year old society girl of Revelstoke, British Columbia, has as her competitor for feminine honors Harriet Hansen of Seattle." Ivind Nilson won his second championship in a row with a jump of 124 feet, setting a new record. Nels Nelsen jumped 143 feet, which did not count as he touched his hands to his skis. Chris Bakken won the four-mile cross-country race, Revelstoke's Allen Grandstrom was second and Hans Otto Giese of Friesberg, Germany, was third. "The women's showing was considered exceptional," as Harriet Hansen finished seventh in twenty-seven minutes and sixteen seconds and Elsa Graff finished eighth.[22]

Elaborate plans were made for the 1924 tournament on July 4, the day Norway's Prince Olav reached his majority, an event celebrated "with flying colors in blazing sunshine….For the first time in 700 years, Norway had an heir apparent of her own. From this date the constitution gives the prince the right to act as agent in the King's place." Uno Hillstrom, champion of Sweden, entered, along with many other jumpers prominent in the ski world. However, the tournament had to be canceled "owing to the absence of sufficient snow on the ski course."[23]

No more midsummer tournaments were held on Mount Rainier, and the jumping action changed to Cle Elum.

Above: Nels Nelsen, five-time Canadian national champion and world's amateur distance record holder (201 feet), competed at the 1916 Revelstoke Winter Sports Carnival. *Revelstoke Museum.*

Opposite: Ivind Nilson jumping 120 feet at Revelstoke, British Columbia, in 1921. Ivind was the 1922 Boys' Ski Jumping World Champion and brother of Nels Nelsen. (The brothers spelled their last names differently.) *Revelstoke Museum.*

In spite of the success of Olga Bolstad, women were generally not allowed to participate in ski jumping events, with a few exceptions. In the late 1920s and early 1930s, the Genesee, Colorado Winter Carnivals allowed women to jump, although on smaller hills than men. Norwegian "girl-jumpers" performed exhibition jumps in several locations. The Cle Elum Ski Club, Seattle Ski Club and Leavenworth Winter Sports Clubs had

female members, but they did not compete in formal tournaments. It was not until the 2014 Olympics at Sochi, Russia, that women were formally admitted into major ski jumping competitions. It took years of lobbying for the international ski fraternity to recognize that women could successfully compete in what was a male-dominated sport. The early success of Olga Bolstad had been long forgotten.

In 2017, Lowell Skoog, a Mountaineer and founder of the Washington State Ski & Snowboard Museum, celebrated the 100th anniversary of Olga Bolstad's adventures on Mount Rainier by creating a jump and going off it using vintage skis and clothing. The event can be seen on the *Seattle Times* website.[24]

Chapter 2

1925–1930

Ski Clubs Form; Permanent Ski Jumps Are Built; Tournaments Become Institutionalized

*I*n 1921, the International Olympic Committee decided to hold an "International Winter Sports Week" to provide equality for winter sports—excluding Germany because of sanctions imposed following World War I. The first Winter Olympics were held in 1924 at Chamonix, France. The only skiing events were Nordic. Alpine skiing was not allowed until the 1936 games in Garmisch-Partenkirchen, Germany. Publicity about the Olympic Games helped to popularize ski jumping in this country.

CLE ELUM SKI CLUB, 1924–33

Cle Elum, located thirty miles east of Snoqualmie Pass on what is now Interstate Highway 90, was formed when the Northern Pacific Railroad was built from Duluth, Minnesota, through the future town of Cle Elum and then over Stampede Pass to Tacoma, Washington, completed in 1884. A tunnel was completed under Stampede Pass in 1887. Coal was discovered by Northern Pacific engineers near Cle Elum, and in the early 1890s, it became a major coal producing center and an important railroad town. The Sunset Highway over Snoqualmie Pass opened in 1915.

In 1921, the Cle Elum Ski Club was formed, led by John "Syke" Bresko, becoming what has been called the first organized ski area west of Denver, "a skiers paradise" that attracted between one hundred and four hundred

In 1921, John "Syke" Bresko, shown with his wife, Tillie, organized the Cle Elum Ski Club, which sponsored jumping competitions until 1933. *Maybo family, CWU.*

locals every weekend. Legions of local kids learned to ski on the club's hill. The club sponsored carnivals, ski races, jumping competitions and special contests until 1933. Northern Pacific provided access to Cle Elum from Seattle and Yakima, and Norwegian jumpers dominated the events. Seattle and Yakima newspapers publicized the tournaments, stimulating interest in the sport on both sides of the Cascades.[25]

In February 1924, in the start of a ten-year tradition, the Cle Elum Ski Club held a ski carnival on Lincoln's birthday. Eleven jumpers entered, watched by 1,200 to 1,500 people. Two jumpers gave an exhibition using only one ski. Four professional jumpers competed, all from west of the mountains. Seattle's John Holden jumped eighty-three feet, the longest of the day. Renton's Arthur Ronstad, winner of the contest on points, "thrilled the spectators during one of his leaps when he struck the course sideways due to the wind and rode over a hundred feet on one foot, nearly straightening up, only to fall after a great effort. He was roundly applauded."[26]

The 1925 Cle Elum carnival was "the greatest outdoor frolic ever held." More than four hundred spectators watched one hundred contestants compete in ten contests—gliding races, cross-country race, goose fashion glide, amateur and expert ski jumping and obstacle courses on the club's ski runs (Rocky Run, Camel's Hump, Devil's Dive and Hell's Dive). Cle Elum's Victor Laurent won the jumping event. The "long and difficult" ladies cross-country race was won by Zoe Connell. After the contests finished, "the courses were thrown open to the public and skiing indulged in until a late hour."[27]

The 1926 Cle Elum tournament was publicized in the Fredrick and Nelson Department Store in downtown Seattle and by the *Seattle Times*, although its geography was off: "Ski Jumpers to Have a Big Day at Ellensburg." More than six hundred people witnessed the ten-event program, which included amateur and expert jumping events and obstacle courses. Bremerton's Rudolph Leonard won the expert jumping event, with jumps of ninety-four and ninety-three feet. Tony Sandona, "the human tumbleweed," captured second place on the Hell's Dive course after remaining upright, a performance judged by all to have been an accident. Russ Connell entered the ladies gliding course, dressed as Mysterious Miss Hanson of Alaska, "fully

This scene from an early Cle Elum Ski Club tournament shows the club's shelter, as well as spectators watching a jumper descending the hill. *Maybo family, CWU.*

John Bresko demonstrates his jumping technique at an early Cle Elum Ski Club tournament. *Maybo family, CWU.*

ten feet tall, wearing yellow rolled stocking's [*sic*], bedaubed with cosmetics and well gifted in the pursuits of flapperism, but all to no avail so far as the judges were concerned." The club's queen, splendidly impersonated by Chet Laurent, "scooted over the jump and made a beautiful ride to the end of the course amid wild cheers."[28]

In the fall of 1926, the Cle Elum Ski Club built a ski lodge on the ridge one and a half miles north of town, on forty acres of land leased from the Northwestern Improvement Company, "at a nominal sum," replacing a rudimentary hut previously used. The site was at three thousand feet elevation, covered with pine and fir trees and provided a variety of ski runs:

> *There are short, gentle slopes for the beginner, and then the courses range upward in length and steepness and difficulty to such an extent that even the most expert jumpers admit that they "get thrill aplenty" out of it. Two of the most difficult parts of the course are Hell's Dive which only those of great experience dare attempt.*

A two-story twenty-two-by-forty-foot lodge was built from native pine logs, with eight-foot-long windows providing a commanding view of the ski course. The lower floor was one large room with a large rustic fireplace. The upstairs was divided into dormitories for men and women. The club's ski jump was on the top of a ridge north of town, reached by a steep two-mile hike hill through the snow.[29]

The growing interest in ski jumping was reflected by the number of articles published in local newspapers. The *Seattle Times* of March 1, 1927, noted that "winter sports, particularly ski-jumping, have captured the visitors at Longmire Springs and the Paradise Valley," even though the sport was only inaugurated in Rainier National Park three weeks before. A remodeled course permitted jumps of thirty and forty feet. From 1,200 to 1,500 visitors visited the park each weekend, 50 percent more than the previous year.

Publicity for the Fifth Annual Cle Elum Ski Tournament in 1928 noted that "[a]s a spectacle, ski jumping has few equals. It is a form of sport which the average person might enjoy vicariously. Jumping from 100 to 120 feet and landing on the toes of Scandinavian snow shoes is a thrilling experience." A crowd of four thousand attended "one of the biggest events of its kind ever staged in this part of the Northwest." Carl Solberg and Sigurd Hansen both jumped seventy-six feet for the expert A Class event, but Sigurd Hansen won.[30]

Twenty-six U.S. men and women competed at the 1928 Winter Olympic Games in St. Moritz, Switzerland. The jumping competition took place on a seventy-meter jump built for the games. Thirty-eight competitors from thirteen countries entered. U.S. jumper Anders Haugen had the best mark in training, giving hopes for a medal. Norway dominated the games, with its athletes winning fifteen medals, including gold and silver in ski jumping. The United States finished in second place, with its athletes winning six medals.[31]

The 1929 Cle Elum Ski Carnival showed off the club's new large jump, which increased the level of competition. Ingle Sneeva, a Norwegian ski expert, came to Cle Elum to give "useful hints on skiing and jumping." He leaped 100 feet off the new jump, which would have been double had the snow been in better condition. "The jump is the best and largest he has seen in the United States." The three thousand spectators saw fifteen jumpers compete on "one of the few natural courses on the coast and what skiers and spectators alike acclaim will be the greatest ski course in the Pacific Northwest." Olaf Locken from Mount Vernon set a distance record of 165 feet from the "gigantic runway" and won the Class A event, followed by Sigurd Kragness, Ralph Follestad and Harry Kragness.[32]

NEW SKI CLUBS FORM AND HOLD ANNUAL TOURNAMENTS

In the late 1920s and early 1930s, new ski clubs formed centered on ski jumping, built ski jumps and hosted tournaments that initially attracted Northwest jumpers and, later, the world's best jumpers. Annual tournaments were hosted by the Northwest's major clubs: Cle Elum until 1933; Seattle Ski Club's events at Beaver Lake on Snoqualmie Pass and later at the Milwaukee Ski Bowl; Leavenworth Winter Sport Club's site in Eastern Washington; and Cascade Ski Club's hill on Mount Hood. Other ski clubs were formed that also hosted occasional tournaments.

In November 1930, the Pacific Northwestern Ski Association (PNSA) was organized by six ski clubs to sponsor regional jumping and cross-country competitions and coordinate calendars: Cle Elum Ski Club, Seattle Ski Club, Leavenworth Winter Sports Club, Bend (Oregon) Skyliners, Hood River Ski Club and Portland's Cascade Ski Club. The PNSA established standards for ski instructors and pioneered testing. Its original charter included Nordic events, not Alpine, and it promoted competition rather than recreational skiing. Previously, each ski club staged its own championship events, but there was no regional tournament. The PNSA affiliated with the National Ski Association and granted formal sanctions for Northwest tournaments. Its charter was changed to include Alpine skiing in the fall of 1933 in recognition of the growing interest of slalom and downhill events.

Seattle Ski Club

In 1929, the Seattle Ski Club was formed by Norwegian immigrants. Reidar Gjolmie arranged to lease one acre of land from the Northern Pacific Railroad Land Company by paying property taxes. The club initially used an abandoned construction camp as a clubhouse, utilized by the Milwaukee Road when it built its tracks over Snoqualmie Pass in 1909.

The club built its ski jumping hill at Beaver Lake, an uphill hike from Snoqualmie Summit, using the natural slope of the hill for the inrun and outrun. Famous ski jumper Olav Ulland described the difficulty of getting to the site in a masterpiece of understatement: "It lays about 3/4 of a mile uphill from the Sunset Highway and the hike to the jumps is not one to encourage attendance." The club was incorporated on February 4, 1930, by Reidar Gjome, C. Stang Andersen, Peter H. Hostmark, Olce Hatlemark and Enoch Andersen. The club had two hundred members, which included titleholders from other nations. In January 1931, the *Seattle Times* reported that the Seattle Ski Club was the nucleus of "decidedly thrilling winter meets" and that its members were "expert skiers, some of the most foremost in the world today." The club built a clubhouse in summer 1931 and rebuilt its ski jump into one of the most challenging in the country—according to the *Seattle Times*, it had "one of the steepest landings in the world, a hill three or four degrees steeper than the famous Holmenkollen Hill in Norway."

The Seattle Ski Club was the center of ski jumping in Western Washington in the 1930s and 1940s, and most of the state's well-known Norwegian ski jumpers were members, including Olav Ulland and Gustav Raaum (both of whom were inducted into the U.S. Ski and Snowboard Hall of Fame). The club sponsored annual tournaments of national importance, attracting the world's best jumpers, who set national distance records. The Seattle Ski Club took over management of the Milwaukee Ski Bowl jumps after World War II. The club hosted tournaments until the early 1950s, when it turned into a cross-country facility, including the jumping events for the 1940 National Four-Way Championships, national championships in 1941 and 1948, and the Olympic tryouts in 1947.[33]

Leavenworth Winter Sports Club

Leavenworth is a historic Great Northern Railroad town on the eastern slopes of the Cascade Mountains. In 1893, Great Northern completed its line from Minnesota over Stevens Pass to Seattle. A tunnel through the Cascades was completed in 1900, replaced by a longer one in 1929. In 1925, the Stevens Pass Scenic Highway opened. From 1893 to 1925, Leavenworth was Great Northern's Cascade Division headquarters, and its switchyard handled one thousand cars per day. In 1922, the *Leavenworth Echo* reported that the Chelan County Athletic Club of Leavenworth was organizing a winter festival to include ski jumping, skating and sledding.

Several sources discuss the club's history, including longtime Leavenworth Winter Ski Club supporter Earl Little, who described the club's history in a 1953 interview.[34]

On November 16, 1928, Walter Anderson, a U.S. Forest Service employee who won a silver cup at the 1928 Cle Elum tournament, published an article in the *Leavenworth Echo*, suggesting that an outdoor sports club be formed and a nearby hill located where members would "clear a strip for a ski course and toboggan slide." This resulted in the formation of the Leavenworth Winter Sports Club on November 18, led by Anderson and Milt Cloke. Club minutes indicate that a ski course was located on private land on Wheeler's Hill not far from the present ski area, on Railroad Avenue (now Ski Hill Drive). Twenty-three sportsmen cleared and cut brush on November 18, donating twenty-seven days of labor to the club. Those who could not work contributed $60.50. A small ski jump was built where a natural knoll formed a takeoff. On January 4, 1929, one hundred people turned out for the opening of the club's ski course and 1,600-foot-long toboggan slide, where a "good house" obtained from Northern Pacific was located. Local residents showed up to "downhill glide" and sled on January 11 and 25 and February 1. The *Leavenworth Echo* noted that five hundred people turned out—"Only a few dared to tackle the 'big ski course,' but many tried the amateur jumping course." The toboggan course took twenty-four seconds to negotiate, and young people were learning to jump, led by Walt Anderson. On February 10, 1929, the club held its first tournament, attended by one thousand spectators, with prizes for the best ski jump and fastest toboggan run; admission was twenty-five cents. The tournament was won by Sig Hansen from Ione, Washington (1913 world champion), with a jump of 65 feet; Walt Andersen was second and was given a life membership in the club. "The big ski course was pronounced one for experts only and some of the visitors did not wish to venture upon it," according to the *Leavenworth Echo*.[35] Sig Hansen spent the winter taking care of the course and building interest in skiing.

The success of the 1929 tournament led the club to develop a permanent facility. The club located a new area on forest service land, one-fourth of mile from its first site, where the Leavenworth Ski Area is located today. Sigurd Hansen supervised the building of a fifty-meter jump with a small trestle, where the present Class B hill is located. In 1930, the club obtained a forest service special-use permit to build a ski area:

> *Interest from* [its] *first tournament propelled the club to request a Forest Service special use permit to build and maintain two ski jumps, two toboggan runs, a parking area, a clubhouse and associated outbuildings. Issued in March 1930, the permit granted the LWSC's 33.12-acre site and permission to clear timber from the hillsides for ski jumps and toboggan runs. The first ski jump…a 50-meter Class B hill, opened that same year.*[36]

Leavenworth's 1929 tournament took place at the club's first site on Wheeler Hill, one-fourth of a mile from present ski area. *Wes Sauer family.*

Fascinated spectators watch a skier go off a small man-made jump at an early Leavenworth tournament. *Stan Harrison Collection.*

For 1931, the area around the fifty-meter jump was cleared, and a new jump was built farther up the hill. However, its trestle "was so flat that jumpers lost speed before the takeoff, and the jumps were far under the 200 feet hoped for," according to Little. The next year, the tournament was moved back to the B jump, which was unsatisfactory. The townspeople "determined to build a jump better than any other in the Northwest," resulting in the club's large seventy-three-meter ski jump, first used in 1933. It was the middle of the Depression and there was no money, so nearly everyone in town donated something—"work, material, a team of horses. Those who couldn't work put in money to hire someone who could." The jump's trestle was 240 feet long, made of poles from 16 to 32 feet long and more than 5,000 board feet, all "carried up that hill on someone's back." The jumping hill was built for $300, using donated labor, which would have cost $6,000 if the club had to pay for its construction and $20,000 in 1953:

> And what a hill. It's 375 feet high from the bottom of the landing slope to the start of the in-run....The foot of the landing slope is 700 feet away in distance from the start. The average slope is over 53 per cent. It is 300 feet down the in-run from the start to the take-off. The take-off is 12 feet above the start of the landing hill....Five thousand cubic yards of dirt and 125 yards of rock were moved and blasted by 30 boxes of dynamite.[37]

In 1932, brothers Hermod and Magnus Bakke from Lyngdahl, Norway, moved to Leavenworth, where they worked for the U.S. Forest Service and played major roles with the Winter Sports Club for decades. In 1933, Hermod "redesigned the big hill at Leavenworth....Hermod worked day and night for two days of back breaking work to prepare the hill," according to his biography in the U.S. Ski and Snowboard Hall of Fame.

After 1933, the Leavenworth jumping hills were improved almost yearly. The hills were reconfigured several times in the 1930s. A Class A jump was built in 1939. For 1950, Hermod Bakke "undertook a massive project on Leavenworth Hill to conform to National Ski Association standards," making three-hundred-foot jumps possible. The Class A jump was rebuilt in 1956— as the original wooden scaffolding had deteriorated and a heavy snowfall caused it to collapse—allowing the club to host national championships in 1959, 1967, 1974 and 1978.

In 1936, with the help of the forest service and Civilian Conservation Corps (CCC), and with Magnus Bakke acting as foreman, the ski club improved its grounds. Forty acres were cleared, and a two-and-a-half-story ski hut was built out of rock from Hatchery Creek and rustic logs. Its warming room had a 9-foot fireplace, a small lunchroom and caretaker's quarters. In 1936, Seattle's Ben Thompson designed a 1,500-foot slalom course at the ski area. In 1938, famous Norwegian ski jumper Olav Ulland taught skiing at Leavenworth, and cross-country trails were added. By 1940, the club had installed a rope tow and lights for night skiing. Ultimately, the site had two warming huts, several jumping hills and a variety of ski runs and trails. The 1960 U.S. Olympic team trained on Leavenworth's jumping hills.

Much of Leavenworth cooperated to make club tournaments successful. Residents packed the jumping hills by foot and on skis and brought snow from the mountains during low snow years that was placed onto the jumping hills. Generations of kids learned to ski and jump on the club's hills and competed in events up and down the Cascades, seeking a prized high school letter in skiing. Leavenworth became one of the premier sites for competitive jumping, reached by Great Northern trains and hosting tournaments until 1978. The jumping site was named Bakke Hill to honor Hermod and Magnus, who were inducted into the U.S. Ski and Snowboard Hall of Fame in 1972, along with Earl Little.[38]

Portland's Cascade Ski Club

In 1927, the Mount Hood Ski Club was organized, built a ski jump on the east side of Mount Hood's Multorpor Mountain (a contraction of Multnomah, Oregon and Portland) and held a tournament in February 1928. Later in 1928, the club split up and the Cascade Ski Club was organized. Ole Haugen secured the rights for a ski jump at Multopor, near the village at Government Camp. Haugen and his brothers built a ski jump on a natural hill with a "cribbage of timbers used to sustain the takeoff geometry." The Cascade Ski Club held its first tournament on January 6, 1929, won by Hjalmar Hvam, a native of Kongsberg, Norway, who moved to Portland in 1927 and was a cofounder of the club. Hvam won the club's tournament on December 23, 1929, with an eighty-four-foot jump, watched by 1,100 enthusiasts.[39]

In November 1930, the Cascade Ski Club helped form the Pacific Northwestern Ski Association, and it hosted the PNSA's first sanctioned jumping championship in 1931. In 1931, the club borrowed $1,000 to reshape its jumping hill, creating Class A, B, C and D jumps. The Class A jump had a shallow takeoff angle and sharp knoll, dropping quickly to a very steep landing hill. A clubhouse was built in fall 1931. In 1934, the club adopted the new sports of slalom and downhill skiing. In 1937, the CCC built a lodge at Multopor, and a rope tow was installed. In 1944, the club purchased fifty-five acres south of Government Camp. A new clubhouse was built in 1955, financed by its members. The club's last ski jumping program was held in March 1971.

John Elvrum competed for the club in the early 1930s, becoming one of the country's best jumpers, until he moved to California. Hjalmar Hvam was a longtime club member and an outstanding four-way skier and Nordic-combined specialist who invented and patented one of the first safety release bindings. Hvam was inducted into the U.S. Ski and Snowboard Hall of Fame in 1967, and Elvrum followed in 1968.[40]

Other Washington Ski Clubs

In 1927, the Mount Baker Ski Club was formed to take advantage of the new Mount Baker Lodge, built by the Mount Baker Development Company and which opened on July 14, 1927, as well as a new highway built for $800,000. The L-shaped lodge was 210 feet long, resembled a Swiss chalet and had one hundred rooms, each with hot and cold water and a telephone. Its fifty-by-ninety-foot dining room seated 300. The club held a tournament in 1930 that included some of the best ski jumpers in the Northwest and Canada and another in 1931, featuring uphill, downhill and cross-country races. A fire destroyed the lodge in August 1931, setting back skiing for years. The club held a two-day slalom tournament in May 1935, where 130 skiers competed in front of 2,000 spectators. In 1946, the Mount Baker ski area was expanded, and a new lodge and chair lift were constructed. The Fjeld Ski Club built a new ski jump more than three hundred feet high close to its lodge and hosted tournaments on Razorbone Hill for a number of years.

The Spokane Ski Club was formed in 1929, initially skiing on Browne Mountain. In 1932, club members built a lodge on the lower slopes of Mount Spokane on eighty acres leased from A.P. Lidner. Huge peeled logs two feet in diameter were used to construct the seventy-two-foot-long lodge, and bricks for the fireplace and chimney came from the old Diamond Watch Mine. The club later purchased property on Mount Spokane, which was improved for skiing.

The ski club hosted jumping tournaments on a hill above Wandermere Golf Course in 1933, 1934 and 1938, each year plagued by low snow amounts. A tournament was held in 1936 at the Ski-Mor ski area on Browne Mountain, sponsored by another organization. A rope tow was installed on Mount Spokane for the winter of 1936–37, in anticipation of hosting the PNSA championships in downhill and slalom racing. In 1942, the PNSA jumping championship tournament scheduled for Spokane was canceled because of war-related transportation conditions and held at Mount Baker instead. In 1948, the club built a ski jump near its lodge on Mount Spokane and held Esmeralda Tournaments from 1948 to 1953, a tournament at Wandermere in 1954 and its last one on Mount Spokane in 1955. Spokane Ski Club jumpers Arnt Ofstadt and John Ring tried out for the 1936 U.S. Olympic team. Helge Sather, who originally competed for Leavenworth and later for Spokane, was one of the country's top ten jumpers.[41]

The Ellensburg Ski Club formed in 1930 and put on its first competitive jumping event in January 1932 in Robinson Canyon, eight miles from the city, under the guidance of Carl Solberg, a former national champion and famed in Europe. It had a unique feature: spectators could sit in their automobiles to watch the jumps. There were Class A and B jumps, good for 175 feet. Helge Sather of Leavenworth won the Class A event with a long jump of 132 feet, with Carl Solberg of Ellensburg placing second.

The 1933 Ellensburg tournament attracted 30 competitors from Northwest clubs. An improved Class A jump was good for jumps up to 300 feet. Ole Tverdal of Seattle won the Class A event with a jump of 117 feet. Helge Sather was second, and Leavenworth's Hermod Bakke had the longest jump of 122 feet. The 1935 Ellensburg Ski Club tournament attracted nearly 200 students and faculty from the local college. In January 1938, the tournament attracted 28 jumpers and 1,500 spectators and was won by Hermod Bakke.[42]

In 1937, the Yakima Winter Sports Club opened a new ski area on the American River, forty miles from town. Its opening tournament featured one-class jumping, downhill and slalom events that attracted many top competitors. Four members of the 1936 U.S. Olympic team competed: Don Fraser, Darroch Crookes, Grace Carter and Skit Smith, along with a young skier with a future, Gretchen Kunigk (later Gretchen Fraser). The Seattle Ski Club sent fourteen members; Washington Ski Club, ten; University of Washington, five; and The Mountaineers, three. Organizers were concerned that five thousand attendees would jam the highway to the meet. Ole Tverdal won the jumping contest, and Hermod Bakke was second. The club was admitted into the Pacific Northwestern Ski Association in 1937. The 1938 tournament featured Class A and B jumping, downhill and slalom races. In 1939, the club enlarged its jumping hill, giving it a length of 150 feet. However, because of a lack of snow, the tournament was held at Quartermile Hill on the west side of Chinook Pass. In 1939, Yakima businessmen started a program to provide free ski lessons for high school students at the American River Ski Bowl. The PNSA championships in slalom and downhill were hosted by the Yakima Ski Club in February 1940.

Chapter 3

1930–1933

Jumpers Compete in a Circuit of Tournaments; Washington Skiing Is Recognized Nationally

*B*y 1930, ski jumpers had a circuit of tournaments to choose from: Cle Elum; Beaver Lake on Snoqualmie Pass; Leavenworth; and Mount Hood. Ski clubs improved their hills, making longer jumps possible. Washington's skiers and ski areas were recognized nationally. Clubs used a common rating system: Class A (elite), Class B (top status not yet earned), Class C (under eighteen years of age) and Veterans Class. The competition to set new distance records excited sports fans throughout the country.

Ski jumping was dominated by tough Norwegian immigrants who drove on icy roads to the events, often on successive weekends, to compete for the glory of the sport since there were no monetary prizes. Competitors had to hike long distances up hills to reach the jumps, carrying heavy wooden skis, and then climb steep scaffolds to reach the takeoff. After each jump, they repeated the process. After tournaments ended, competitors typically entertained audiences by performing stunts such as simultaneous jumps or somersaults. The best ski jumpers were celebrities, much like professional quarterbacks are today.

Tournaments attracted thousands of hardy spectators who traveled long distances by car or train, hiked up steep hills through the snow to reach the jumping sites and stood outdoors for hours, often in snowstorms. Webb Moffett, who operated the Snoqualmie Summit Ski Area, said that "[t]housands of people used to hike up from the highway at Snoqualmie to Beaver Lake to watch those crazy Norwegians fly through the air at competitions put on by the Seattle Ski Club. After the meet, it was always a

thrill to watch the jumpers come down, straight-running Municipal Hill by leaping from hillock to hillock."[43]

The Seattle Ski Club's first tournament at Beaver Lake in 1930 was the first annual Pacific Coast Ski Championships, and it attracted thirty-three entrants, including Ole Hegge of the Bardu Ski Club of Norway, 1927 King's Cup winner. Buses carried spectators from Seattle to the summit for $3.00 to see the "air-hoppers" (admission $0.25). Parking was half an hour walk from the jumping hill. The tournament was won by Erling Thompson of the Seattle Ski Club. E. Finsberg of Kent had the longest jump at 151 feet.

At the 1930 Cle Elum tournament, Conway's Olaf Locken leaped 165 feet in a special exhibition, "the longest standing jump executed in the United States this year," thrilling three thousand "intrepid spectators who trudged up the snowy mountainside to the event." Ivan Finsberg of Cle

Opposite: This map shows the ski jumping circuit between Leavenworth, Cle Elum, Mount Hood and Beaver Lake on Snoqualmie Pass. *From the* Seattle Times, *February 7, 1930.*

Above: "Ski jumpers have none of the conveniences fans get. Torger [Tokle] has to climb up to slide down." *Wicken, California Ski Library.*

Left: The 1930 Cle Elum tournament offered a variety of events, including amateur and expert jumping, Ladies' Gliding, Rocky Run and Hell's Dive. *Maybo family, CWU.*

Below: Seattle's Harold Dalsbo flies like a bird at the 1930 Cle Elum tournament. *Maybo family, CWU.*

46

The First Annual Leavenworth Tournament, in 1930, attracted a large following, shown by the number of cars in its parking lot. *Stan Harrison Collection*.

Spectators line up along the jumping hill at the First Annual Leavenworth Tournament, 1930. *Lee Pickett photo, UW Special Collections*.

A jumper poses on the lip of the takeoff at the 1930 Leavenworth Winter Sports Club Tournament. *Lee Pickett photo, UW Special Collections.*

Elum had the longest jump, 150 feet, but the event was won on form points by Howard Dalsbo with a jump of 119 feet. Ole Helge was second and Olaf Locken third.[44]

Nels Nelsen, the "world champion jumper" from Revelstoke, British Columbia, who held the world's distance record of 240 feet, won the 1930 Leavenworth tournament in front of a record crowd of 3,500 spectators. Vancouver's Fred Finkenhagen, who had the longest jump of 108 feet, was second, and Leavenworth's Sigurd Hansen was third.

1931: RIDE THROUGH A COAL MINE AT CLE ELUM; REGIONAL TRYOUTS FOR U.S. OLYMPIC TEAM; NEW LODGE AND JUMP AT SNOQUALMIE PASS

On January 25, 1931, the *Seattle Times* described how popular skiing had become. "Seattle and its slightly less pretentious friends, Portland and

Vancouver, have discovered winter in seven or eight places; the western *haut monde* migrate every weekend in cars and gets its fill of skiing....And everyone skis." The Seattle Ski Club uses an abandoned construction camp on Snoqualmie Pass, where it "built a timber jump with one of the steepest landings in the world—a hill three or four degrees steeper than the famous Holmenkollen Hill in Norway." Its tournaments attract two or three thousand people.

The road over Snoqualmie Pass was kept open for the first time during winter 1931. By 1934, the entire highway had been paved, offering better access to the mountains. Ski tournaments attracted better ski jumpers and larger crowds.

Alf Engen, part of a group professional ski jumpers, challenged his competitors early in 1931 by setting a new professional world's distance record of 243 feet at Big Pines, California. "Sliding down the 700-foot runway of the new jump, the world's highest, at an estimated speed of ninety-five miles an hour, Engen glided off the brink and made a perfect landing." He broke Henry Hal's record of 229 feet set at Quebec in 1925. Alf emigrated from Norway in 1929 and joined a professional ski jumping tour with his brother Sverre, Sigurd Ulland, Lars Haugen, Einar Friedbo and others, becoming one of the country's most accomplished skiers. Alf won the National Professional Ski Jumping Championships from 1931 through 1935, setting two world professional jumping records. Big Pines was Southern California's best-known ski jumping venue. It opened in 1924, and a ski jump was built in 1929, later replaced by a bigger one in 1931, one of the country's largest. Its tournaments drew up to thirty thousand people, and a number of distance records were set there.[45]

In the early 1930s, three jumpers from Vancouver, British Columbia, began competing in Washington tournaments—Nordal Kaldahl, Tom Mobraaten and Henry Solvedt, known as the "Three Musketeers." All were born in Kongsberg, Norway, immigrated to Vancouver and trained together but joined different ski clubs. Kaldahl won the Vancouver city combined title in 1931 and 1934 and the 1933 Pacific Northwest jumping championship. Mobraaten won the Vancouver city combined title in 1933 and the Western Canada championships in 1935 and 1939 and was on the 1936 Canadian Olympic team.

There was an intense battle for jumping supremacy in the early 1930s between Nordal Kaldahl and John Elvrum from Trondheim, Norway, who competed for Portland's Cascade Ski Club. Kaldahl worked as a pipefitter on Vancouver's drydocks and was a power jumper, usually described in

"The Three Musketeers of B.C."—Tom Mobraaten, Nordal Kaldahl and Henry Solvedt—competed in Washington in the 1930s. *Hollyburn Heritage Society.*

Left: John Elvrum, from Portland's Cascade Ski Club, battled Nordahl Kaldahl for jumping supremacy in the early 1930s, using an elegant style though often over-jumping hills going for distance. *Wicken, California Ski Library.*

Right: Nordahl Kaldahl was a power jumper and Canadian champion, often described by his strength and enthusiasm, who won many tournaments in Washington. *Hollyburn Heritage Society.*

terms of his strength and muscular build and enthusiasm: "[E]lectrically-muscled bit of skiing dynamite; whooping wildman." Elvrum had an elegant style, jumping "as if he had steel springs in his legs and wings on his shoulder blades," although he was known for overjumping hills to gain more distance.

The Third Annual Leavenworth Tournament in January 1931 featured stars from Washington, Oregon and British Columbia, who competed on the "newly constructed hill for the Class A competition." A new toboggan slide, "with mile-a-minute" thrills, and an ice skating carnival were added attractions. Jumpers from Vancouver, British Columbia, won the top three spots in the Class A competition in a blinding snowstorm, witnessed by four thousand spectators. Nordal Kaldahl was first, Fred Sinkenhagen second and A. Haugen third.

At the Cascade Ski Club's 1931 tournament on Mount Hood, twenty-four jumpers entered the Class A event, twenty-seven in Class B and twenty-six in the cross-country race. More than ten thousand spectators attended, cars were parked for five miles along the highway and one thousand cars were turned back because of lack of parking space. Portland's John Elvrum won the Class A event. Seattle's Howard Dalsbo placed third in the Class A event.[46]

The Coal Mine at Cle Elum

The Eighth Annual Cle Elum Tournament in 1931 offered an exciting new development: a ride through a coal mine to get to the jumping site.

After the 1930 tournament, club organizers realized that they had to provide better access to the jumping site, which was a "rather strenuous" two-mile hike up a steep hill to the top of a ridge north of town. In 1931, sleds pulled by tractors took spectators to the entrance of a coal mine, where they rode in mine cars through Coal Mine No. 7's tunnel three quarters of a mile up the mountain in ten minutes, followed by a half-hour walk to the ski jump. The cars were covered with canvas carpeting "so as not to get the natty ski costumes of the ski beauties smudged"—one dollar from the railroad station (round trip) and fifty cents for admission to the tournament. Spectators were told, "Do not wear dress shoes and rubbers"—instead, wear hiking boots or a good pair of galoshes. Ladies should wear

Tractors hauled spectators to a coal mine's entrance for a ride through the tunnel at the 1931 Cle Elum tournament. *Maybo family, CWU.*

trousers or short street skirts. A tam or toque would do for head gear "that is not too good a target for a snowball," and a sweater or cruiser coat would complete the outfit. The jumping hill was 352 feet from the takeoff to the bottom of the hill, and a 100-foot scaffold would "provide the bullet-like speed necessary for long, spectacular jumps."[47]

Seven trains filled with ski fans arrived from Seattle and another from Yakima. Others drove over Snoqualmie Pass, the first time it was kept open for winter travel, and Cle Elum experienced its first winter traffic jam. In a blinding snowstorm that obscured the runway, Portland's John Elvrum jumped 128 feet to win the Class A event. Leavenworth's Olaf Locken, who set the course record the prior year, was second. Five thousand spectators cradled their hot dogs and hot chocolate trying to stay warm in the snowstorm.[48]

Ski Tournament
WINTER CARNIVAL
Cle Elum ▾ Sunday ▾ February 15
Eighth Annual Tournament—Cle Elum Ski Club

· Spectacular ride through parts of two coal mines to ski course by electric tram.

Special Northern Pacific Train to Cle Elum—
Lv. Seattle 7:30 a. m. Ar. Cle Elum 10:45 a. m.
Lv. Cle Elum 5:30 p. m.

ROUND TRIP FARE $3.50
From King Street Station

Reserve Your Tickets Now at any Northern Pacific office

Northern Pacific Railway

Spectators taking the Northern Pacific to the 1931 Cle Elum tournament could ride through a coal mine to get within a half-hour walk to the ski jump. *From the* Seattle Times, *February 2, 1931.*

Seattle Ski Club Builds Lodge, Improves Its Ski Hill and Holds Regional Olympic Tryouts

In 1931, the Seattle Ski Club hosted the regional tryouts in ski jumping and cross-country for the 1932 Olympic Games at Lake Placid, New York. Milwaukee Road provided special trains to its Hyak stop east of Snoqualmie Pass, with buses transporting spectators back to the summit. The *Seattle Times* warned that it was a "short hike from the Summit to the jump of less than a mile, and although the trail was not difficult or steep, attendees were warned against wearing low shoes or oxfords."[49]

The tournament attracted seventy stars from Western Canada and the Pacific Northwest. The thirty-one jumpers entered in Class A included the champion of Canada, twenty jumpers from British Columbia and competitors from Portland, including the Northwest champion. The jumping hill had a "45 degree pitch...so steep none but the best will attempt it."

SKI JUMPING

The World's Most Spectacular Sport

SEATTLE SKI CLUB
Annual Tournament and Tryout
for the
OLYMPIC WINTER GAMES

Under Auspices of
The National Ski Association of America

SNOQUALMIE PASS SUMMIT

SUNDAY, MARCH 1
AT 1:00 P. M.

Milwaukee Special Train Leaves Seattle 9 a. m.
Buses Leaves 3rd and Virginia
Automobile Highway to Summit in Perfect Condition

ADMISSION $1.00	CHILDREN FREE
Refreshments at Tournament Hill	

CHAMPIONS OF WESTERN CANADA
AND PACIFIC COAST TO COMPETE

Milwaukee Road promoted the 1931 Jumping Tournament and tryouts for the U.S. Olympic team for the 1932 Winter Games, featuring the "world's most spectacular sport." *From the Seattle Times, February 26, 1931.*

Eighteen competitors entered the grueling ten-mile cross-country race that stretched "from the Summit at Snoqualmie to the vicinity of Source Lake" and back, "winding through woods and open stretches under snow-laden trees and cliffs." The tournament was "amazingly successful," with a crowd of ten thousand watching the cross-country race and five thousand viewing the jumping. However, it "was not an Olympic test for American jumping," as "the tournament failed to yield a solitary candidate for next winter's Olympic games," according to the *Seattle Times* of March 2, 1931.

The jumping event was won by John Elvrum, who leaped 170 and 180 feet with almost perfect form, winning his match up with Nordal Kaldahl. However, Elvrum was not a U.S. citizen, and "that counted him out of the Olympic tryouts," although his 180-foot jump set a new hill record. Nordal Kaldahl was second, but he was Canadian. "The only American jumpers in the tournament were one or two in the Class B, whose performances were not particularly hot." Vancouver skiers were first and second in the cross-country event, Harold Smedja followed by Harold Balavik, and Portland's Hjalmar Hvam was third. Norwegian jumpers won the top ten places in the competition. Later in March, the Seattle Ski Club said that it planned to lengthen the takeoff and broaden the landing of its jump for next year, so "real records will be made."[50]

In May 1931, the Seattle Ski Club appropriated $7,000 to improve its facility on Snoqualmie Pass—$6,000 to construct a new clubhouse and the rest to refurbish the takeoff and correct the pitch of its jumping hill. The new lodge, completed in the fall of 1931 on land leased from Northern Pacific, was a three-story structure "with a pitched roof sheer enough to edge off the heavy winter snow," noted the *Seattle Times* of October 18, 1931. The first floor had a large lounge with the customary mountain fireplace. The second floor had a big receiving lounge, convertable to a dining room, with a kitchen in the back. The third floor had a sleeping lounge for two hundred people.

Seattle Times reporter Ken Binns wrote that "all summer long, a diligent crew graded and regraded, took out stumps" and smoothed its bumps, giving Beaver Lake's Big Hill "the sheerest pitch of any in America":

> *The architects who packed the course with stiff banks of snow weren't interested in degrees horizontal. They chose the most violent pitch on the mountain-side at Summit, built a log take-off, then began the more delicate process of anticipating where a good skier should land. Having discovered that point…they fooled him. They stepped back about ten paces and built another precipice.*

When a jumper reached the point of "the trickery of the architects" while flying off the jump, "[r]ight where he begins to drop they have thoughtfully removed the earth. In the case of Snoqualmie, nature assisted materially by providing another hill. So the skier continues to drop. It is this drop which materially adds yards to the ultimate distance the jumper acquires in his medal-seeking." The Beaver Lake inrun is 400 feet, compared to 1,400 foot at Ogden, Utah. With a 1,400-foot runway, "our jumpers would be landing in Canada….They'd be jumping 300 feet and killing themselves."[51]

1932: Kaldhal–Elvrum Competition Heats Up; Cle Elum's Giant New Jump; Northwest Competitors Face National Jumpers

The battle for America's longest jump intensified in 1932. Alf Engen broke his own professional distance record set in 1931 by jumping 257 feet at Big Pines, California. It was the second-best official jump ever recorded, after Sigmund Ruud's jump of 265.74 feet in 1930 at Davos, Switzerland.[52]

Ken Binns described the heated rivalry between Nordal Kaldhal and John Elvrum, where Elvrum often overjumped hills in his effort to win:

> *This Kaldahl-Elvrum ski jumping feud promised to last until John Elvrum, the smooth Portlander, either beats Nordal Kaldahl, the British Columbia ace, or jumps off the edge of the world. Elvrum is down to Kaldahl this year, and he's tumbled himself into a hospital once and almost a second time with*

his daring leaps in an effort to beat his rival. Such do-or-die rivalry really deserves success, but Kaldahl is a hard lad to beat with his smooth consistency on the tiny ribbons of wood that catapult him to championships.[53]

The "precipitous slope" of Beaver Lake's big hill attracted twenty-one Class A and twenty-seven Class B jumpers in January 1932 to the Seattle Ski Club's Northwest Invitational Tournament, where the quality of the jumpers and snow conditions compared favorably to those at the Lake Placid Olympics. Binns continued:

Fifty skiers, all able, some brilliant, is an amazing field. And the fifty and more assured of jumping will represent the greatest array of skiers you probably could find in any one section of the United States.... They seem to flock to the Washington country. They were indulging in sardonic chuckles today at the expense of Lake Placid, N.Y, scene of the Winter Olympic Games, if they get any snow. "Why don't they come out here," the skiers declared. "Here they can have snow within easy riding distance of Seattle."

Kaldahl beat Elvrum for Class A honors, in a blinding snowstorm, with a jump of 170 feet—11 feet longer than Elvrum's best, using different jumping styles:

Both held the sweeping crouch as they screamed down the takeoff, but as they reached the lip their styles arbitrarily changed. Elvrum, using the aero-dynamic manner—a diving leap, head stretched to the ski tips, arms literally strapped to his sides, nose-dived ahead, seemingly a part of the narrow blades of hickory which flung him forward. Kaldahl, a short, compact bundle of skiing fire, took a higher leap, body more erect, arms falling in cadence.

Both might go to the national ski jumping tournament at Lake Tahoe, where they could finish one-two.[54]

Later in January 1932, John Elvrum was injured at Mount Hood, breaking his nose and his collarbone when he overjumped the hill. Elvrum was straining to outdo the 189-foot jump of Hjalmar Hvam. Elvrum jumped 210 feet, on a hill designed for a 190-foot maximum jump, landing "far out into the soft snow, past the pitch of the hill, to land in a tangled, whirling, gyrating knot." He got up but collapsed walking back to the

A jumper sails through the air at the 1932 Seattle Ski Club tournament at Beaver Lake, where local skiers competed on equal terms with the best national athletes. *Museum of History and Industry.*

lodge. The injury would likely keep him from competing at the National Ski Championships at Lake Tahoe.[55]

At the 1932 Leavenworth tournament, both its Class A and B events were conducted from the same hill, but a "65-foot tower with three starting platforms and a well-pitched landing" had been built. The tournament featured two former national champions: Sigurd Hansen of Ione (1913) and Carl Solberg of Ellensberg (1915). However, for the second year in a row, Nordal Kaldahl won the tournament. In spite of his injuries, John Elvrum competed "to fight it out with Kaldahl" but fell as he overjumped the hill. Harold Belsvik was second and Helge Sather of Leavenworth third.[56]

The 1932 Olympic Games were held February 4–15 at Lake Placid, New York, the first held in the United States. Lake Placid's ski jump was built in 1917, using the natural slope of the hill. Its Olympic jump was built in 1927, with a steel tower that was raised to seventy-five meters for the competition. The only skiing events were Nordic (jumping, cross-country and combined). U.S. athletes won the most medals, followed by Norway and Canada.

Most of the snow had melted when the ski jumping event occurred. Norway's Birger Ruud won the gold medal, Hans Beck silver and Karre Wahlberg bronze. Sigmund Ruud was seventh. "Americans performed well in ski jumping," according to Anson in *Jumping Through Time*. Norwegian immigrant Casper Oimoen from South Dakota, winner of three national championships, was the highest U.S. jumper, placing fifth, followed by Peder Falstad (thirteenth) and John Steelt (fifteenth). Roy Mikkelson, originally from Kongsberg, did not place.[57]

New Giant Cle Elum Jump

In February 1932, the Cle Elum Ski Club hosted the Pacific Northwest Ski Jumping Championships. Its "mighty new ski jump" was described by Ken Binns in the *Cle Elum Echo-Miner*:

> *You never saw such a hill. They took the old hill and buried it under a convincing mass of lumber. They shafted a jumping tower far into the stratosphere, at an almost inconceivable pitch. The tower jerked up into the heavens at a 46-degree angle, 117½ feet above the comparative level of the takeoff. The landing dropped at a 46-degree pitch, 194½ feet from the takeoff to the flat. It exceeded in ferocity even the Seattle Ski Club's precipice.*

The steep scaffolding helped make Cle Elum's giant new jump the "biggest and baddest in the west and maybe even the whole world." *Maybo family, CWU*.

Cle Elum's jump was "one of the most hazardous in the world, 6% steeper than any in Norway," according to the *Seattle Times*. *Maybo family, CWU.*

This image shows the lower portion of Cle Elum's jump and the tower where tournament judges stood to evaluate the jumpers' form. *Maybo family, CWU.*

The tournament also featured a cross-country race, and awards were given for the best combined skier in jumping and cross-country, the best jumper and the best cross-country skier. The five-mile cross-country course challenged competitors with "ups and downs," where proper waxing was critical, as well as "quick hair-raising jumps" that required "grinding pain-ignoring nerve. When you see that lad come running cross the line, you see a lad with gameness. Cross-country skiing is not for the chickens." Northern Pacific would bring five hundred spectators to the tournament, with a "diner in the string of cars, calculating increased appetites en route....Go by rail—safe, warm, comfortable." Round trip from Seattle was $3.50. Trucks would take spectators to within a forty-minute walk of the jump.[58]

In 1932, Alf Engen sent a telegram to the Cle Elum Ski Club, saying, "I am a professional and have arranged to jump in several tournaments this winter which offer some very attractive monetary rewards but, should you, however, make an offer which will make it worth my while to come to your city, I shall be very glad to jump upon your hill."[59] Alf never jumped at Cle Elum, but he did compete in other Washington tournaments.

The 1932 Cle Elum tournament featured "the jumping duel that is rapidly becoming a skiing epic—the fight of John Elvrum, Northwest jumping champion, to outjump, outperform, that compact bunch of Dominion dynamite—Nordal Kaldahl." Just 41 contestants competed in front of 3,500 spectators. John Elvrum had the longest jump of 202 feet, a Northwest record, on a hill designed for 190-foot jumps. For the third tournament in a row, Elvrum overjumped the hill, fell in a whirling tangle of snow and skis, broke a ski and did not jump again, losing the jumping title to Ole Tverdal of the Seattle Ski Club. Portland's Hjalmar Hvam won the combined jumping and cross-country championship. The PNSA president said that local jumping "ranked with any in the United States."[60]

Northwest Ski Stars Compete Against Their National Counterparts

The national championships were held at Lake Tahoe in late February 1932. They were the first held west of the Rockies and attracted the nation's best jumpers and cross-country skiers, most of whom were from the East or Midwest. Olympic Hill was designed and built in 1930 by Lars Haugen from Telemarken, Norway, who designed the jump at Big Pines. The tournament had jumping events and, for the first time, 18km and 50km cross-country races for men and a three-mile cross-country race for women. It was "the coming out event party for Tahoe winter sports," according to Ingrid Wicken.

Before the tournament, "Northwest skiing received small recognition in the East." However, in the 18km cross-country race, Portland's Hjalmar Hvam beat Connecticut's Magnus Satre (three-time national cross-country champion) by fifty seconds. Hvam also won the Class B jumping event and the National Combined Championship, putting Northwest skiing the map. The Class A tournament was won by Anton Lekang ("big blond Viking from the Norway Ski Club of New York"), narrowly beating John Elvrum, although Elvrum had the longest jump of 198 feet. Sigrid Stromstad Laming won the ladies cross-country race, becoming the first National Ski Association women's champion. She was listed as a Class C jumper, for "exhibition only."[61]

The national ski stars who competed at Lake Tahoe came to the Northwest to participate in the 1932 Seattle Ski Club tournament at Beaver Lake in early March. It attracted seventy-four skiers—"there never was such a brilliant display of jumping talent," including six who were internationally famous, all of Norwegian descent: Anton Lekang, Norway Ski Club, New York, 1932 national champion; Casper Oimoen, Canton, South Dakota, former national champion; Magnus Satre, Salisbury, Connecticut, three-time national cross-country champion; Ottar Satre of Salsbury, Connecticut ("one of the best combined jumpers in the U.S."); Roy Mikkelson, Norge Ski Club, Chicago, 1932 U.S. Olympic team member; and Guttorm Paulsen, Norge Ski Club, Chicago, one of the best combination men in the world. They would compete with the best of the local jumpers, including John Elvrum and Nordal Kaldahl.[62]

Magnus Satre, "Satre the Magnificent," won the 17km cross-country race in a twenty-five-man field in an "astonishing time" of eighty-four minutes, eight seconds. Elvrum finished second and Al Johansen of Vancouver, British Columbia, third. Roy Mikkelson won the jumping event with jumps of 176 and 175 feet, beating Anton Lekang, who came in fifth. Nordal Kaldahl jumped 195 and 202 feet in practice, but snowfall limited the jumps during the competition, so the competitors jumped for style points not distance. Kaldahl took third in the jumping competition and Elvrum fourth. Elvrum won the combined championship, for Northwest bragging rights. Guttorm Paulsen was second and Magnus Satre third.[63]

In mid-March 1932, at the Cascade Ski Club's tournament at Mount Hood, the national ski stars were "invincible in the special jumping event," with Roy Mikkelson winning the title, Anton Lekang coming in second and

Guttorm Paulsen third. However, Northwesterners took three of the top four places in the combined: John Ring of the Bend Skyliners, followed by Magnus Satre and Portland's John Elvrum and Hjalmar Hvam.[64]

After the tournament, the national stars praised skiing in the West. Roy Mikkelson wrote, "I also want to tell you that after the trip out in the West, I don't like Chicago. I didn't like it before. But now I can understand why it is so bad." Anton Lekang said that the Pacific Northwest

> *in the near future will be the center of the ski sport in America, owing to excellent hills where most wonderful ski courses can be developed, to the abundance of snow in the mountains, good roads to them, and the favorable temperature for enjoying ski sport. Already now the Pacific Northwest seems to be more ski-minded than any part of the country.... The most amazing experience on the whole trip west was the great number of excellent skiers in the states of Oregon and Washington.*

Portland's John Elvrum "ranks with the best in America. He has marvelous form. He usually makes the longest jumps at their meets in the Northwest. But the whole Northwest is alive with skiers who are just as good as any, east or west."[65]

In December 1932, it was announced that Portland's John Elvrum and Hjalmar Hvam would compete in the National Ski Association meet in Salisbury, Connecticut, in late January, 1933. Seattle was not sending a competitor, as it lacked a skier who finished high enough to compete with the nation's skiing elect.

1933: NEW LEAVENWORTH JUMP; LAST CLE ELUM TOURNAMENT

By 1932, Roy Mikkelson had moved to Northern California, where he became the leading jumper for the Auburn Ski Club, winning eleven club tournaments.

In 1933, the Spokane Ski Club hosted a jumping competition on a hill above the Wandermere Golf Course, fifteen minutes from the city center, where previous winter carnivals featured ice skating and hockey. Seattle engineer Peter Hostmark designed a Class A jump and laid out the hill's specifications. The hill was 700 feet long, with a thirty-four-degree angle of steepness, for jumps up to 185 feet. Parking was available for one thousand cars.

Opposite, top: Seattle engineer Peter Hostmark examines the jumping hill he designed at Wandermere for the 1933 Spokane Ski Club tournament. Hostmark designed many of the Northwest's ski jumps and was a tournament judge. The tournament was a huge success; twenty-five thousand spectators caused a huge traffic jam, and the last cars arrived just before the end of the jumping. *Ty A. Brown/Jerry Numbers, Libby Collection.*

Opposite, bottom: The 700-foot-long Wandermere hill had a thirty-four-degree angle of steepness, for jumps up to 185 feet. *Ty A. Brown/Nu Art Studio of Spokane, Lawrence Numbers.*

Above: A competitor finishes his jump at the 1933 Spokane Ski Club tournament, watched by thousands of spectators. *Ty A. Brown/Jerry Numbers, Libby Collection.*

Invitations were accepted by every major ski club in the Northwest, giving the club a "brilliant representation at its opening tournament." Two Seattle experts were judges: Peter Hostmark and Allen Granstrom. Because of the lack of snow, unemployed men were hired to haul snow in from surrounding areas and spread it over a layer of straw on the landing hill. Huge piles of hay were placed at the end to stop the jumpers. The tournament was a resumption of "the tremendous jumping rivalry which has thrilled a dozen skiing crowds" between Nordal Kaldahl and John Elvrum. Kaldahl spent the summer "in rigorous training working in the Canadian woods and playing soccer every Sunday," according to the

Seattle Times of January 13, 1933. The tournament was a huge success, with twenty-five thousand spectators causing a huge traffic jam—the last cars arrived just before the end of the jumping.

A strong crosswind handicapped the competitors. Class A jumpers used the Class B jump for their first jump but could use the big jump for their second. Elvrum had the longest jump, but Kaldhal won the tournament on form points, a decision that upset the jumper from Portland so much that he skipped the Pacific Northwest Championship tournament on Snoqualmie Pass later that year. The Spokane Ski Club was admitted into the Pacific Northwest Ski Association two weeks after its first tournament.[66]

Tom Mobraaten made his debut at the Portland Winter Sports Carnival at Mount Hood, winning the jumping event against a "brilliant Northwest field." Hjalmar Hvam was second but won the combined cross-country and jumping title.[67]

In January 1933, the Seattle Ski Club's Third Pacific Northwestern Ski Association Championship Tournament at Beaver Lake featured cross-country racing and ski jumping. The *Seattle Times* noted, "Field caliber

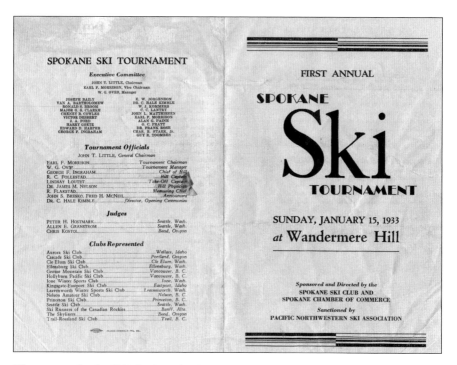

The program for the 1933 Spokane Ski Club tournament shows that every major ski club in the Northwest sent competitors, providing a "brilliant representation." *Maybo family, CWU.*

highest noted in this nation…making the skiing world eye the tournament with amazement." Of the fifty-four Northwest entrants, four "rank high in the national yearbook.…Nowhere, it seems, this side of Norway, are there so many able skiers, not even in the northern Middle-Western states." Spectators were told that "heavy clothing and boots are recommended. French heels on feminine shoes are discouraged, and dancing pumps aren't at all successful." Snoqualmie Summit was a two-hour drive from Seattle, and the jumping venue was "a trifle less than a mile from the Summit, up a well packed trail."

The tournament was swept by the "Three Musketeers" of British Columbia in front of four thousand spectators. The Class A event was won by Nordal Kaldahl, the "iron-muscled" jumper who showed nearly perfect form in his jumps of 159 and 185 feet. Tom Mobraaten finished second in the jumping, followed by Henry Solvedt. Portland's Hjalmar Hvam won the cross-country event, followed by Mobraaten, who won the combined jumping and cross-country title. John Elvrum did not compete, as he "was irked by the ruling of the Spokane judges during the big tournaments two weeks ago which awarded the championship to Nordal Kaldahl over the Norwegian star."[68]

New Leavenworth Jump

The 1933 Leavenworth tournament showed off the club's new big jump on what was later named Bakke Hill. Hermod Bakke, a Norwegian immigrant who moved to Leavenworth in 1932, "redesigned the big hill in Leavenworth," working "day and night for two days of back breaking work to prepare the hill, and then jumped at the Leavenworth meet the next day." The new hill was built to the "exact specifications of the famous Lake Placid slide in New York State" and paralleled the old hill. After four successful tournaments, the club "discarded its old hill [and] built a new one.…With a critical point of 73 meters, it was one of the largest ski jumps of the whole country." The old jump was

> *a perfect form hill…but this year's is another—a new one fifty feet removed from the old, with a longer, steeper landing slope and a higher takeoff.… The hill is 375 feet high from the start to the bottom of the landing slope, or as high as an average thirty-story building. It is possible for a jump of 300 feet to be completed. Possible, not probable, as the world's record is 267 feet.*

The Leavenworth hill is one jumpers and spectators will love, being right on the edge of town. "There's a 100-yard walk to it. All other hills in the Northwest entail some hiking."[69]

The tournament's entry list included "practically every Class A and B jumper in the Northwest…which gives Leavenworth the finest field of jumpers in America." The field could outscore those jumping at the national championships—"the Northwest has that many good tournament skiers." John Elvrum, "the Babe Ruth of Northwest skiing," had overjumped three hills the prior year, "breaking three sets of skis and cracking up himself each time." Many predicted that he would not come back to compete in 1933, but "they figured not on the Portland jumper's hardiness. Not only did he come back, but he jumped better than ever before this winter."[70]

Two of the Three Musketeers from Vancouver took the top places. Tom Mobraaten "defeated a magnificent crowd [of five thousand] on a magnificent hill," beating forty-two competitors. Henry Solvedt was second and Haakon Albinson of the Ellensburg Ski Club third. The anticipated Elvrum-Kaldahl battle was not a factor, as both spilled. However, Elvrum jumped 201 feet, which was a new hill record and was the longest jump in the country in 1933. Peter Hostmark, PNSA judge, said that "those jumps gave verification to your claim that here in the Northwest lies the bulk of the skiing talent in America."[71]

Last Cle Elum Tournament

For its tenth annual tournament in 1933, the Cle Elum Ski Club arranged for trucks to take spectators to within five city blocks of the jump. The tournament's program included a description of how ski jumping was judged and information regarding the club's new jump. Competitors get two jumps in the event and are judged first for form and then for distance, each rating being equal:

> *Form is based on correct ski position from the time the skier leaves the top of the tower until he passes the flags at the end of the course. A jumper's skis, in the air, should be close together, parallel, in the same plane and gradually become parallel to the landing slope also. In a perfect leap every movement of the jumper shows complete mastery of his body and skis at all times.*

Cle Elum Ski Club, Inc.
Tenth Annual Tournament
Sunday, February 19, 1933

SKI CLUB
CLE ELUM, WASH.

Competing Clubs

CASCADE SKI CLUB	Portland, Oregon
CLE ELUM SKI CLUB	Cle Elum, Wash.
ELLENSBURG SKI CLUB	Ellensburg, Wash.
GROUSE MOUNTAIN SKI CLUB	Vancouver, B. C.
HOLLYBURN SKI CLUB	Vancouver, B. C.
LEAVENWORTH WINTER SPORTS CLUB	Leavenworth, Wash.
SEATTLE SKI CLUB	Seattle, Wash.
SKYLINERS	Bend, Oregon
VANCOUVER SKI CLUB	Vancouver, B. C.

Left: The program for the 1933 Cle Elum tournament listed the nine Northwest ski clubs that sent members to compete. *Maybo family, CWU.*

Below: Cle Elum's 1933 program described how ski jumpers were scored and the history of its giant new jumping hill. *Maybo family, CWU.*

CLASS B—JUMPING

NAME	CLUB	1st	2nd
John Leed	Princeton		
Robert Hvam	Cascade		
John Anderson	Cascade		
Myron E. Jones	Cascade		
Ernest Wintenute	Grouse Mountain		
Jack Abramson	Grouse Mountain		
M. Billingsley	Vancouver		
Wally Baker	Vancouver		
Mickey Mitchell	Vancouver		
Fred Zevart	Cle Elum		
Pete Marta	Cle Elum		
Chester Laurent	Cle Elum		
Leif Flak	Seattle		
Arvid Helby	Seattle		
Martin Tverdal	Seattle		
Laddie Plouse	Cle Elum		
J. Bird	Leavenworth		
Bjorne Paulson	Skyliners		
Olaf Skjersaa	Skyliners		
Ole Ring	Skyliners		
Einar Hermansen	Cascade		
Herman Fahner	Cascade		
Dwight Bradshaw	Ellensburg		
Carl Solberg	Ellensburg		
Erling Johnson	Leavenworth		
Walter Anderson	Leavenworth		
Benton Alley	Leavenworth		
Halvor Hagen	Ione		
Reibar Aspaas	Ione		
Swen Hansen	Ione		
Jack Hays	Yakima		

HOW SKI JUMPING IS SCORED

All jumpers are scored on each of the two jumps but the longest jumps do not necessarily win the contest. The jump is judged, first, for form, and second, for distance. Each rates equally. Form is based on correct ski position from the time the skier leaves the top of the tower until he passes the flags at the end of the course. A jumper's skis, in the air, should be close together, parallel, in the same plane, and gradually become parallel to the landing slope also. In a perfect leap every movement of the jumper shows complete mastery of his body and skis at all times.

Interesting Information Regarding Cle Elum's New Ski Hill

Cle Elum's new Ski Hill was reconstructed during the summer and fall of 1931 at the cost of $5,000, to give the hill a "perfect curve" that would permit distance leaps in safety. To achieve this goal, 120,000 feet of lumber and 60,000 feet of rustic timber procured on the grounds were necessary in the construction of bridge work below the take-off in addition to building of a tower 117 feet higher in elevation than the take-off., The bridge gives a perfect parabolic curve with a pitch of 38 to 43 degrees at the point the jumper alights to glide down the runway. The width of the bridge work is 68 feet at this point to insure safety.

The tower has a pitch of 46 degrees decreasing to 15 degrees as it nears the take-off. The timber for this work was donated by the Northwestern Improvement Co., shippers of the famous Cle Elum-Roslyn coal.

The best place to view the Jumping Events is from the plateau below the take-off. Follow the trail from the lodge, indicated by the signs.

PRIZES

Tournament prizes will be awarded at the Hotel Travelers Banquet at 5:30, Sunday evening, on the day of the Tournament.

The tournament program continued, noting that the ski hill was reconstructed in 1931 at a cost of $5,000, donated by local merchants, and using 120,000 feet of lumber and 60,000 feet of timber from the site. The hill had "a perfect curve" to permit long jumps in safety. A tower 117 feet higher than the takeoff was built, with a pitch of forty-six degrees, decreasing to fifteen degrees as it nears the takeoff. A 68-foot-wide bridge below the takeoff gave a "perfect parabolic curve with a pitch of 38 to 43 degrees at the point the jumper alights to glide down the runway."

A four-way fight was expected between Nordal Kadahl and John Elvrum, who battled each other all year, and Vancouver's Tom Mobraaten and Henry Solvedt. However, a winter storm and gusty wind interfered with the tournament. "The biggest ski hill in the United States drew only 2,500 spectators in near blizzard conditions." The takeoff was judged too dangerous, so the takeoff nose was broken down to make the jump safer. Nordal Kaldahl won the event in spite of gale-force winds that "made

Spectators on the difficult two-mile uphill hike from Cle Elum to the ski jumping site, 1933. The unwillingness of spectators to make the hard trek to the summit was one of the main reasons the ski club abandoned the hill. *Maybo family, CWU.*

A blizzard and high winds at the 1933 Cle Elum tournament caused officials to modify the jump's takeoff to make it safer. *Maybo family, CWU.*

skiers clutch the hand rail at the top." Henry Solvedt was second and Ole Tverdal third.[72]

The 1933 tournament was the Cle Elum Ski Club's last. Competition had increased as new ski clubs formed, and the difficulty in getting from Cle Elum to its jump, an arduous thirty- to forty-minute uphill walk, was an insurmountable obstacle. "The unwillingness of spectators to make the hard trek to the Summit was the reason the ski club abandoned the hill."[73]

"Girl Ski Jumpers"

Female ski jumpers made the news in 1933, the first time since Olga Bolstad took the Northwest by storm in the 1920s. Johanna Kolstad, a nineteen-year-old "Norway ski girl," who was "the holder of numerous women's ski-jumping titles," had "performed creditably against men in Norway, but banning of mixed contests there caused her to come to the United States for competition." Kolstad arrived here in October 1932 and participated at the Norge Ski Tournament in early 1933, where she jumped 125, 136 and 128 feet in an exhibition.[74]

The Pacific Northwestern Ski Association allowed Kolstad to compete at the Pacific Northwest Championships:

> *And now, into that extremely masculine sport of ski-jumping, drops two fair damsels! Johanne Kolstad and Hilda Baskerud, 19 years old each, startled conventional Oslo by entering the tournament in that Norwegian*

"Girl ski jumpers" show off at the 1930 Leavenworth Winter Sports Club tournament. *Lee Pickett photo, UW Special Collections.*

CAN SHE JUMP!

Johanna Kolstad, Norwegian girl ski jumper, was the exhibition star at yesterday's Seattle Ski Club annual home tournament at Summit, Snoqualmie Pass. She made leaps of 118 feet twice with a shortened takeoff and in sticky snow.

Brushing Up Their Technique
* * *　　* * *　　* * *　　* * *
They'll Take Big Jump, Soon

Left: "Girl ski jumper" Johanna Kolstad making an exhibition jump at 1933 Seattle Ski Club tournament. *From the* Seattle Times, *March 13, 1933.*

Right: Seattle Ski Club women ski jumpers ready for the club's tournament at Beaver Lake. *From the* Seattle Times, *February 19, 1931.*

> *city. Tournament officials permitted them to compete. They placed in the final standings. But the shock to Ski Officialdom was too much. They were barred from later competition with their masculine rivals....Girl ski jumpers, even in Norway, are very rare. It's particularly a male sport, and a dangerous one. Girls don't fit in it too well.*[75]

The tournament would include "girls' and women's gliding," but only Kolstad appeared, and she made an exhibition jump. Ole Tverdal won the tournament, beating Tom Mobraaten, Nordal Kaldahl, Helge Sather and Henry Solvedt. Johanna Kolstad later appeared at the Cascade Ski Club's annual tournament on Mount Hood, making exhibition jumps of 131 and 130 feet. In April, Kolstad leaped 152 feet and tied for first place in tournament at Mount Shasta.[76]

The Cle Elum Ski Club, Seattle Ski Club and Leavenworth Winter Sports Club had women ski jumpers, but they were not allowed to compete in tournaments.

Chapter 4

1934–1936

Ski Jumping Grows in Popularity but Is Challenged by the Emergence of Alpine Skiing

The Spokane Ski Club's 1934 tournament at Wandermere presented "a scene more suggestive of spring than winter." Six carloads of snow were imported from the Cascades on Great Northern trains, and 250 truckloads were transported to the jumping site. Nordal Kaldahl did not compete, but his rival was there. John Elvrum, "who jumps as if he had steel springs in his legs and wings at his shoulders blades," won the club's second tournament, "fighting cross-winds that even aviators took notice of yesterday, winds that flipped aloft the slats of many less agile jumpers." Elvrum was followed by Vancouver's Tom Mobraaten and Henry Solvedt and Leavenworth's Hermod Bakke and Helge Sather.[77]

The Seattle Ski Club's Fourth Annual Jumping Championship at Snoqualmie Summit in early February 1934 featured ski jumping, a cross-country race and the first slalom race sanctioned by the Pacific Northwestern Ski Association, showing that Alpine skiing was becoming popular. There were more than one hundred entrants, despite efforts to limit the field—"We do not need inexperienced jumpers.…Motorists stopped by traffic on the pass should park their machines, purchase tickets from the ticket sellers who follow traffic down the highway, and get free transportation to the Summit in the buses the ski club has retained for the tournament." The jumping competition was won by Henry Solvedt, and Nordal Kaldahl finished second. Tom Mobraaton won the combined racing and jumping championship. Hamish Davidson of Vancouver, British Columbia, won the slalom race featuring thirty-eight competitors, which was "a test of racing skill which

Left: The poster for the 1934 Spokane Ski Club tournament promised "daring jumps by Western champions." *Maybo family, CWU.*

Below: Trucks brought snow that was packed onto the jumping hill for the "snowless" 1934 Spokane Ski Club tournament at Wandermere. *Ty A. Brown/Ziegler family.*

Above: Snoqualmie Pass was crowded by five thousand cars parked on the highway during the 1934 Seattle Ski Club tournament, which featured ski jumping, a cross-country race and the first slalom race sanctioned by the Pacific Northwestern Ski Association. *Washington State Archives.*

Left: Tom Mobraaten of Vancouver, British Columbia, jumping at the 1934 Seattle Ski Club tournament at Beaver Lake, where he won the combined championship. *Wicken, California Ski Library.*

proved to be unexpectedly strenuous and spectacular." Attendance was huge, and there were five thousand cars parked on the highway.[78]

At the 1934 Big Pines California Winter Sports Carnival, distance records were shattered, and two members of the Portland's Cascade Ski Club turned in remarkable performances. John Elvrum won the tournament with a 240-foot jump, a new amateur distance record, bettering the Olympic record by 8 feet and the American record by 16 feet. Roy Mikkelsen of Auburn, California, jumped 234 feet, also breaking both records, and finished second. Hjalmar Hvam placed third and jumped 242 feet in an exhibition, which did not count as a record. The Cascade Ski Club lost its dominant competitor, as Elvrum was offered a job by the Arrowhead Springs Corporation to work at a small ski resort in California's San Bernardino Mountains that later became Snow Valley.[79]

Leavenworth's Annual Pacific Northwest Championship Tournament in 1934 included ski jumping and cross-country racing. The jumping event was held on Leavenworth's "long and steep and dangerous" hill, said to be "the world's most perfect hill" where one could "drive all the way." A lack of snow required "artificial aid," so trucks hauled snow to the ski hill, and the entire community turned out with apple boxes that were filled with snow, hauled up the hill on ropes and dumped on the jump. A conveyor system brought the empty boxes back to the bottom of the hill. Tom Mobraaton swept the tournament, becoming combined champion, Class A jumping champion and cross-country champion. Falls took Nordal Kaldahl and John Elvrum out of contention—Elvrum again overjumped the hill going for distance. Five thousand spectators watched the first "Apple Box Tournament," said to be the "finest competitively and best managed the Northwest has ever seen."[80]

ALPINE SKIING BEGINS TO CHALLENGE SKI JUMPING

By the mid-1930s, Alpine skiing was beginning to grow in popularity, raising concerns that it would displace ski jumping as Washington's premier winter sport.

In January 1934, the Seattle Park Department opened a ski area at Snoqualmie Summit, the Municipal Ski Park, after a Civilian Conservation Corps crew cleared the hill and built a warming hut, making downhill skiing available to the public. Weekly slalom races were held at Paradise

Valley on Mount Rainier, introducing Alpine skiing to the Northwest. In February, the Seattle Ski Club's tournament featured the first slalom race sanctioned by the PNSA, along with ski jumping and cross-country races. The first Silver Skis Race was held on Mount Rainier in April 1934, a virtually uncontrolled downhill from Camp Muir at 10,000 feet to near Paradise Lodge at 5,500 feet—it would become the Northwest's most iconic race. In the spring of 1935, the National Downhill and Slalom Championships and Olympic team tryouts was held on Mount Rainier, attracting the country's best skiers.

In September 1934, the Washington Ski Club was organized to focus on competitive Alpine ski racing and "enter all competitions on the Coast as far as possible." Membership was open to any person over eighteen, "white, and a citizen of the United States of America." The club sponsored most of the competitive Alpine races until World War II.[81] The Pacific Northwest Ski Association amended its bylaws to recognize the "tremendous growth in the popularity of slalom and downhill racing....Slalom and downhill racing are entitled to equal recognition with jumping and cross-country." Alpine skiing was added to the Pacific Northwest championships, and a four-way combination championship would start the following year, with equal weight given to each branch of competition. This was a significant step for the PNSA, whose activities had been limited to Nordic everts.

The PNSA issued a warning about the sport:

> *Unless juniors eager to learn ski jumping of the better variety are located, groomed and developed, ski jumping two or three years from now will go into serious decline.*
>
> *It has become increasingly apparent with the development of slalom and downhill racing that jumping—a fine and daring ski sport, safe only for the most adept—would inevitably decline unless a program were sharply defined to built it up. The bulk of Class A jumping rests with those Norwegian youths comparatively fresh from the old country. Class B has seen casual development among the American born, but not enough.*

Class B events had been held on Class A hills, which were "too severe a test for the younger and more inexperienced jumper. Unwilling to refuse, they took the huge hills, some with a lump in their throats." The coming year, PNSA would encourage slalom and downhill racing, and clubs would construct courses where they have never been before.[82]

The Seattle Ski Club's 1935 tournament at Beaver Lake featured jumping and a slalom race, with parallel courses for men and women that would be "a conditioner for prospective entries in the National downhill and slalom championships at Rainier National Park." Spectators should "[w]ear boots and two pair of woolen socks." The jumping, featuring twenty competitors, was moved from the Big Hill to the Class B hill because of icy conditions. Portland's Hjalmar Hvam won the jumping event, viewed by two thousand spectators. "The brilliant Hermod Bakke of Leavenworth, who doubtless will be sent by the Leavenworth Winter Sports Club to the Olympic jumping trials at Salt Lake March 3, took second." In the slalom, which had forty-eight entrants, Darroch Crookes of the Washington Ski Club won, despite a time handicap due to a missed set of flags.[83]

In April 1935, the National Downhill and Slalom Championships and Olympic tryouts were held on Mount Rainier for men and women, attracting the best skiers in the country. Hannes Schroll, an Austrian teaching at Badger Pass at Yosemite, won the slalom, downhill and combined events, beating the favorite, Dartmouth's Dick Durrance. Sisters from Tacoma won titles—Ellis-Ayr Smith the women's National Downhill title and Ethelynne "Skit" Smith the women's National Slalom title and the Combined National Championship title. A teenager, Gretchen Kunigk from Tacoma, who would later make her mark in ski racing as Gretchen Fraser was "watching in awe from the sidelines."[84]

The 1935 Leavenworth tournament was the PNSA Championship in jumping and cross-country skiing, as well as the sectional Olympic tryouts. The entire town turned out to make the meet successful. Federal funds were used to hire twenty-seven men to work on the hill for twenty-three days; they "perfected the runout at the bottom of the hill. They smoothed it perfectly. We planted ten pounds of dandelion seed on the hill....Our jumpers can jump on four inches of snow," according to the *Seattle Times*.

Washington Ski Club's team included several candidates for the Olympic cross-country trials: Don Fraser, Alf Moystad, Hans Otto Giese and Darroch Crookes. Hermod Bakke won the jumping event with jumps of 200 and 201 feet in a wind that "twisted him from side to side in the air," on a course "where 1,500 pounds of rock salt had broken the ice into a shifting, treacherous bed, and the least sideslope sent jumpers tumbling." He won the right to compete at the Olympic Games tryouts at Salt Lake. Five thousand spectators saw the event, with five hundred coming on a Great Northern special ten-car train that was "jammed to the roof." Vancouver's Henry Solvedt won the eleven-mile cross-country race and

The newspaper shows Leavenworth's Hermod Bakke jump at Beaver Lake in 1935 and discusses the $50,000 WPA plan to make the summit into a major national ski jumping center with a grandstand, a cabin and a 225-foot jump designed by Seattle's Peter Hostmark "comparable to the magnificent ones in Norway." *From the* Seattle Times, *December 8, 1935.*

placed fourth in the jumping, winning the combined title. Don Fraser finished a disappointing tenth in the event's "historic langlauf" or cross-country race. Fraser said that the "Norwegian lads…passed me as though I was standing still" with their "amazing shoulder strength."[85]

At the U.S. Olympic jumping tryouts at Salt Lake City on March 3, 1935, the top four finishers were Sverre Fredheim of Minneapolis; Roy Mikkelsen of Auburn, California; Casper Oimoen of Anaconda, Montana; and Einer Fredbo of Salt Lake City. Northwest jumpers finished out of the money. Helge Sather and Hermod Bakke of Leavenworth finished tenth and eleventh, respectively. Spokane jumpers Arnt Ofstadt and John Ring were twelfth and twentieth, respectively. Hjalmar Hvam fell on both of his jumps.[86]

In 1935 and 1936, the Works Progress Administration discussed plans to spend $50,000 to transform Seattle's Municipal Ski Park on Snoqualmie Pass into one of the country's main ski jumping centers. A 225-foot jumping hill, designed by Peter Hostmark, would be "the most modern one this side of the huge Olympic take-off at Lake Placid, New York," and comparable to the magnificent ones in Norway, with a cabin and a grandstand. Unfortunately, WPA funds were "slashed in 1936 and 1937," and the Snoqualmie project was never built. The image here shows how many skiing-related articles appeared in newspapers in the 1930s.[87]

1936: Winter Olympics in Germany; Sun Valley Opens

The 1936 Olympic Games were held in Garmisch-Partenkirchen, Germany, in February. Showing how strong our skiing was, five Washington skiers went to Europe with the Olympic teams for the games: Seattle's Don Fraser, Darroch Crookes and Grace Carter and Tacoma sisters Ellis-Ayr and Ethelynne Smith. These Olympics featured Alpine skiing for the first time, with a single combined downhill and slalom event, along with the traditional Nordic events. Men and women competed in Alpine events, but only men were allowed in Nordic events.

In the jumping competition, watched by 100,000 spectators, Norway's Birger Ruud won the gold medal, Reidar Andersen won bronze and Sweden's Sven Eriksson took silver. U.S. jumpers finished eleventh (Sverre Fredheim) and twenty-second (Roy Mikkelson). Ruud nearly had an unprecedented double Olympic event win in jumping and Alpine skiing. In the combined dowhilll/slalom event, Birger won the downhill by 4.4 seconds but missed a gate in the slalom and placed fourth, out of medal contention. The U.S. team manager said, "Our men probably tried too hard for distance. Certainly they showed that longer training on the actual hill is necessary when meeting the competition of men who, by aid of much practice under very competent coaching, have developed a nearly flawless style."[88]

The 1936 Leavenworth ski jumping tournament was won by Ivind Nilson of Revelstoke, British Columbia, with his teammate Hans Gunnerson taking second, in front of 5,500 spectators, who braved extreme weather. The Great Northern special train surpassed all records, with fourteen cars "jammed to the doors." The jumps at the tournament were the longest made in the country that year.[89]

On February 13, 1936, a tournament scheduled for Bend, Oregon, was transferred to the Spokane Ski Club because the hill was not completed. Slalom and downhill races were held at the Spokane club's lodge and ski jumping at

Ski-Mor, a small resort on the east side of Browne Mountain. Hjalmar Hvam won the jumping event, defeating Helge Sather and Arnt Ofstad.[90]

The Northwestern Ski Jumping Championships, hosted by the Seattle Ski Club, was dominated "by lads of Norwegian descent," with Nordal Kaldahl, Ivind Nilson and Hans Gunnarson of Canada competing against Hermod Bakke, Heige Sather, Hjalmar Hvan and Ole Tverdal. "Kaldahl is the color of the tournament…of any tournament. A whooping wildman, his performances over a four-year period have been epic." The tournament was postponed after a snow slide closed the Snoqualmie Pass highway, killing two men in a car, burying a bus with twenty passengers (who survived) and derailing a Milwaukee Road train. At the rescheduled event, Hermod Bakke won the combined jumping and cross-country title, and Howard Dalsbo completed "the perfect circle of Northwest Championships" by winning the jumping event.[91]

Norway's 1936 Holmenkollen competition attracted 450 entrants and fifty thousand spectators, including King Haakon VII, Queen Maud and Crown Prince Olaf. Reidar Andersen, Birger Ruud's "compatriot and

Sun Valley's Ruud Mountain ski hill, with a forty-meter jump, was designed by Alf Engen and Sigmund Ruud and built in 1937, with a chairlift for skiers. It was Sun Valley's center for ski jumping and slalom racing. *The Community Library, Ketchum, Idaho.*

Alf Engen shows perfect form while jumping at Sun Valley's Ruud Mountain. *Charles Wanless photo, Engen family, Marriott Library.*

perennial rival…captured the coveted King's Cup." Sweden's Sven Erikksen "just nosed out Ruud for the runner-up position."[92]

In 1936, the Federation Internationale de Ski (FIS) established specifications governing the design of ski hills to establish uniformity throughout the world. It emphasized safety and provided a standard accepted in international competition ever since. Ski jumpers competing in different countries could find predictable hill conditions, taking away home hill advantages.[93]

In December 1936, the Union Pacific Railroad opened its Sun Valley Resort, built for $1,250,000 in the remote mountains of Idaho. It was the pet project of Averell Harriman, UP's board chairman, and was the country's first destination ski resort, with an ultra-modern lodge, chair lifts invented by UP engineers and a ski school with Austrian instructors that made skiing sexy. The resort attracted skiers from all over the world and became the country's skiing center.

In summer 1937, Alf Engen and Sigmund Ruud located and designed a forty-meter ski jump at Sun Valley, and a chairlift was installed on what Harriman named Ruud Mountain. Harriman hired Engen as a sports consultant, which included representing Sun Valley in competitions from 1937 to 1948, where he achieved great success in both Nordic and Alpine events. Engen won the National Amateur Jumping Championships three times, set three national distance records and was the 1937 Canadian national jumping champion and 1946 national open champion. Alf won National Amateur and Open Classic Titles (jumping and cross-country), two National Four-Way Championships (Washington, 1940, and Sun Valley, 1941) and the 1942 National Open Slalom-Downhill Combined. In 1940, Alf was awarded the American Ski Trophy from the National Ski Association. In 1950, he received the Skier of the Century Award. Alf was inducted into the U.S. National Ski and Snowboard Hall of Fame in 1959.

Chapter 5

1937–1938

Norwegians from Kongsberg Dominate Competition; Washington Tournaments Attract the World's Best Jumpers

For the 1937 Cascade Ski Club's tournament on Mount Hood, CCC crews had removed 1,500 cubic yards of dirt to provide a hill that would accommodate 225-foot jumps. John Elvrum won the tournament with jumps of 185 and 183 feet. Elvrum represented the Viking Ski Club of Los Angeles but was a "Norwegian boy who made his name" as a member of the Cascade Ski Club. Harry Tregellus from the Viking Ski Club was second, Leavenworth's Hermod Bakke third and Ole Tverdal of the Seattle Ski Club fourth. The senior event was won by Seattle's Howard Dalsbo.[94]

For Leavenworth's 1937 Northwest Ski Jumping Championship, its "already tremendous ski jump" had been improved to offer a larger maximum capacity while becoming safer. The changes were based on "the latest information on construction of inruns and takeoffs." A new trestle was built for the takeoff, 14 feet back from the crown of the landing slope, raising it 8 feet and increasing the maximum jump from 250 feet to about 265 feet. With a retarded takeoff and an 8-foot higher start, the jump was safer than before. Also, 4 feet were cut off the crown of the landing, opening up the hill for both spectators and jumpers, and a new higher judges' tower was built. "The curve is such that the jumper is making speed from the very start to the takeoff without any loss such as we had before." The Class B tower, inrun and takeoff were "entirely new, built all in one scaffold," according to the *Seattle Times* of January 25, 1937.

LEAVENWORTH

again invites you on the Great Northern Ski Train (on time, this time) to its

INTERNATIONAL SKI JUMPING TOURNAMENT

SUNDAY, FEB. 6

Remember . . . no climbing, no walking; whisked by bus right to the 250-foot hill itself.

Great Northern used a ski jumper to advertise its ski train for Leavenworth's 1937 International Jumping Tournament. *From the* Seattle Times, *November 17, 1937.*

Tournament contestants included Caspar Oimoen of Anaconda, Montana, five-time national champion, 1936 Olympian and holder of the American amateur jumping record of 257 feet; Vancouver's Tom Mobraaten, prior Northwest champion and 1936 Canadian Olympian; Hermod Bakke, defending Northwest champion; Einar Fredbo of Anaconda; and Ole Tverdal of Seattle. "Despite a blinding snowstorm," Spokane's Arnt Ofstad won the championship with jumps of 192 and 186 feet, followed by Einar Fredbo and Leavenworth's Helge Sather, who had the longest jump of the day, 194 feet. The event was watched by 7,000 spectators, including 2,000 from Seattle, 1,800 of whom traveled on three special Great Northern trains with forty-four cars. The railroad had been swamped by the last-minute rush of people wanting to ride the ski trains.[95]

The 1937 National Ski-Jumping Championship tournament on Ecker Hill outside Salt Lake City in February was a memorable one. Eighty-one contestants entered in four classes, including four jumpers from the Northwest: Arnt Ofstad of Spokane, Ole Tverdal of the Seattle Ski Club and Helge Sather and Hermod Bakke of Leavenworth. The four would get the thrill of their lives, jumping against Norway's Sigmund Ruud, who had jumped "the unbelievable distance of 324 feet," as well as other Norwegian stars. According to the *Seattle Times*:

Five young Norsemen will resume, in the tense atmosphere of a national ski-jumping tournament tomorrow, a friendly rivalry they left off as boys in Norway more than ten years ago. Since the days when they skimmed together down the steep slopes outside of Oslo, the five separately reached top ranking in the sport. Four of them have won trophies in hundreds of tourneys in their adopted America, and the fifth, still a resident of Norway, holds the unofficial world ski-jump record.

The five Norsemen were Sigmund Ruud (1928 Olympic silver medal winner, one of the world's greatest jumpers), Alf Engen (national champion), Sigurd Ulland (California champion), Roy Mikkelson (1935 national champion and 1936 U.S. Olympic team member) and Einar Fredbo (national champion runner-up in 1935). Sigmund Ruud came from Norway "to see if the boys could jump like they used to when they were small." The five would have plenty of competition from George Kotlarek of Duluth, Minnesota, present champion, and two-score jumpers of similar caliber.[96]

"Winner Forced to Record Leap in Close Battle" in "the greatest ski jumping duel in American history," said the *Seattle Times*. Alf Engen defeated Sigmund Ruud "by the extremely thin margin of 226.3 points to 224.6, but he had to set a new American competitive distance record of 245 feet to do it." Engen broke the 242-foot record set by John Elvrum in 1934. The margin between Ruud and Engen was in distance, as Ruud outscored Engen on form. Einar Fredbo was third, Sverre Fredheim fourth and Sigurd Ulland fifth. Hermod Bakke was the highest Northwest finisher at eighth: "The Engen jump was a masterpiece of symmetrical power....When his skis touched the snow and his feet instinctively shifted to the telemark position he used to regain balance, there wasn't a perceptible margin between the landing hill and dip....Only a great jumper could have ridden it." After the tournament, Engen said the highlight was "to have been able to watch Sigmund Ruud ski" and described the life of a ski jumper:

> *It's just plain work, mixed with thrills induced by the knowledge that you might break your neck at any time. It's fun jumping even as far as 200 feet. But when you try to go any farther than that, the possibility of serious injury is so great that most of the joy is taken out of the sport. But still, when you get by the first two or three tournaments of the season, you become used to it—and well—I guess I get a kick out of it anyway.*

The Ruud/Engen competition would continue at the Seattle Ski Club tournament in March.[97]

However, in August 1937, the National Ski Association announced that outdated distance sheets were used at the National Ski Jumping Championships and that a study of the sheets found an error. Sigmund Ruud was the national champion instead of Alf Engen.[98]

The Seattle Ski Club's 1937 tournament at Beaver Lake was a showdown of jumpers from Kongsberg, Norway, who would "wage such a duel as Norway would enjoy." Entrants included Alf Engen (national ski jumping champion, who had broken more records in America than any other skier and had jumped 287 feet), Sigmund Ruud ("one of the greatest skiers ever offered the world by that skiing nation," who had jumped 334 feet), Sverre Kolterud ("greatest four-way combined skier in the world"), Tom Mobraaten (Canadian Champion), Hjalmar Hvam (former National combined champion), Corey Gustafsson from Portland and Nordal Kaldahl from Wells, British Columbia. The *Seattle Times* noted:

> *The Ruud-Engen-Hvam-Kaldahl-Kolterud rivalry will live long. The Kongsberg jumping style—grand form plus great distance—had been made famous through two generations. It is particularly distinctive. It calls for pronounced forward lean, a distinctive arching of the body from the hips… aerodynamic jumping, the technicians call it…something like a glider leaving a hill, to soar.*

Above: Leavenworth's Helge Sather jumps at the 1937 Seattle Ski Club tournament at Beaver Lake, where California's Sigurd Ulland beat Sun Valley's Alf Engen for the title. *Wicken, California Ski Library.*

Opposite: Skiers pack Beaver Lake's jumping hill for the next competitor at a Seattle Ski Club ski tournament. *Wicken, California Ski Library.*

Alf Engen had the longest jumps and set a new hill record of 210 feet, but Sigmund Ruud won the tournament on form points. Sverre Kolterud finished second, followed by Engen, Ole Tverdal of Seattle, Helge Sather of Lynwood, Arni Ofstad of Spokane and Hjalmar Hvam. The "greatest ski jumping tournament the Seattle Ski Club has ever held" was watched by three thousand spectators.[99]

After the tournament, the competitors performed exciting exhibition jumps, freed from the rigors of being judged on their performances, but the "exhibition double jumps gave the crowd more of a thrill than it wished." Sigmund Ruud and Sverre Kolterud performed a spectacular double exhibition jump of 217 feet. Ruud's speed "was tremendous," and he was thrown toward the crowd when he landed. Ruud "threw himself flat on the snow, skidding, ski-first into a woman spectator. She had the wind knocked out of her, but recovered." Ruud had only torn ligaments. Hjalmar Hvam was also hurt doing a double jump with Tom Mobraaten, when he "fell hard, hit his face with his ski and suffered cuts on his forehead and nose."[100]

OLAV ULLAND MOVES TO SEATTLE TO COACH SKI JUMPING

In 1937, the Pacific Northwestern Ski Association arranged for the Norwegian Ski Association to send one of its top ski skiers to coach Washington's young jumpers. Norway's famous ski jumper Olav Ulland was selected and came to Seattle in late December 1937, initially on a four-month visa. He taught ski jumping for the Seattle Ski Club and Leavenworth Winter Sports Club and competed in tournaments.

Ulland was from Kongsberg, the ski jumping capital of the world, and began jumping at age four. He competed for Norway from 1929 to 1936, placing high in a number Holmenkollen tournaments, setting a hill record of 50.5 meters in 1930. He won a number of titles in the early 1930s and was on the 1932 Norwegian Olympic team, although he was hurt and did not compete. Olav was the first to break the 100-meter mark by jumping 103 meters at Ponte di Legno, Italy, in 1935. He coached the Italian team at the 1936 Olympics. Olav's brother Sigurd Ulland moved to the United States in the late 1920s, moved to California in 1930 and in 1932 joined a professional ski tour with Alf Engen and others. Sigurd became one of the country's most successful ski jumpers.

Olav Ulland became a member of the Seattle Ski Club and a mainstay of Northwest skiing. He was inducted into the U.S. Ski and Snowboard Hall of Fame in 1981, "remembered as an outstanding ski jumper who set records, ski jumping coach, official and promoter and a skiing retailer who was at the founding of the key organizations in the industry," according to his bio in the U.S. Ski and Snowboard Hall of Fame. He was also inducted into the Washington Sports Hall of Fame and the Northwest Ski Hall of Fame.

1938: Ruud Brothers Tour the Country

As a demonstration of Norwegians' dominance of ski jumping, Birger and Sigmund Ruud toured the United States in the winter of 1938 to promote ski equipment in the American market. The tour was so significant that it was the subject of a master's thesis by Kristofer Moen Helgrude for the University of Oslo in 2003: "Are Norwegian Americans 'Born on Skis'?: Exploring the Role of Skiing in North America Ethnic Identity in the 1930s through the Adventures of Sigmund and Birger Ruud."

Birger was called the world and Olympic jumping champion—his record "is nothing short of amazing." The *Salt Lake City Tribune* noted that the Ruuds were "mighty little men…who had the precision of machines," and if they became any better, they would no longer be classified as "genus homo." The *American Ski Annual* of 1938–39 noted that of all foreign skiers who competed in this country's tournaments, "Birger and Sigmund Ruud… deserve credit for having done more toward developing, promoting, and stimulating the American people to be ski minded, than any other skiers in the world." Both brothers were inducted into the U.S. Ski and Snowboard Hall of Fame in 1970.

The Ruuds participated in eight exhibitions and tournaments all over the country, including the Seattle Ski Club's tournament at Snoqualmie Summit in March. At Fox River Grove, Illinois, the brothers jumped in front of thirty thousand spectators, and fifty-seven thousand attended a night exhibition at Chicago's Soldier Field. The First Annual Southern California Open Ski Meet was held at the Los Angeles Memorial Coliseum. A giant ski jump was built from a web of steel that soared 60 feet above the Coliseum's rim and a long wooden runway with a forty-degree pitch, designed for 170-foot jumps. Ice was ground up to make snow, which was packed on the runway. Birger and Sigmund took first and second in front of twenty thousand spectators.[101]

A giant ski jump is being built at the Los Angeles Memorial Coliseum, where Birger and Sigmund Ruud competed in 1938. *Wicken, California Ski Library.*

Spokane's "snowless" tournament of 1938 was held at Wandermere, sponsored by the Wandermere Ski Association. The jump had been improved by adding a 40-foot tower to increase the speed from the starting point, and the landing zone was extended to improve the crash zone. Spokane's snowless winter made conditions challenging, with "a barren hillside on which imported snow and cracked ice had been packed for the jump. A strong and gusty cross wind almost blew the jumpers from the thirty-foot path, banked with sand on either side and provided with a pile of straw at the end." Alf Engen won the competition "under most trying conditions," with a long jump of 177 feet, in front of eight thousand spectators. Following Engen were John Leed, Copper Mountain, British Columbia; Tom Mobraaten, Princeton, British Columbia; Ole Tverdahl, Vancouver, British Columbia; and Hermod Bakke, Leavenworth.[102]

Reidar Gjolme's two sons (Reidar Jr. and Harold, known as "Tass") showed that they were jumpers with a future. In 1938, Tass Gjolme won the High School Championship tournament and the Leavenworth High School tournament, and the Gjolme brothers led Garfield High School to its fourth consecutive skiing championship. Hans Otto Giese, who was in charge of ski tournaments for Seattle high school students, said, "Those boys…are getting better. Much better."[103]

In 1938, Leavenworth's ski jump was called the "greatest in the Pacific Northwest." Fourteen Class A jumpers entered the tournament, including Birger Ruud (world champion); members of the 1936 Olympic team Casper Oimoen (five-time national jumping champion) and Jimmy Hendrickson; and Sigurd and Olav Ulland, "Norway's first team." Three Great Northern trains brought 1,500 spectators from Seattle and Everett to the tournament. More than 5,000 spectators watched Sigurd Ulland win the event with a long jump of 233 feet, beating Birger Ruud and his "famed brother Olav." *Seattle Times* ski writer Ken Binns said that Leavenworth was crammed so full of people for the tournament that "when you try to eat, you may be taking someone else's ham sandwich."[104]

The 1938 National Ski Jumping Championships in Brattlesboro, Vermont, were won by Sigurd Ulland of the Lake Tahoe Ski Club, "one of the all-time jumpers and current world title holder," who beat "a sparkling

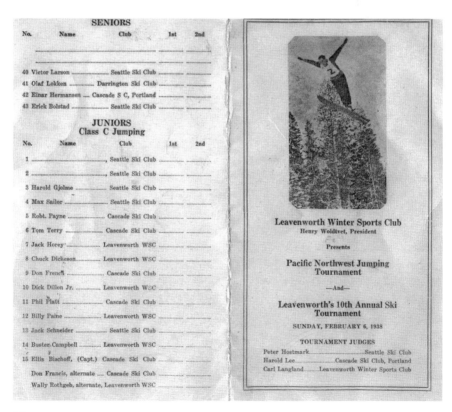

This program used at the 1938 Leavenworth tournament listed the young jumpers who competed in the Class C event. *Ty A. Brown.*

BIRGER RUUD TO JUMP AT SUMMIT

Eyes Closed, Head Down, Sigurd Soars

Ulland Wins Leavenworth Tournament

Where Leavenworth left off yesterday on its huge jumping hill, Seattle Ski Club picks up today with an announcement designed to startle even the most blase of skiers:—

Birger Ruud, world's champion, will headline its jumping list, March 6, at Summit, Snoqualmie Pass!

He and his brother, Sigmund, will jump, too, against the man who won yesterday's Leavenworth competition in blinding snow—Sigurd Ulland of Lake Tahoe, Calif., brother of Olav, the sensational jumper who is teaching Northwest juveniles how to jump.

It was a typical Leavenworth tournament yesterday . . . typical in its preparation and its performance.

Five thousand saw it. But they saw the Class A competition through a snowy blur. Snow began to fall at the conclusion of the B competition, won by Ed Martinson of Darrington; and as the crowd climbed slowly to the master hill, it came down heavier.

Ulland, in defeating his famed brother and winning the Class A championship with amazing leaps of 233 and 230 feet, was jumping blind, literally.

When he pushed off at the start for the high-speed descent to the takeoff, he timed his run and closed his eyes.

When he thought it about time to reach the takeoff, he opened his eyes against the bite of the flying snow long enough to take a powerful leap.

When he was in the air, he closed his eyes again.

When he thought he was about ready to land, he opened them.

On both jumps, he was scarcely a yard above the snow when he opened his eyes to see just where he was.

His style was powerful and beautiful. On form points, the three judges—Peter Hostmark, Harold Lee and Carl Langland, scored him high.

Second award went to Einar Fredbo, Seattle Ski Club, third place winner in last year's national championship at Ecker Hill, Salt Lake.

His unique beauty of form, and two jumps of 216 and 200 feet, put

LEAVENWORTH RESULTS

CLASS A

	1st Jmp.	2nd Jmp.	Points
S. Ulland, Lake Tahoe	233	230	226.75
Einar Fredbo, Seattle	216	200	212.60
Olaf Ulland, Norway	209	190	213.45
O. Tverdal, Seattle	220	192	210.70
Caspar Oimoen, Anconia	209	203	207.85
H. Bakke, Leavenworth	200	176	202.65
J. Hendrickson, Wiscon.	216	161	198.80
H. Sather, Leavenworth	209	189	195.70
Arnt Ofstad, Spokane	194	146	195.60
T. Knudsen, Darrington	179	142	191.50
Leif Flak, Seattle	188	125	189.50
Art Granstrom, Spokane	161	139	180.20
O. Skjersaa, Bend, S. L.	170	110	176.60
Jesse Baird, Leavnwth.	101-F	..	..

EXHIBITION

Otto Lang, Seattle	114	92	..
Hjalmar Hvam, Cascade	188	110	..

CLASS B RESULTS

Ed Martinson, Dar.	110	111	214.4
Dan Kjosnos, Leaven.	98	101	205.0
John Magnussen, Seat.	101	97	204.1
Ole Amoth, Bend S. L.	96	107	203.1
Elton Blaiser, W. S.	100	99	201.5
Walter Hagen, Wand.	105	107	199.9
Dave Anderson, Wand.	101	97	196.2
Martin Tverdal, Seattle	101	92	194.5
Reidar Gjolme, Seattle	93	96	193.3
E. Klinger, W. S. C.	91	99	192.7
A. Johnson, Norheim	84	81	177.3
O. Rotegaard, Cascade	105	102-F	156.
John Ellertson, Dar.	108	113-F	156.
Cecil Morris, Cascade	100	93-F	129.8
B. Oppegaard, Leaven.	203	100	129.3
J. Melby, unattached	89	96-F	128.6
Roy Nerland, Seattle	100-F	..	..
Knute Frolich, Seattle	101-F	..	..
F. Zetsvelse, Ellensburg	101-F	..	..
C. Zevart, Ellensburg	96-F	..	..
Joe Leif, Darrington	101-F	..	..
Ted Rystad, Norheim	107-F	..	..
E. Pasquan, Cle Elum	96-F	..	..
O. Bettine, Cle Elum	91-F	..	..
R. Folestad, Jr., Seat.	89-F	..	..
Birger Rian, Seattle	81-F	..	..
Otto Rosand, Wand.	101-F	..	..

JUNIOR RESULTS

C. Dickenson, Lavnwth.	81	90	215.5
Harold Gjolme, Seattle	73	81	205.1
D. Dillon, Jr., Leaven.	73	76	194.8
Jack Scheleider, Seattle	70	76	188.2
B. Campbell, Leaven.	73	71	187.7
J. Horey, Leav.-W. S. C.	64	70	183.6
H. Hansen, Bremerton	67	70	181.4
Billy Payne, Leaven.	73	73	179.7
Max Sather, Seattle	64	67	166.
Dan French, Cascade	52	53	148.6
Ellis Bishoff, Cascade	49	50	148.5
Charles Boggs, Leaven.	43	48	140.1
Tom Terry, Cascade	43	44	134.5
Phil Platt, Cascade	43	62	120.1
Wally Rothgeb, Leaven.	67	76-F	112.0

SENIOR RESULTS

Victor Larsen, Seattle	113	116-F	163.0
Erik Bolstad, Seattle	107-F	107	116.5
O. Lokken, Darrington	100-F	116	82.

F—Fell.
*Jumped outside the competition.

Sun Apollo Takes Caliente Feature

AGUA CALIENTE RACE TRACK, Mexico, Monday, Feb. 7.—(AP)—Sun Apollo and Full Tilt fought it out in the stretch in the $800 El Cajon Handicap yesterday with Sun Apollo crossing the wire to win by a nose. The Darb was third. The race was over a mile and 70 yards and was run in 1:46.4. Sun Apollo paid $4.20, $3.60 and $3.

Unable to hold his eyes open against the beating of a heavy fall of snow, Sigurd Ulland of Lake Tahoe, Calif., still jumped powerfully at Leavenworth yesterday, to distances of 233 and 230 feet and the Leavenworth championship. He closed his eyes when he started, opened them on the takeoff, closed them in the air, opened them as he was about to land, far down the slope.—A. P. photo.

News of Sigurd Ulland's win at the 1938 Leavenworth tournament is overwhelmed by news that Birger Ruud would compete at Beaver Lake. *From the* Seattle Times, *February 7, 1938.*

international field." Ulland set a new hill record of 214 feet, breaking Alf Engen's mark of 212 feet set three years before. Birger Ruud, who was ineligible to compete for the amateur title because he promoted ski equipment, scored the highest in the meet and won the National FIS open championship, followed by Ulland. Third was a tie between Paul Bietila,

University of Wisconsin skier, and Sverre Fredheim of the Central Ski Association. Alf Engen of Sun Valley was fourth. Bietila's finish, just behind the Ruud brothers, was impressive since he was still a college student. Bietila was one of three famous brothers born in Ishpeming, Michigan, who competed on equal terms with the Norwegians. Paul was tragically killed in a jumping accident in 1939. All three Bietila brothers were later inducted into the U.S. Ski and Snowboard Hall of Fame.[105]

California's Sigurd Ulland (Olav's older brother), the 1938 national jumping champion, often competed in Washington. *Wicken, California Ski Library.*

The Ruud brothers were the big attraction at Washington's biggest event of the year, Seattle Ski Club's Championship tournament at Snoqualmie Summit, featuring a "truly an amazing field of jumpers." The Seattle Ski Club had previously attracted "mighty fine skybusters," but never any "whose names were as great as the Ruud brothers," according to the *Seattle Times* of March 7, 1938.

Seven of the sixteen jumpers in the Class A contest were from Kongsberg and proudly displayed white *K*s on their red sweaters, a symbol of their hometown: Birger and Sigmund Ruud, Olav and Sigurd Ulland, Rolf Syverrtsen, Tom Mobraaten and Hjalmar Hvam. Several of them were raised within a block of one another. Nels Eie also entered, a "powerful jumper" and world intercollegiate champion who out-jumped Birger in the Eastern Championships earlier in the year. Alf Engen had set the hill's record of 210 feet the prior year. Milwaukee Road ran special trains to its Hyak stop, and buses brought passengers back to Snoqualmie Summit, where a crowd of ten thousand could be handled.

Sigmund Ruud said that he and his brother had jumped in seven tournaments around the country, "and this one will be the first on natural snow. They had to haul it in every place else." Since Birger's name had been used to endorse ski equipment, he was not an amateur, so the tournament had to be an "open" one to allow him to compete. Three times before in international competition, Birger received perfect scores of 20 in tournaments, which was unheard of.[106] Matt Broze was one of the competitors at the 1938 tournament. He competed in a number of tournaments through the Northwest, winning the 1940 Silver Skis race on Mount Rainier. His son, Matt Broze, provided the photographs seen here, taken by his father at the 1938 event.

Top: Birger Ruud waxes his skis at the 1938 Seattle Ski Club tournament at Beaver Lake. *Matt V. Broze family.*

Bottom: Sigmund Ruud and his brother Birger were the stars at the 1938 Seattle Ski Club tournament. *Matt V. Broze family.*

Birger Ruud won the Seattle Ski Club tournament with point scores of 19 and 19.5 out of a possible 20 points, under very difficult conditions—more treacherous than the judges had seen in years. The Big Hill was "cold to the point where skis failed to break the crust on either the in-run to the take-off, or the out-run to the flat." At the end of his "meteoric" descents in front of four thousand spectators, Birger "didn't come to a casual, christying stop. No. He somersaulted." Olav Ulland was second and Sigmund Ruud third, barely beating Einar Fredbo, "Seattle Ski Club's great stylist." After the tournament, the Ruud brothers "topped the greatest day in Seattle Ski Club history with a perfect double jump, both off the takeoff together, and landing in unison, 196 feet down the hill."[107]

Above: After Birger Ruud made a flawless jump to win the 1938 Beaver Lake tournament, he "didn't come to a casual, christying stop....He somersaulted." *MOHAI.*

Right: Birger and Sigmund Ruud entertained the crowd by doing a double jump after the 1938 Beaver Lake tournament ended. *From the* Seattle Times, *March 7, 1938.*

THE RUUDS LOOK DOWN ON THE CASCADES

That is Sigmund 'Ruud, left; three times a member of the Norwegian Olympic team; and that is Birger Ruud, right, twice Olympic
Games winner and last year's champion ski jumper. They did
a double jump at Big Hill, Summit, yesterday, after Birger had won
the club's jumping championship. They jumped 196 feet.—A. P. photo

Olav Ulland and Nils Eie performed another double jump at Beaver Lake, 1938. *Matt V. Broze family.*

During the 1938 tournament, several competitors stayed at a cabin on Snoqualmie Pass. Birger Ruud drew a picture of a ski jumper on a cabinet door, which appears above his signature, and signed it along with Niles Eie and Olav Ulland. A friend of the author's, Hedrick Hanson, left messages in Norwegian that are translated as follows.

> *Birger Ruud: "The boys' best thanks."*
> *Nils Eie: "Unforgettable memory."*
> *Olav Ulland: "The best wishes in the future from your pupil. You will go*
>   *a long way."*
> *"Thanks from me" (thanks for the stay).*

The Ruud brothers traveled to Sun Valley to compete at the 1938 Harriman Cup, which were the Combination National Jumping and National Downhill and Slalom Championships. They were all-around skiers and planned to compete in the downhill and slalom events. Birger had nearly won an Olympic medal in downhill in 1936 and was one of the world's top

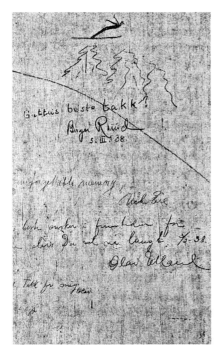

Left: Birger Ruud made this drawing on a cabinet door at the Snoqualmie Pass cabin where he and other jumpers stayed in 1938. *Hedrick Hanson.*

Below: Alf Engen, Nels Eie and Birger Ruud do an impressive triple jump at Ruud Mountain, Sun Valley, 1938. *The Community Library.*

Above: Olav Ulland and Portland's Hjalmar Hvam did a tandem somersault at Mount Rainier after the 1938 Silver Skis Race. *Tacoma Public Library.*

Left: Olav Ulland, who came to Seattle to coach ski jumping in late 1937, jumps at Mount Rainier in 1938. He is wearing a red sweater with a white *K* on it, showing that he was from Kongsberg, Norway, a small town that produced many world-class jumpers and was known as the ski jumping capital of the world. *Kirby Gilbert.*

five in downhill racing. However, both were hurt and could not race, and Dartmouth's Dick Durrance won his second Harriman Cup.

Birger Ruud won the jumping tournament at Sun Valley's Ruud Mountain, which was designed for 40-meter jumps, with a leap of 48 meters, a new record for the hill, in spite of having torn chest muscles. Alf Engen jumped 47 meters in competition, Sigurd Ulland 46.5 meters and Dick Durrance 45.5 meters. Engen made a "giant leap" of 50.5 meters before the competition started that was described in the *Sun Valley Ski Club 1937–1938 Report*:

> *But it remained for the great Engen to crown the year's jumping on Ruud Mountain. In one mighty leap, not counted in competition but official none-the-less, Alf soared down the hill 50.5 meters!…"It was more than the law can possibly allow on a 40-meter course!" And without a doubt it will stand as Ruud's all-time record!*

The 1938 Silver Skis race on Mount Rainier in late March was canceled because of high winds, disappointing a crowd of 8,400. Instead, a slalom race was held instead that was won by Portland's Hjalmar Hvam; Olav Ulland finished fifth. After the race, Olav Ulland and Hvam entertained the crowd by doing a side-by-side somersaults on their skis.[108]

Chapter 6

1939–World War II

Competition for the Longest Jump Intensifies; Alf Engen–Torger Tokle Rivalry Captivates the Nation

In 1939, two Norwegian ski jumpers came to the United States who would dazzle the country—one famous and the other a virtual unknown. Both competed in Washington and were later inducted into the U.S. Ski and Snowboard Hall of Fame. Reidar Andersen was a highly successful ski jumper. He was a Nordic-combined skier, member of the 1932 Norwegian Olympic team and three-time winner of the King's Cup at Holmenkollen (1936, 1937 and 1938), where in 1937, competing against 450 jumpers in front of fifty thousand spectators, he beat Birger Ruud. Andersen won the bronze medal in the 1936 Olympics and set a new distance record in Europe of 344 feet in 1939. He toured America in 1939, winning every jumping tournament he entered, eighteen in the United States and Canada, taking one hundred trophies home. Andersen won the amateur downhill title at Sun Valley's 1939 Harriman Cup. He was inducted into the U.S. Ski and Snowboard Hall of Fame in 1971.

Torger Tokle from Lokken Verk, Norway, moved to New York City, where he worked as a carpenter and joined Norway Ski Club. Unlike his peers, he did not have an overwhelming jumping career in Norway, although that quickly changed. Within twenty-four hours of his arrival, Tokle won a tournament at New York's Bear Mountain, setting a new hill record. He next jumped at Lake Placid in an FIS tryout tournament, winning the Class B event and getting higher scores than well-known jumpers. In the FIS competition, he asked to compete in Class A. Tokle tied with Reidar Andersen for first place, jumping sixteen feet longer than Andersen, and beat two members of the

1936 U.S. Olympic team, Sverre Friedheim and George Kotlarek. This was a remarkable result for a skier new to this level of competition.

Tokle was virtually invincible before World War II, winning forty-two out of forty-eight tournaments in which he competed, setting three American distance records and attracting huge crowds. He was inducted into the U.S. Ski and Snowboard Hall of Fame in 1959. He was known as a power jumper who, according to Anson, "displayed a sense of timing and power that carried him swiftly down the hill. His powerful, and precisely-timed takeoffs provided him with a sufficient distance point to capture victories over more stylish jumpers.…In the history of winter sports, there have been few athletes who…so completely dominated the years in which they participated."[109]

Newspapers used colorful descriptions for Tokle. The *Seattle Times* of December 28, 1941, said that he was a "long range bomber of ski jumping… the spring-legged little Norwegian who shoots for the moon every time he zooms from a ski-jumping hill, the 'umph' boy." Alf Engen's battles with Torger Tokle were legendary.

New National Distance Records Are Set—Two on One Day; Norway's Crown Prince Skis on Mount Rainier

The 1939 Leavenworth tournament, the club's thirteenth, lacked snow so "[t]he whole town of Leavenworth pitched in to transfer snow from the golf course and carry it in apple boxes to the Class A jump." The tournament was won for the second year in a row by Sigurd Ulland of Lake Tahoe, California, in front of four thousand spectators. Ulland had a long jump of 249 feet, a mark that was a new American distance record in competition. Sigurd's brother Olav Ulland was second; Johnny Leeds of Copper Mountain, British Columbia, third; and Hermod Bakke fourth. Only the Class A event was held because of the lack of snow. Leavenworth had never seen a jumper who had such takeoff power as Sigurd Ulland. "As he left the high takeoff, he catapulted himself high in the air, then floated." Sigmund stayed in Leavenworth to practice, as he was headed to the national championships at St. Paul, Minnesota, where he would jump against Alf Engen and Reidar Andersen.[110]

However, later that day, Sigurd Ulland learned that his "friendly enemy," Alf Engen, took the new distance record away from him, as Alf jumped 251

Left: Great Northern trains brought spectators to the 1939 Leavenworth tournament, and cars and trucks took them to the ski hill, located north of town. *Wes Sauer family.*

Below: Leavenworth residents spread snow brought in from surrounding hills in apple boxes at the 1939 "Apple Box Tournament." *Ted Price Collection, Greater Leavenworth Museum.*

feet at the Thirteenth Annual Big Pines, California Winter Sports Carnival, bettering his own mark of 245 feet set in Utah in 1937. Reidar Andersen jumped 265 feet in an exhibition, which did not count, but he won the tournament on form points. Another jumper was seventeen-year old Ella Gulbrandsen, who along with Johanna Kolstad was touring the United States. Ella made several exhibition jumps. The 1939 Carnival was the last major tournament held at Big Pines, which had been one of Southern California's best-known sports areas as Alpine skiing grew in popularity.[111]

The 1939 National Ski Jumping Championship at St. Paul, Minnesota, in early February, was won by Reidar Andersen ("whose handsome appearance has won him acclaim as the Adonis of ski jumpers") with jumps of 193 and 197 feet and "almost perfect form." Sun Valley's Alf Engen was second. Defending champion Sigurd Ulland was fifth. Seattle's Ole Tverdal competed in the Class C event but failed to place. Paul Bietila, a twenty-year-old University of Wisconsin student from Ishpeming, Michigan, the national collegiate champion, fell doing a practice jump and later died from pneumonia. Bietila was inducted into the U.S. Ski Hall of Fame in 1970, joining his two brothers.[112]

In late February 1939, Alf Engen, "the powerful Sun Valley, Idaho, skier," won a new title as the National Combined Jumping and Cross-Country Champion. In the specialized event of Class A jumping, Engen lost to his rival, Reidar Andersen, although Andersen did not compete in the combined competition. Seattle's Olav Ulland was second in the jumping, Engen was third and Tom Mobraaten fourth. After the tournament, the competitors performed several spectacular dual leaps in an exhibition, averaging two hundred feet each, with two pairs of jumpers in the air at the same time. Engen and Andersen formed one pair and Ulland and Oimoen the other. "A series of these double twin leaps was followed by a 'beautiful' diamond jump led by Oimoen, with Engen and Andersen paired, and Ulland flying almost on their heels, forming a diamond of four pairs of skis in the air together."[113]

In 1939, tournaments were held at a new ski jump built on Pine Mountain at Iron Mountain, Michigan, a WPA project with a massive 148-foot tower, the tallest in the country, often called the highest artificial ski slide in the world. The competition for the longest jump intensified. The Ulland-Engen distance marks were put to rest by Bob Roecker of Duluth, Minnesota, who set a new American record of 257 feet at Iron Mountain, beating Alf Engen in the tournament.[114]

The Seattle Ski Club's Northwest Championship Tournament on Snoqualmie Summit in March 1939 was headlined by national champion

New national distance records were set at Iron Mountain, Michigan's jump, said to be "the highest artificial jump in the world." *Author's postcard.*

Sigurd Ulland. It was an "open tournament," so Sigurd's brother Olav Ulland could compete, since he could not jump in an amateur competition as a ski instructor. The tournament had the best field of Class A jumpers seen that year. Reidar Andersen was missed, but with "Sigurd Ulland and Olav… and the other sixteen Class A jumpers, you have a tournament. A GREAT tournament." The Class B jumpers were good enough to be competing in Class A soon. "Tass Gjolme will be ready for 'A' competition almost before you know it." A few years before, the Class B jumpers wouldn't consider going off the Big Hill. "And if they HAD gone off it, most of them would be scared stiff. Now they're clamoring for Big Hill competition."[115]

Vancouver's Tom Mobraaten won the Class A event in front of three thousand spectators who braved a heavy snowfall. Sigurd and Olav Ulland "fought out a brotherly battle for second place," with Sigurd winning "in spite of a knee injury that kept him from walking down stairs. He had to hop on one leg—but he could still jump." "But the spectacular performance of two score juniors captivated the crowd." The Class B jumping event was won by Harold (Tass) Gjolme, who two weeks previously had won the junior jumping event at Leavenworth and was promoted to Class B. "He learned his skiing at Seattle Ski Club under the diligent eye of his father, Reidar Gjolme."[116]

In April 1939, Reidar Andersen won the Fjeld Ski Club tournament at Mount Baker, beating Olav Ulland and Tom Mobraaten. Andersen stayed in the Northwest to race in the Silver Skis Race on Mount Rainier, where he finished third behind Sun Valley ski instructors Peter Radacher and Arthur Schlaffer despite having an injured shoulder.[117]

In May 1939, Norway's Crown Prince Olav and Princess Martha visited the Northwest on a trip to strengthen ties between the two countries on the eve of World War II. Prince Olav was a well-known sportsman who began skiing at age two and had won contests in both ski jumping and sailing contests, including a gold medal in sailing at the 1928 Olympics. Their visit included skiing on Mount Rainier, accompanied by their Norwegian-American hosts, which included Tacoma's Gretchen Kunigk, who later married 1936 Olympian Don Fraser and won gold and silver medals in skiing at the 1948 Olympics in Switzerland.

After a formal lunch at Paradise Inn, the prince and princess started the climb to Alta Vista. The prince wore "an old, gray pair of knickers, a cap that had seen better days, and a slightly battered jacked" and used "a pair of shiny, new, steel-edged skis" he was given. There was a "certain horrible fascination about the idea of a Crown Prince landing on his neck in a snowbank at any speed over fifteen miles an hour." The prince skied with a "mile-eating Norwegian langlauf stride." When the prince reached the summit, he showed his humor while smoking a cigarette. He was asked when he thought a war would begin in Europe and answered dryly, "They needn't start it for me." When the party returned, the prince and princess "were enthused over the mountain, the surrounding scenery and the skiing. Prince Olav said it was all much different from Norway, but just as good."[118]

In November 1939, skiers flocked to an Indoor Ski Tournament at Seattle's Civic Ice Arena, offering ski jumping and slalom competitions, with matinee and evening shows—general admission forty-two cents and children fifteen cents. "For the first time in Western ski history, a sanctioned ski meet will be held within the confines of a building, though that is stretching the truth a bit. Because of the size of the jumping hill, the competition must…start outside and then come popping through the window," noted to the *Seattle Times* of November 10 and 11, 1939. The entry list was headed by Sun Valley Ski School director Friedl Pfeiffer, Olav Ulland and Nordal Kaldahl. More than eleven thousand attended the two-day event. "Carpenters had erected, on the Stadium side of the Ice Arena, a spidery scaffold. It rose to the roof of the enormous building, and from its peak, cascading down toward a canvas-covered window, was the in-run of a ski jump." Skiers

Norway's Crown Prince Olav skis with Tacoma's Gretchen Kunigk Fraser at Paradise Valley, Mount Rainier, May 1939. *National Nordic Museum.*

pushed one-hundred-pound blocks of ice up the hill, converting them into corn snow, which was spread out for the jumpers and slalom racers to pack. Ulland said the jumping hill, designed by Peter Hostmark, "is splendid…. We all like it." Olav Ulland dominated the jumping competition; Nordal Kaldahl of Wells, British Columbia, was second; and Ole Tverson was third. Friedl Pfeifer won slalom honors, and Sigurd Hall of Seattle was second.

Left: The Seattle Ski Club held an Indoor Jumping Tournament in the fall of 1939 and 1940. *From the* Seattle Times, *November 13, 1940.*

Right: Olav Ulland did a somersault off the ski jump at the 1939 indoor tournament, narrowly missing the ceiling. *From the* Seattle Times, *November 11, 1939.*

The *Seattle Times* published a picture of Olav Ulland performing "veritable miracles," somersaults off the jump after the tournament, during which his skis hit an overhanging girder eighteen inches above his head every time. Ulland said, "I'll do a somersault if you'll buy me a new pair of skis every time I break one."[119]

In 1938, inspired by Union Pacific's Sun Valley resort, the Milwaukee Railroad opened the state's first modern ski resort, the Milwaukee Ski Bowl, at Hyak east of Snoqualmie Pass. It was accessible by train from Seattle in two hours, had the state's first overhead cable lift (a J-bar called a Sun Valley–type lift without chairs), a modern ski lodge and lighted slopes for night skiing. The *Seattle Times* offered free lessons for Seattle high school students to learn "controlled skiing." In 1939, world-class ski jumps were built at the Ski Bowl for the jumping events of the National Four-Way Championships, to be held in Washington in March 1940.

Opposite: The world-class jumps at the Milwaukee Ski Bowl were designed by Peter Hostmark for the 1940 National Four-Way Championships. *Wicken, California Ski Library.*

Right: The judge's tower was next to the ski jumps on Olympian Hill at the Milwaukee Ski Bowl. *Wicken, California Ski Library.*

The jump was the culmination of a three-year dream of Peter Hostmark, president of the Pacific Northwestern Ski Association and a product of Norway's Institute of Technology, who had immigrated to Seattle in 1927. Hostmark, a "national authority on ski jumping and the design of jumping hills," designed the new jumps as an $18,000 project for the Milwaukee Road to attract "the world's greatest ski-jumpers. Seattle and the Pacific Northwest may rightfully claim one of the most tremendous jumping hills in the United States." The Class A jump could sustain leaps of 285 feet, and the Class B jump permitted jumps of 195 feet. "The big jump has already been pronounced one of the finest in the world." "The inrun has a fine natural curve; is unlimited because of [the] timber free slope above the hill and may thus be modified for varying snow conditions." The ski area was easily reached by train and will likely be called "skiing deluxe."[120]

ALF ENGEN AND TORGER TORKLE BATTLE FOR JUMPING SUPREMACY

The second generation of Seattle ski jumpers made their presence known in 1940. "Gjomle Ski Champ, Seattle Youth Takes First," noted the *Seattle Times* of January 2, 1940. At the Sun Valley Intercollegiate Ski Meet over the the Christmas holidays, Reidar Gjolme's two sons led the University of Washington ski team to the collegiate championship. Harold (Tass) won the combined title in the four-event tournament by winning the jumping event on Ruud Mountain, finishing second in the downhill, fourth in the cross-country and sixth in the slalom, leading to "a hands down victory in the four-event meet." Reidar Jr. won the downhill.

From 1940 until World War II, there were a number of epic battles for new distance records between Alf Engen (skiing for Sun Valley) and Torger Tokle (Norway Ski Club of New York), a rising jumping star. Engen began 1940 by winning an Invitational Ski Jumping Tournament on Ecker Hill outside Salt Lake City, beating top-notch rivals including Roy Mikkelson of Auburn, California, and Gordon Wren of Steamboat Springs, Colorado.

For the 1940 Pacific Northwest Championship Tournament at Leavenworth, the jumping hill had been improved by CCC workers, who raised the knoll and dropped the transition, meaning that earth was added to the bulging part of the landing hill and the "dip" deepened. The Leavenworth Winter Sports Club leveled a challenge to the Ski Bowl's giant new jumping hill. "I'll bet we get greater distance on our hill....We've not been asleep, you know." The tournament pitted Sigurd Ulland, 1938 national jumping champion who set a distance record of 248 feet at Leavenworth in 1939, against Alf Engen, who jumped 251 feet the same day. Sigurd Ulland moved to Leavenworth in 1940 and was in charge of maintenance of its "great jumping hill." Engen won the tournament, jumping 252 feet, a new hill record and thought at first to be a new national distance record, but it did not exceed Bob Roecker's jump of 257 feet. Tom Mobraaten was second and Sigurd Ulland third. The tournament chief said they would give Alf a bigger hill the following year—"How about two-eighty?"[121]

The biggest tournament of 1940 was the National Four-Way Ski Championships in Washington, with the downhill and slalom events held

Alf Engen set a new hill record of 252 feet at Leavenworth in 1940. *Wicken, California Ski Library.*

at Mount Baker, the cross-country at Snoqualmie Pass and jumping at the Milwaukee Ski Bowl. The *New York Times* of March 13, 1940, noted that the tournament featured "the country's foremost all-around skiers…in the most difficult of all national championships." There were two stories to the tournament. First, the competition between Alf Engen and Seattle's Sigurd Hall, a Norwegian immigrant who was a well-known climber and mountaineer but was new to competitive Alpine skiing. Second was a battle in the jumping event between Alf (who competed in all four events) and Torger Tokle (who only competed in jumping).

Sigurd Hall won the downhill race at Mount Baker after starting in twenty-seventh place. Sverre Engen was second and Alf third. Sverre won the slalom, and Hall finished third and led in the total point standings, slightly ahead of Alf. Both Alf and Hall were accomplished cross-country skiers, and they finished one place apart in the competition: Engen was fourth and Hall fifth. The title would be determined by the jumping competition, where the inexperienced Sigurd would compete against Alf, one of the country's best jumpers.

The jumping event was held on the giant new ski jump built at the Milwaukee Ski Bowl, designed to take advantage of the hill's natural slope.

Engen won the jumping event on form points, although Tokle had the longest jump. Showing that he was an all-around skier, Alf Engen "the stocky skiman from Sun Valley went off with the works," becoming the National Four-Way Champion. His brother Sverre was second, Sigurd Hall third and Portland's Hjalmar Hvan fourth. The newsreel boys expressed disappointment that they only had one spill to film in the jumping event, and the rest rode out their leaps.[122]

Hall's third-place finish against competition was impressive, showing that he was one of the best four-way competitors in the country. Sigurd Hall was tragically killed in April 1940 in the Silver Skis Race on Mount Rainier when he skied into rocks in a fog bank, becoming the first death in a sanctioned ski race in the country. His death led to a reexamination of the rules governing downhill races.[123]

Sun Valley hosted the 1940 national championships in Downhill and Slalom Combined and Jumping Championships in March. Dick Durrance won the combined title and his third Harriman Cup, gaining permanent possession of the prize. Alf Engen did not fare well in the Alpine events (finishing sixty-fourth in the downhill) but won the jumping event, pressed closely by a strong rival, Gordon Wren of Steamboat Springs, Colorado. Alf won the ski jumping tournament at Estes Park, Colorado, in June 1940, beating Gordon Wren, where snow had to be trucked in from the Rocky Mountain National Park for the tournament.

In November 1940, the Second Annual Northwest Indoor Jumping Tournament was held at Seattle's Civic Ice Arena. "A giant man-made hill, risen overnight after expert jig-saw placement of 10,000 lineal feet of tubular steel and 30,000 feet of lumber, is ready to thump beneath its blanket of snow." Fifteen Class A jumpers

Opposite: Milwaukee Road took spectators to the 1940 National Four-Way Championships at the Milwaukee Ski Bowl to see "thrills in every jump." *From the* Seattle Times, *March 14, 1940.*

Above: Alf Engen beat Torger Tokle on form, although Tokle had longer jumps; Alf became the 1940 National Four-Way Champion. *From the* Seattle Times, *March 18, 1940.*

competed, including Alf Engen, national jumping and four-way champion, and Olav Ulland, defending champion. The jumpers would "pour down the seventy feet of ice in-run from a high tower outside the arena's south wall, through a twelve-foot window, and 'umph' from the takeoff to soar out over the slope." Even though he had never jumped indoors, Engen won, beating Howard Dalsbo of Seattle and Olaf Rodegaard of Portland. Ulland fell on his second jump but pleased the crowd "with two of his hair-raising somersaults from the takeoff of the indoor hill." The indoor course only had a one-hundred-foot runout, which "is hardly enough and some of the boys took a beating as they swished down off the giant man-made jumping slope."[124]

In December 1940, Alf Engen was awarded the American Ski Trophy by the National Ski Association as the "amateur who furthest promotes skiing in the United States through sportsmanship and performance." On December 22, 1940, the *New York Times* named Dick Durrance, Alf Engen and Torger Tokle as Skiers of the Year.

1941: THREE DISTANCE RECORDS SET IN ONE MONTH

For the 1941 ski season, a Class C jump was built at the Milwaukee Ski Bowl to provide "junior skiers of Seattle and vicinity an opportunity to learn the art of ski-jumping on a small, appropriate hill." The Washington Ski Club ran the jumping program, which provided long-needed jumping instructions for juniors.[125]

On February 9, 1941, at Iron Mountain, Michigan, Alf Engen jumped 267 feet to set a new North American distance record, although he lost to Walter Bietila on form points. Showing the level of competition that existed, two hours later at Leavenworth, Torger Tokle exceeded Engen's distance, setting a new record of 273 feet. The *Seattle Times* of February 10 commented, "Too bad Alf."

Torger Tokle was out to set a new North American ski jump record at Leavenworth in 1941. He was excited to hear that the jump's takeoff had been pushed back 8 feet, making 260 feet a conservative estimate of the hill's capacity. On February 9, Tokle had a "mighty leap of 273 feet," setting a new North American record. The jump was so long that Tokle almost overjumped the hill and landed on the flat. "Tokle Outjumps Engen," the headline read: "Needless to say, 5,500 mouths were agape and official measurers scurried breathlessly to their steel measuring tapes as Tokle rode out his prodigious jump....Tokle's leap was supreme, longest jump ever recorded in North American amateur competition." This set the stage for the face-off between Tokle and Engen at the upcoming Milwaukee Bowl tournament.[126]

Showing the intense competition between the two men, Alf requested that the ski jump at Salt Lake's Ecker Hill be changed to permit longer

A student discovers that learning to jump is not easy, on the Class C hill at the Milwaukee Ski Bowl. *Milwaukee Road Historical Society.*

jumps. Alf wanted to keep the American distance record in Utah. Alf and his brothers were always willing to do the work necessary to modify Ecker hill—extending the inrun, moving the takeoff further up the hill and reshaping the landing hill to increase safety. In 1934, Engen soared 296 feet in an exhibition and, in 1939, jumped 281 feet in practice, neither of which was official. The hill's takeoff was moved back 40 feet "to prepare for an assault on the world's ski jumping record during the national combined championships," held in February 1941. Engen retained his combined cross-country and ski jumping championship but only jumped 236 feet, as a bright sun had turned the snow into slush.[127]

Excitement was high for the national jumping championships at the Milwaukee Ski Bowl on March 3, 1941. *Seattle Times* writer Chick Garrett said that Tokle had an edge in distance and Engen in form, but he was putting his money on Alf.

Tokle worked as a carpenter in New York, requiring climbing miles of stairways, developing his legs "to have the snap of steel springs." Engen was in top condition from his work with the forest service in Utah and was eighteen pounds lighter than the prior year. Alf was the country's top competitor in both Nordic and Alpine events and was training for the Four-

Left: Torger Tokle out-jumped Alf Engen to win the 1941 Leavenworth tournament, setting a new national distance record of 273 feet. *From the* Seattle Times, *February 10, 1941.*

Below: Tournament judge Peter Hostmark presented the winner's trophy to Torger Tokle at the 1941 Leavenworth tournament. *Wicken, California Ski Library.*

A MILLION THRILLS

7

U.S. NATIONAL JUMPING TOURNAMENT at SNOQUALMIE SKI-BOWL

MAR. 2nd

IT will be a great day in U.S. skiing annals—packed with breathtaking thrills! American and Canadian jumpers will soar from Olympian Hill's towering crest in "all-out" attempts to shatter the history-making 273-ft. record. Will they make it? Plan to be right on the spot—and SEE!

Ride to the Bowl swiftly, comfortably aboard Milwaukee Road's Electrified SNOW TRAINS. View the tourney from "ringside" vantage—the Big Hill is directly opposite the Lodge with its fine lounge, sun veranda and all-day food service. Special train service to take care of all comers.

LEAVE SEATTLE Union Station **9:30 A. M.**
Returning, Leave Bowl 4:30 P. M. or Immediately After Tournament.

● **ROUND TRIP ADULT FARE... $1.25**
Children under 12, 65c Round Trip
WASHINGTON SKI CLUB TOURNAMENT CHARGE, 75c EXTRA
Children under 12, 35c

ON MARCH 2, ONLY, persons arriving at Bowl by private automobile may enter. For each person entering Bowl by automobile the admission fee will be 50c, and the Washington Ski Club Tournament Charge 75c extra. Children under 12, half rate. Limited parking space, no charge.

For Additional Information:
City Ticket Office: 4th & Union, EL. 6600; Union Station, 4th & Jackson, EL. 6941; Department and Sporting Goods Stores

The **MILWAUKEE ROAD**

Milwaukee Road trains offered rides to the 1941 National Jumping Championships, where spectators would experience a "million thrills." *From the* Seattle Times, *February 24, 1941.*

Way Championships later in March at Sun Valley and the National Downhill and Slalom Championships in Aspen. He would likely be acclaimed "America's greatest all-around skiman." Although Engen and Tokle were fierce competitors in tournaments, there was a strong sense of camaraderie between them. The *Seattle Times* of February 27, 1941, had a picture of Alf and Torger enjoying a breakfast at the home of Peter Hostmark, one of the judges at the tournament. Can you imagine, these days, the top two competitors in a major national sporting event having breakfast with one of the people who would judge their performances?

Tokle's new record made him a favorite, but the competition was tough. Last year's winner, Alf Engen, had a jump of 267 feet at Iron Mountain, Michigan, which was exceeded only by Tokle's jump at Leavenworth. Two Bietila brothers from Ishpeming, Michigan, would give Tokle a fight. In mid-February, Eugene Wilson of the Duluth Ski Club beat Tokle at a meet. Before the tournament, Tokle jumped an amazing 276 feet, exceeding the 273-foot North American record, although it did not count since it was done in practice.

Tokle, "the human sky rocket from New York," jumped 288 feet to set his second North American distance record in less than a month, winning the tournament and usurping Alf Engen's throne as national champion. Alf Engen was second and Art Devlin third. Tokle, "the powerful-legged little Norwegian gambler," took a chance on his second jump. After his first jump, he led Engen in both distance (by 27 feet) and form. Rather than play it safe, he gambled and soared to a new national distance record, almost falling and losing the tournament: "For a moment as Tokle came down hard on the landing slope after his prodigious second leap, his skis sought to escape from under him, and almost did. But Torger ruled his boards…and rode out his history-making jump," noted the *Seattle Times*.

Above: Dick Dillon of the Leavenworth Winter Sports Club competing at the 1941 National Jumping Championships at the Milwaukee Ski Bowl. *MOHAI.*

Left: A jumper soars toward the Milwaukee Ski Bowl lodge at the 1941 National Ski Jumping Championships. *MOHAI.*

Left: Sun Valley's
Leon Goodman
flies over spectators'
heads at the 1941
National Ski Jumping
Championships.
MOHAI.

Below: Torger Tokle
won the 1941
National Jumping
Championships, setting
a new national distance
record of 288 feet,
his second record in a
month. *From the* Seattle
Times, *March 3, 1941.*

TOKLE NEW JUMP CHAMP

THERE GOES THAT RECORD!

Ski Leaper Gambles, Makes Record Flight Of 288 Feet for Title

By CHICK GARRETT

A new North American ski-jumping distance mark of 288 feet was blazed across the sky at Snoqualmie Ski Bowl yesterday when Torger Tokle, human skyrocket from New York, usurped Alf Engen's throne as national champion, but that was just part of the drama-packed story.

All the sports world loves a gamble, and 5,500 winter sports fans gasped and cheered when the powerful-legged little Norwegian gambled aplenty with the most coveted honor in American jumping, the national title, and won.

For a moment as Tokle came down hard on the landing slope after his prodigious second trap, his skis sought to escape from under him, and almost did.

But Torger ruled his boards there on giant Olympian Hill; he rode out his history-making jump and those 5,500 fans swallowed the catches in their throats and "loved" the little guy who risked everything to give them what they had come by auto and train to see—a record-busting flight.

Took Chance

It was a daring gamble. Facing his second jump, Tokle held a wide edge on Engen, the defending champion, in both distance points and form points.

He soared 266 feet on his first jump, 27 feet farther than Engen, and in form, where the defending champion was expected to build an advantage, Tokle held the edge. The conventional thing to do was "play her safe," Tokle didn't.

His 288-foot ride over Olympian Hill made the national ski-jumping championships a complete success and came as an expressive "Thank you" to the weather man, who ended three worrisome days of nothing but rain by providing clear

TALL HUSKIES WILL GET CALL IN FINAL SERIES

Northern Division

	W.	L.	Pct.	Points For Agst.
W. S. C.	12	7	.618	440 537
Oregon State	7	5	.583	436 383
Oregon	7	7	.500	507 538
Washington	5	9	.357	521 691
Idaho	4	11	.314	502 573

GAMES THIS WEEK
Tomorrow—Idaho vs. O. S. C. at Moscow.
Wednesday—Idaho vs. O. S. C. at Moscow.
Friday—Washington vs. Oregon at Seattle; W. S. C. vs. O. S. C. at Pullman.
Saturday—Washington vs. Oregon at Seattle; W. S. C. vs. O. S. C. at Pullman.

Southern Division
(Final Standings)

	W.	L.	Pct.	Points For Agst.
Stanford	10	2	.833	556 461
California	6	6	.500	466 457
U. C. L. A.	6	6	.500	517 489
U. S. C.	2	10	.167	454 566

By GEORGE M. VARNELL

Although the brackets are filled for the final Northern and Southern series to determine the Pacific Coast Conference basket-

sailing out over Olympian Hill at Snoqualmie Ski Bowl, 21-year-old Torgre Norwegian-born New Yorker, is shown in midflight of the 288-foot jump that | broke his own North American record, won him the National Ski Jumping Tournament title yesterday. He lost a few points on form on this jump.—A. P. photo by Paul Wagner.

Bob Riley of Ithaca, Minnesota, won the Class B event, Ralph Bietila the Class C event and Helge Sather of Spokane the Veterans event.

Showing the level of competition, several jumpers exceeded the Olympic Hill's previous record of 234 feet, and three exceeded 257 feet, which up to the prior month was the national distance record: Alf Engen jumped 262 feet, Walt Bietila 260 feet and Roy Laramie 258 feet. Six jumpers at the tournament were later inducted into the U.S. Ski and Snowboard Hall of Fame: Torger Tokle, Alf Engen, Arthur Devlin, Walter and Ralph Bietila and Olaf Ulland. After the tournament, Tokle said that if the takeoff was moved back 30 feet, he could jump 325 feet, and he could jump 400 feet "on the proper sort of hill."

Before the tournament, the Olympian Hill's takeoff had been set back twelve feet to make longer jumps possible—a controversial move. Some jumpers said that lengthening hills for "a few of the headline distance boys would not only be dangerous, but would work a hardship on the rest of the field, and in short time discourage the upcoming crop of ski jumpers." Tokle was seen as the "problem boy," given his desire to keep jumping hills around the eighty-meter size. "If they start building hills for Tokle alone, ski-jumping will suffer."[128]

Later in the year, Alf Engen showed that he was the country's best Alpine and Nordic skier, winning the 1941 Nordic-Combined Championships (jumping and cross-country) and his second consecutive National Four-Event Combined Championships at Sun Valley. Alf placed fourth in the slalom and won the jumping contest, displaying "his supremacy in the air overwhelmingly....Alf Engen won the Four Way Combined Championships by an impressive manner."[129]

The *Wenatchee Daily World* of December 3, 1941, published an article, "Leavenworth May Not Stage Famous Jumping Tournament," looking at the future of the annual meet. The draft, increasing popularity of Alpine skiing and competition from other tournaments had reduced the number of big-name competitors available. Torger Tokle set a national distance record at Leavenworth that year and then set another record at the Milwaukee Ski Bowl the following month. Without major improvements to the Leavenworth hill, the new record was out of reach. Club officers believed that ski jumping at Leavenworth had reached its zenith.[130]

Olav Ulland Describes Ski Jumping
in Washington

In April 1941, Olav Ulland's description of ski jumping in Washington was published in the *Seattle Times*:

> *The rapid development of ski-jumping the past twenty years has been due to the improved construction of jumping hills. In the early days, the takeoff was built in the middle of an evenly graded slope with the result that the vertical fall was much too great in comparison with the distance jumped. On this type of hill, very little speed could be used and the landing on a 100-foot jump was very difficult.*
>
> *Later the takeoffs were placed on the knoll of the hill and jumping distances naturally increased. And, as the takeoffs were pushed further and further back from the knoll itself, engineers began constructing hills scientifically. Thus, the jumper was enabled to cover flat ground by going forward at high speed before he dropped down into the landing hill, and the vertical fall in proportion to the distance jumped was much less than on the old hills. With the landing hill and takeoff constructed correctly, according to the curve of the jumper's flight through the air, the later-day jumpers could go into the landing slope at a smaller angle which made it possible to stand on really long-distance jumps.*

Ulland believed that ski jumping suited American youth, as no thrill compared to "sailing through space on a pair of hickory boards":

> *Ski jumping in the Pacific Northwest had a rosy future....We have all the natural requirements in terrain and small hills for beginners may be easily constructed at all of our popular skiing grounds. We have medium-sized hills for the more advanced jumpers and two of the largest and best-constructed hills in the country easily within our reach. But energetic and purposeful work must be undertaken by our jumpers and ski leaders if the Pacific Northwest is to have the place in American ski jumping that it should have.*

The Northwest had no Class A jumpers in the 1941 national championships, after traditionally having a strong field. They had grown older and were in the Veterans Class, so "we are now practically without A class representation." Class B jumpers failed to step up to the next level, necessary "if they are to compete on near-equal footing with jumpers from the East and Middle West." They performed under par in the national meet because the hill was too big for them. It was thought that Northwest clubs should hold more meets—five meets per season was "not enough to make tough competitors out of our boys."[131]

In the fall of 1941, Olav Ulland joined forces with Scott Osborn, "veteran Northwest downhill and slalom performer" and outstanding racer at the University of Washington, to start a sporting goods store in Seattle, Osborn & Ulland, after retailer Eddie Bauer loaned them money. Ulland's career in retailing was acknowledged when he was inducted into the U.S. Ski and Snowboard Hall of Fame in 1982.

Chapter 7

World War II Interrupts Skiing; Skiers Serve in the Military

*A*fter the Japanese bombed Pearl Harbor on December 7, 1941, and war was declared on Japan and Germany, things changed dramatically. The year 1942 was a transition period, as the country began gearing up for war and normal peacetime activities were winding down. Some ski tournaments continued, but mobilization for war began to affect skiing.

Olav Ulland ("topnotch ski-jumping instructor in the Pacific Northwest") and the Seattle Ski Club took over the program to train the next generation of Washington ski jumpers from the Washington Ski Club. A free junior jumping class was held on Sundays at the Milwaukee Ski Bowl on the Class C jump next to the big Olympian Hill. Ulland said that ski jumping requires an early start and expert coaching and that this program would develop all-around skiers.[132]

Torger Tokle continued his winning ways. He won the first jumping event of the year at Bear Mountain, New York, winning the Franklin D. Roosevelt trophy for the third time. Tokle skied in the invitational downhill race and had the fastest time but was disqualified for knocking over two obstacles.

In late January 1942, Torger Tokle, "the human airplane," competed against twenty of the country's best jumpers at the Seattle Ski Club's Invitational Open Jumping Tournament at the Milwaukee Ski Bowl. Tokle was "a gambler who shoots at the hill mark virtually every time he hits the inrun—and has 19 hill records to this credit." He would be challenged by "stylists" Reidar Andersen, Birger Ruud and Alf Engen. Sverre Friedheim was "as smooth velvet to gunny sack on form alone." The Canadian hotshots

Tom Mobraaten, Art Johnson and Karl Baadsvik "are no country cousins in the flying business." The Milwaukee Road charged $2.31 for a round trip and tourney admission. Admission was $1.50 for those who drove, with funds going to the Red Cross War Fund. Alf Engen was ruled "out of jumping" by the U.S. Ski Association because he was listed as the "All-American champion" in an advertisement for skates named after him.[133]

Tokle won the Milwaukee Ski Bowl event, as he "outsoared, outperformed and outscored" the other jumpers. His jumps of 248 and 263 feet were "beautiful to behold as he twice reached for the clouds," and "critics who had been labeling Mr. Tokle as strictly a powerhouse leaper, one who sacrifices form for distance, ducked their noggins and blushed yesterday." However, no new record was set because of unfavorable weather conditions. Tokle said that Olympian Hill was too big that early in the season, as jumpers "haven't our legs, and we're not ready for the biggest ski-jumping hill in the country in January.…Tokle stoutly maintains a 300-foot leap is possible on Olympian Hill as takeoff and landing slope stood yesterday." Tom Mobraaten was second and Art Johnson third. After the tournament, Sverre Fredheim, who finished fourth in the Class A event, left for the national ski jumping championships at Duluth, Minnesota, where he would wear Washington Ski Club colors. Fredheim was the top American ski jumper in the 1936 Olympics as well as the PNSA champion.[134]

The Fourteenth Annual Leavenworth Tournament was held in early February 1942. No Great Northern trains ran to the event because of wartime transportation demands. Olav Ulland arrived at Leavenworth five days early to condition his legs for a serious title threat. Tom Mobraaten won with a long jump of 245 feet. Howard Jensen from Chicago was second and Olav third. John Ellerson of Stanwood provided the day's main thrill when he lost a ski in midair after the takeoff, landed safely on his one ski after a jump of 208 feet and finished out his run before spilling.[135]

In February 1942, a PNSA downhill and slalom tournament sponsored by the Spokane Ski Club was canceled because of transportation difficulties caused by the war and lack of snow. The jumping competition was held and was won by Sverre Fredhiem of the Washington Ski Club, who defeated Norge Ski Club's Howard Jansen.

There was a surprise at national jumping championships, held in early February 1942, at Duluth, Minnesota, for the twelve thousand spectators. A nameless Norseman called "Ola" beat Torger Tokle. His name was kept secret because he was a member of the Free Norwegian Air Force training in Canada and his family in Norway might suffer if the Nazis knew his identity.

"He won a decision over Tokle this week which has got the bookmakers muttering in their beards." Tokle was a "muscle jumper," and the Nameless Norseman was a jumper of grace and refinement. "Ola" could not match Tokle on distance but won on form points. Ola also beat Tokle at the Eastern Ski Jumping Championships. Olav Ulland said that Ola would not have beaten Torger on a bigger hill, but when Tokle gets beaten on any jumping hill, "it's enough to set the wires clicking."[136]

Torger Tokle won other tournaments in 1942, including the Twenty-First Annual Sno Bird's Invitational Championship in Lake Placid, New York. Arthur Devlin was second. Fourth and fifth places were won by two Norwegian Air Corps entries from Canada—one known as "Ola," who held the U.S. Eastern and National Titles, and the other as "Sigurd."

In early March 1942, Torger Tokle, "the Norwegian carpenter from Brooklyn," won the tournament at Iron Mountain, Michigan, in front of a crowd of twenty thousand, setting a new American distance record of 289 feet and breaking the hill's distance record of 267 feet set by Alf Engen in 1941. "Although he had one cracked ski, his new mark was one foot longer than his prior record set at the Milwaukee Ski Bowl in 1941." Engen finished fourth. Tokle said he "outjumped" the hill by 19 feet. Art Devlin jumped 287 feet but fell. In late March 1942, Tokle won a tournament at Salt Lake City, beating Alf Engen, Art Devlin, Gordon Wren and Corey Engen. Tokle's dream of a 300-foot jump was set back by "sticky snow."[137]

A jumping exhibition was held on Sun Valley's Ruud Mountain after the 1942 Harriman Cup, featuring Alf Engen (who had won the national two-way combined championships the previous weekend at Yosemite), Torger Tokle and Art Devlin. "It started out as an improvised and casual exhibition to end in a dazzling and record-breaking performance." They moved the takeoff back 25 feet to enlarge the hill, to get more than the hill's design limit of 150 feet, and then "records toppled left and right like the pins in a bowling alley.…Tokle, demonstrating the traditional Norwegian jumping school, an elegant, effortless and far reaching float through the air, set a new hill record of 188 feet." Alf Engen jumped 175 feet. The jumpers finished by jumping in group formations from two to eight in the air at one time.[138]

Tokle enlisted in the Tenth Mountain Division in October 1942, and his last jump as a civilian was at Steamboat Springs, Colorado, in March 1943.

Washington's ski areas played important roles during World War II. Army Mountain Troops trained at Mount Rainier from 1940 to 1942, and the Pacific Northwest Ski Association and local ski clubs taught skiing to local military personnel. Sahalie Ski Club led the efforts, bringing servicemen

Top—America's outstanding jumpers reveal their individual styles. L to R—*Art Devlin, Alf Engen and Torger Tokle*

Left—*Art Devlin balances on the mountain tops*

Right—*Torger Tokle, holder of the American Jumping Record of 289 feet*

page 9

The jumping skills of Art Devlin, Torger Tokle and Alf Engen were shown in the *Sun Valley Ski Club Annual*, 1942. *The Community Library.*

to their lodge on Snoqualmie Pass and teaching them the sport. Most had never seen snow before.

In the fall of 1940, a full year before the United States entered World War II, the army began training what were known as ski troops and testing winter equipment at Mount Rainier, using soldiers from existing units at Fort Lewis. When the country entered the war on December 8, 1941, the Eighty-Seventh Infantry, Mountain Infantry Battalion, was activated at Fort Lewis and trained on Mount Rainier, becoming the first formal unit of mountain troops. In 1942, the army decided to expand the number of its mountain troops, and Camp Hale, Colorado, was established as a larger training facility, where about fifteen thousand soldiers were stationed. In the fall of 1942, the Mountain Training Center (MTC) moved to Camp Hale.[139]

The war's impact was seen in October 1942, when the Leavenworth Winter Sports Club announced that it would not hold its 1943 tournament and instead contributed $1,000 to buy war bonds. In December 1942, the Office of Defense Transportation ordered railroads not to run sports specials for the duration of the war. Milwaukee Road decided not to operate the Ski Bowl so it could commit its resources to the war effort.

Webb Moffett, who acquired Ski Lifts Inc. in 1941, the company that operated the ski area at Snoqualmie Pass, described how the Summit Ski area survived during the war:

> *With the outbreak of war in 1941, the future appeared rather dismal. Rainier was set aside for the training of mountain troops, Mt. Baker was closed for the duration, and, the most critical problem for everyone was gas rationing....Even the Milwaukee Bowl, which had been very popular by virtue of the ski trains, had to close down for lack of rolling stock. Curiously, it was gas rationing that saved Snoqualmie. People still wanted to ski and they could pool their five gallons of gas a week, jam-pack their cars, and drive the shorter distance to Snoqualmie. Business quadrupled the first year, and Snoqualmie grew with more and more rope tows.[140]*

In early December 1942, Sun Valley announced that it would close for the duration of the war. The closure affected 625 Union Pacific employees, Otto Lang's Ski School of 10 instructors and 1,000 skiers with holiday reservations, 500 from the Seattle area.

Some organized events were held in 1943. Leavenworth hosted a "hastily arranged informal" tournament with "all the color and class of the championships." Most of the Northwest's crack jumpers attended, and proceeds went to the Camp Little Norway Association at Toronto to aid young Norwegians training there. Olav Ulland jumped 265 feet in practice and would compete against Hermod Bakke, Helge Sather, Arnt Ofstad and others. Dick Durrance, national downhill and slalom champion, "who has not jumped for some time," was expected. Durrance was working for Boeing Aircraft Company in Seattle during the war.[141]

In January 1944, Lieutenant Walter Bietila, "one of the famous skiing family of Ishpeming, Michigan," beat Sergeant Torger Tokle of Camp Hale, Colorado, on form points in the indoor Norge Ski tournament in Chicago. Tokle won the Class A jumping competition at the Thirty-First Annual Steamboat Springs Winter Sports Carnival in February 1944 for the second year in a row. Tokle also competed in slalom and jumping events in Aspen later that month.[142]

Most of the country's best skiers served in the military, many in the Tenth Mountain Division, where their skills could be put to use. Olav Ulland served for twenty-eight months with the U.S. Army Signal Corps in Alaska's Aleutian Islands, where he taught soldiers to ski on Mount Moffett's Adak Ski Hill, on Adak Island. From 1943 to 1945, there was a rope tow at the site, and a tracked vehicle was also used. Ulland's article "Skiing in the Aleutians" was published in the *American Ski Journal* of 1946; in it, he noted:

> *In order to give the boys something to do, the Army promoted sports in a big way, and along these lines, I was handed the detail of promoting and instructing skiing for the Alaska Communication System, and the job was later enlarged to include the whole base....Quite a number of the pupils learned to ski the whole mountain in a steady, controlled run, and those boys enjoyed the exciting pleasures that only skiing can give.*

Peter Hostmark, who designed Northwest ski jumps, served on a special committee established in November 1940 to look into obtaining equipment and clothing for the army's fledgling ski troops, called the Office of Research and Development. During the war, Hostmark was a rescue officer with the American First Arctic Search and Rescue Squadron in Greenland. "An expert skier, Captain Hostmark once went on a dangerous expedition to an isolated region near Spitzenberg, Norway. He started with four companions. Only Captain Hostmark returned." The Search and Rescue Squadron "helped rescue injured American soldiers from the deep snows of Belgium," jumping out of C-47 airplanes with their "sled dogs, drivers and equipment,

During World War II, Olav Ulland taught skiing in the Aleutian Islands, where he was stationed with the army. *Wicken, California Ski Library.*

braving enemy fire, deep snows, and subzero weather to rescue stranded soldiers and take them to base hospitals," saving hundreds of lives.[143]

Alf Engen worked with the army quartermaster, in charge of obtaining equipment for the Army Mountain troops. He was the liaison between the army and factories, helping to set up production lines to obtain needed

131

equipment such as climbing supplies and skis with holes in their tips to make them into sleds. He also he skied with shell-shocked patients at Sun Valley, which served as a Naval Rehabilitation Hospital during the war.

John Elvrum was in the Tenth Mountain Division and served on the Italian front. Art Devlin was a B-24 pilot and flew fifty combat missions in Europe, earning three Purple Hearts and numerous other military honors. Roy Mikkelsen served with the Tenth Mountain Division and was reassigned to the Ninety-Ninth Norwegian American Battalion, which fought across Europe under General Patton. He received a proclamation from Norway's King Olav. Birger Ruud spent the war in Norway, where he was admired for his courageous anti-Nazi stand during Germany's occupation. He refused to cooperate with the Nazis and would not organize ski tournaments under their auspices. He was arrested after he helped stage illegal competitions and spent eighteen months in a concentration camp. When he was released in the summer of 1944, he joined the resistance and used his skiing skills to locate and hide ammunition dropped by British aircraft. In recognition of his contributions, he carried the Norwegian flag in the 1984 Olympic opening ceremony at the age of eighty-two. Reidar Andersen was a part of Norway's Snowballen group, formed to combat Nazi attempts to control Norwegian National Sports.

Torger Tokle was killed in Italy in March 1945, serving with the Tenth Mountain Division. A comrade reported that "he died a hero's death...fighting while disregarding all danger....Tokle was a ferocious and determined fighter. He never once relaxed in the fight against the Nazis." During his short career in the United States, Tokle won forty-two of the forty-eight tournaments in which he competed, broke twenty-four hill records and set three American distance records, two in Washington. In August 1945, the 1944 Citation for Sportsmanship was awarded posthumously to Sergeant Torger Tokle, "the champion ski-jumper who was killed in action last spring." In 1959, Tokle was inducted into the U.S. Ski and Snowboard Hall of Fame.[144]

Chapter 8

1945–1950

Ski Jumping Continues Its Popularity;
Milwaukee Ski Bowl Burns Down and Closes

$\mathcal{S}$kiing resumed and expanded after World War II, as men returned from war and the country hurried to get back to normal life. There was a pent-up demand to resume activities that were enjoyed before the war. Interest in skiing was stronger than ever, and ski areas expanded and were upgraded. Jumping hills were recontoured and redesigned, judging towers were replaced and ski clubs were reorganized. Some prewar stars continued to compete, but others jumped in Senior Classes. The National Ski Association committee on ski hill design interpreted standards in the FIS rulebook, provided guidance regarding the design and building of jumping hills and issued certificates of approval for hills that complied with FIS regulations.[145]

Ski jumping continued its popularity, although the Seattle Ski Club struggled to keep its programs going. In 1946, the Mount Baker ski area was expanded with a new lodge and chair lift, and the Fjeld Ski Club built a new ski jump more than three hundred feet high, close to its lodge, and hosted tournaments on Razorbone Hill. Washington State College built a Class C ski jump on its campus in the fall of 1946. New jumpers emerged beginning in 1947, as Norwegians became exchange students in U.S. schools. The Milwaukee Ski Bowl did not reopen until 1947, so tournaments initially took place at the Seattle Ski Club's Beaver Lake site.

The Pacific Northwestern Ski Association had its first postwar meeting in November 1945, where it agreed on an expanded ski program in slalom, downhill, jumping and cross-county. Olav Ulland urged the association to have more interest in ski jumping.

OLAV ULLAND DESCRIBES WASHINGTON SKI JUMPING AND COMPETES ALL OVER THE WEST

Olav Ulland wrote an article for the 1947 *American Ski Annual*, "Seattle Ski Club Jumping—Past and Present." The Seattle Ski Club's Beaver Lake site on Snoqualmie Pass had an A Hill good for 210-foot jumps, on which the world's best jumpers had competed. Its B Hill was good for 160-foot jumps and C Hill for 90-foot jumps. The club had a smaller practice hill good for 70 feet, but it collapsed during a heavy snowfall in 1945. The Beaver Lake jumps were three-fourths of a mile uphill from the Sunset Highway, and "the hike to the jumps is not one to encourage attendance," as Ulland noted.

The Seattle Ski Club had problems keeping its jumping programs going because of the work it took to keep the hills open, in spite of having a membership of five hundred. Ulland continued: "Huge snowdrifts have to be leveled and the landing hills have to be footstamped carefully to insure a good foundation." Jumpers spent much of the day getting the hills in shape and then had to hurry to get in a few jumps before nightfall. There were too few willing to work, and much of the work was done by the "old timers," who kept the sport alive. Many junior members avoided doing their part, creating discord among those who worked hard. "The boys like to jump, but they do not want to waste half the Sunday preparing the hills," Ulland commented. Jumpers from Norway were growing old, and two-thirds of the Class A competitors should have joined the Senior category years before. The "work horses" were dropping out, and unless some easier training facilities could be found, ski jumping's future around Seattle would be jeopardized.

The A jump at the Milwaukee Ski Bowl had not been used since 1942—a few Sunday jumpers could not prepare such a big hill. The Seattle Ski Club reached an agreement with the Milwaukee Road regarding the use and operation of the Ski Bowl's jumping hills "for some years to come." The club agreed to organize local, national and international tournaments and run a free jumping school for juniors. The club would keep the jumping hills in shape all week using a caretaker. Ulland concluded his article by noting that the area would have "the best possible practice facilities for the Seattle area, ski jumping here has a great future ahead, especially with it accessible by train....Our intentions are to build the annual meet at the Olympic Hill up to be one of the biggest in the country."

Competition in 1946 began with the Fifteenth Annual Leavenworth Tournament, after a four-year war-induced lapse. Many jumpers from the Northwest and Canada who participated before the war appeared, including

Olav Ulland, "the high-flying Norse with steel springs in his legs," won the 1946 Leavenworth tournament, where the crowd approached prewar size. *Wicken, California Ski Library.*

Olav Ulland, Earl Pietsch, Art Johnson, Ole Tverdal, Arnt Ofstad and Art Grandstom. Ulland had been jumping better than ever, and had a 240-foot practice jump. Great Northern would no longer run special trains, and "gone will be the great Norwegian jumper, Torger Tokle, who was killed in

Italy." Carloads of jumpers had driven the 140 miles over Stevens Pass from Seattle on Sundays, "for some much needed practice."

Olav Ulland, "the high-flying Norse with steel springs in his legs," won the 1946 Leavenworth Ski Classic, watched by a crowd of four thousand, approaching prewar size. "The old rivals, Tom Mobraaten and Olav Ulland, were fighting it out in pre-war style, and this time Olav came out ahead with 234–250 feet." Mobraaten was second and Art Johnson third. Olav soon left for the national ski jumping championships at Steamboat Springs, Colorado, where a new hill rated in the three-hundred-foot jump class.[146]

"Feuds Enliven Ski Jump Meet" at the National Ski Jumping Championship at Steamboat Springs, Colorado, in mid-February 1946, according to the *Seattle Times*. The event was a test of eastern versus western jumping:

> *Easterners say Westerners are lacking in jumping form, while the leapers from the Far West say the Eastern entrants are short on nerve.*
>
> *Western jumpers are resentful of talk by Easterners that they are slam-bang riders who gain their distance by speed instead of jumping ability. Easterners…dislike criticism by Westerners that they cover up lack of jumping ability by posing as sticklers for form.*

Art Devlin of Lake Placid and Merrill Barber of Brattleboro, Vermont, believed that Alf Engen took advantage of them in a meet by changing the jump without their knowledge. Some foreign-born jumpers did not like the idea of a trophy being given to the best American-born jumper. Devlin and Barber were precision jumpers who would test their style against the "slam-bang style of Western jumpers." The Seattle Ski Club sent a four-man team: Olav Ulland in Open Class A, Charles Wenger and Ken Christensen in Class B and Ole Tverdal in the Senior event. Olaf was "primed to break the hill mark of 249 feet." Alf Engen, "the daredevil from Sun Valley," jumped 250 feet in practice to lay down the gauntlet.[147]

Alf Engen won the National Open Championship with a long jump of 259 feet in front of six thousand shivering spectators. "His long absence from competition seemed to have little effect on him." Engen competed on borrowed skis but exhibited "graceful displays of form on take-offs and landings." Four competitors beat the hill record of 248 feet. Art Devlin won the National Amateur Championship. Olav Ulland, who fell on one of his jumps, said that Northwest jumpers enjoyed contact with their national competitors: "We learned again what we have to shoot for to reach the standard of the top United States Jumpers. We regret very much that distances are as far as they are between the East and the West, but with faster trains and other means in the offing, we hope to develop a frequent exchange of jumpers in the future."[148]

Olav Ulland next went to Salt Lake City for the Utah Ski Club's Inter-mountain Four-Way Ski Tournament, along with Ole Tverdal and Ken Christensen of Seattle Ski Club and Wilmer Hampton of the Wenatchee Ski Club. Alf Engen announced his withdrawal from competitive jumping for the rest of the season. "I have 20 years of skiing behind me…and I don't think I should jump every weekend." Olav opined that "[t]here's too much stress on distance and not enough on form." In Norway, everyone who watches tournaments is a judge, and if a skier makes the longest jump but falters on the landing, they would all say it was no good.[149]

Olav Ulland won the Cascade Ski Club tournament on Mount Hood in late February 1946 in poor weather that prevented the last four jumpers from making second runs. Spokane's Helge Sather was second, followed by Wilmer Hampton of the Wenatchee Ski Club. Olav's brother Sigmund (thirty-seven-year-old former national ski jumping champion) won the California State Ski Association Championship at the first annual "Snowshoe" Thompson memorial meet.

In early March 1946, the Seattle Ski Club held a Class A, B and C tournament at Beaver Lake. "Virtually the entire cast from the Leavenworth meet will be on hand to oust high-flying Olav Ulland…from his second Pacific Northwest title." Tom Mobraaten, "the ski-jumping stylist" from Vancouver, British Columbia, was the winner; Arnt Ofstad was second and Karl Baadsvik third. Karl Stingl, a downhill and slalom threat, won the Class B event.[150]

In October 1946, the National Ski Association gave the Seattle Ski Club sanction to hold trials to select the U.S. Olympic jumping team for the 1948 Olympics at St. Moritz, Switzerland, after it bid $2,200; a four-man team and two alternates would be chosen. The event would bring "some of the crack amateur jumping talent in the United States, and the meet will be even larger than the nationals held here five years ago." The president of the National Ski Association said that Western Washington's ski terrain was "ideal," the Seattle Ski Club was "a progressive group" and the Ski Bowl had "ideal hills."[151]

In November 1946, Sigurd Ruud wrote to Olav Ulland, informing him that Norwegian and American representatives agreed to exchange skiers the coming winter. The Norwegian Olympic Ski Team would tour the United States for eight weeks, compete in tournaments and be at the Milwaukee

Ski Bowl tournament to select the U.S. Olympic team. Americans selected for the Olympic team would then train in Norway. Gustav Raaum, winner of the prior winter's Junior Holmenkollen Ski Classic, would appear at the Olympic team selection tournament.[152]

1947: Milwaukee Ski Bowl Reopens; U.S. Ski Teams for the 1948 Olympic Teams Are Selected

In the winter of 1947, the Milwaukee Road reopened its Ski Bowl, and competitions were held in Washington to select the U.S. Alpine and Nordic teams for the 1948 Winter Olympics in St. Moritz, Switzerland.

Alpine events began with the Pacific Northwestern Ski Association's Annual Amateur Downhill and Slalom Championships at Stevens Pass in early February. Next was the National Championship Downhill and Slalom event in Ogden, Utah, in late February. The action-packed year ended with the Olympic team tryouts at Sun Valley in March 8 and 9, 1947, followed by the Harriman Cup competition, after which the Olympic Alpine team was to be announced.

The U.S. Olympic jumping team would be selected after a series of events, starting with the Leavenworth tournament in January and a pre-Olympic meet (the Northwest Jumping Championships) at the Milwaukee Ski Bowl on February 16. Final selection would occur after a tournament at the Ski Bowl in March. The events brought the country's best jumpers to the Northwest, and the trials became like a "little Olympics."[153]

There were four ski jumps at the Milwaukee Ski Bowl: the "A-hill capable of 300-foot jumps; the B-hill capable of 240-foot jumps; a C-jump, next to the Class A and B hill, designed for jumps up to 140-feet; and a new beginners hill good for jumps of 50 or 60 feet....It is one of the outstanding jumping hills of the country, having an adjustable takeoff so that skiers, by adjusting their own takeoff, can increase their jumps to high figures," according to Olav Ulland.

The Seattle Ski Club had provided instructions and a competitive program for juniors through the war years. In 1947, Olav Ulland gave jumping lessons to beginners age eleven and over and taught high school and college jumpers at the Ski Bowl every Sunday for eight weeks. "We want to develop jumpers here who will eventually be able to compete on even terms with the best the European countries can offer." He focused on Class B jumpers since several "proved themselves capable of competing on the A Class and very likely some of them will be moved up and the A Class will have the additional jumpers it needs badly," mentioning Leavenworth's Rae Hendrickson, "who's regarded as sure-fire prospect for the United States Olympic Games jumping team."[154]

The 1947 season began at Mount Baker the second week of January. Leavenworth's Rae Hendrickson set a new hill record of 192 feet, bettering the 191-foot record set by Reidar Andersen in 1939, marking Hendrickson as "the man to watch in the Olympic Games jumping tryouts at the Milwaukee Ski Bowl in March." In spite of his jump, he placed third behind Olav Ulland and Tom Mobraaten. Hendrickson, Ulland and Mobraaten out-jumped the hill, and Hendrickson's legs "took a terrific jar on landing"; however, he recovered and sped down the end-run.[155]

On February 2, 1947, the Leavenworth Winter Sports Club's tournament drew national competitors, including Art Devlin of Lake Placid, national ski jumping champion, and Merrill Barber of Brattleboro, Vermont, "top Eastern flier." Fans could see Rea Hendrickson, "the youngster who cracked the record on Mount Baker's Razorbone Hill." More than five thousand watched the meet, mainly from Eastern Washington, since snow slides closed Stevens Pass. Art Granstrom, the Everett Ski Club veteran, "who makes landing on the toughest slopes look easy," won the tournament, edging out Olav Ulland with jumps of 237 and 234 feet.

Art Devlin jumped a "breathtaking" 286 feet at Leavenworth. This would have been a new hill record, since it was 13 feet longer than Torger Tokle's jump of 273 feet in 1941, but it did not count because he fell. Allan Grandstrom, a tournament judge, said that Devlin's jump was the best he had seen in more than twenty years of judging. "I think Devlin is one of the best jumpers in the world." Unfortunately, Devlin overjumped the hill and wrenched his knee. He had to stay off his skis for at least two months and would miss the national championships at Ishpeming, Michigan, and Norway's Holmenkollen tournament. The knee injury would not keep him off the Olympic team, as the rules were elastic enough to provide for that kind of emergency.[156]

The 1947 National Ski Association Championships at Ishpeming, Michigan, experienced bad weather and hazardous winds. A Norwegian jumper competed who would make an instant impact on this country, Arnholdt Kongsgaard, the oldest member of the Norwegian team, who spent two years during the war in a Nazi concentration camp for his work with the Norwegian underground. He had regained his competitive edge the previous year, placed second in the junior Holmenkollen, regarded as the "World Series" of Norway and became Norway's no. 2 jumper. The takeoff on Ishpeming's Suicide Hill had been lengthened by three feet and flattened to keep the riders from gliding too high, where dangerous wind would "throw them for serious spills. With the arch of their jump reduced, it was impossible to get spectacular distance." A crowd of eight thousand "thrilled to the stylists from Norway," as the Norwegian Ski Team competed as part of its national tour. Kongsgaard made two sensational jumps to win the event. Second was Kongsgaard's teammate Ragnar Baklid, followed by Ralph Bietila, Joe Perralt and James Lawson.[157]

On February 16, 1947, the Seattle Ski Club hosted the PNSA Jumping Championships at the Milwaukee Ski Bowl, a prelude to the Olympic Games Trials. Seventeen "Class A cloud-busters" entered, and the meet was won by Joe Parrault, who boosted his Olympic Games stock by making two spectacular jumps. The three thousand spectators ooh'd and aah'd at his performance. Vancouver's Tom Mobraaten was second, Arnt Ofsted third and Olav Ulland fifth. Torger Tokle, who held the hill record, was remembered in a simple ceremony by skiers placing a wreath of flowers over crossed skis at the 288-foot mark on the hill. Perrault had been coached by Tokle when they served in the army's Tenth Mountain Division.[158]

On March 22 and 23, 1947, the final Olympic jumping team tryouts were held at the Milwaukee Ski Bowl, sponsored by the Seattle Ski Club, on "what was probably the biggest and best designed ski-jumping hill available in the United States."[159]

"One of the best jumping fields ever assembled in the history of Northwest skiing" would compete on the giant Olympian hill, "but jumpers from the mid-west, where ski jumping continues to be the leading phase of skiing competition, dominated the list of competitors." Ralph Bietila would compete against some of the "nation's best fliers," including local favorite Olav Ulland, "who always can be counted on for distance." A crowd of six thousand was expected, many riding Milwaukee Road's special trains that cost $3.62, including the entry fee. Torger Tokle's 289-foot national and 288-foot hill mark were expected to be challenged. Alf Engen, "one of the all-time skiing greats from Sun Valley" and co-coach of the 1948 Olympic team, intended to match distances with the invading ski stars, increasing chances that a new record would be set. Twenty-two jumpers competed for a place on the Olympic team, including Leavenworth's Rae Hendrickson. The Norwegian ski team performed in an international ski jumping exhibition.[160]

Left: Olav Ulland's sporting goods store advertised the 1947 PNSA tournament at the Milwaukee Ski Bowl. *Wicken, California Ski Library.*

Right: The 1947 national Olympic jumping tryouts at the Milwaukee Ski Bowl attracted the country's best jumpers and became a "little Olympics." *Wicken, California Ski Library.*

Warm air affected the tournament, making the hill too soft for "real jumping competition," and distances were not "in the extreme brackets that the big jumping hill is good for." However, miracle powder "snow cement" held the hill's snow in perfect condition for two days of competition, where jumpers from the Midwest dominated. Arnhold Kongsgaard was the star of the show. "The spring-legged Norwegian flyer who left a German concentration camp a short two winters ago, boomed 294 feet in an exhibition jump," exceeding the late Torger Tokle's American record by six feet, but the jump was not official since it was not made during a competition.

Joe Perrault from Ishpeming, Michigan, finished first. Walter Bietila and Sverre Fredheim, veterans from the 1936 U.S. Olympic team, finished in the next two places. Six jumpers were selected for the Olympic team: the top three finishers, Gordon Wren (the lone westerner) and Ralph Bietila, giving the family two Olympic team members. Leavenworth's Rae Hendrickson did not place. Art Devlin, who injured his knee at

Gustav Raaum, the junior Holmenkollen champion, is shown jumping at Lillehammer, Norway, in 1946. Raaum came to Seattle in 1947 to compete and study at the UW. He stayed and became a mainstay of Northwest ski jumping. *Chris Raaum.*

Leavenworth, was the sixth to be selected for the team, after earning his berth "with flossy jumping" in other events. Alf Engen, co-coach of the Olympic team, borrowed jumping skis to try the hill and proved that "the old master can still fly," soaring 260 feet. The jumpers left for Sun Valley for two weeks of intensive training. The chairman of the Olympic Selections Committee said, "We're going to have a good team...capable of giving the European teams a real battle all the way."[161]

After the tournament, Gustav Raaum from Lyngdahl, Norway, a member of the Norwegian Ski team, stayed to attend the University of Washington, encouraged by Olav Ulland and others, where he led its jumping team. This was the beginning of an influx of Norwegian jumpers who attended Northwest schools as exchange students. Raaum said that fifty-six Scandinavian exchange students competed on the ski teams at Northwest schools after World War II, forty-one in Washington alone. The Norwegian skiers who competed for UW, including Einar Bekken, Karl Blom, Kristian Guttormsen, Jack Hasse, Tor Heyerdahl, Jan Kaier, Ole Lie, Asbjorn Lundteigen, Christian Mohn, Thor Mjoen, Ole Tom Nord, Knut Olbert, Per Peterson, Edwin Ronnestad, Helge Ronnestad, Kjell Stordalen, Gunnar Sunde, Per Valbo, Per Wegge and Torbjörn Yggeseth.[162]

1948: Norwegians Compete for Jumping Supremacy; Olympic Games Are Held

In 1947, Olav's brother Reidar Ulland, "one of the top cloud-busters in Europe," moved from Norway to Washington and competed for the Seattle Ski Club. Reidar's son Ragnar later became one of the Northwest's outstanding ski jumpers.[163]

In February 1948, Arthur Tokle (Torger's younger brother) won a meet in Salt Lake, representing the Norway Ski Club of New York, his brother's club. UW skier Gustav Raaum finished second, Olav's brother Arne Ulland (who had placed second in the junior category at Norway's Holmenkollen tournament, regarded as the country's "World Series") was third, UW's Kjell Stordalen was fourth and Reidar Ulland was sixth.[164]

The 1948 Olympic Games in St. Moritz, Switzerland, the first held since 1936, were the big skiing story of the year. It was the first to feature a full array of Alpine events, with three men's and three women's skiing events. Alf Engen and Walter Prager, Dartmouth's longtime coach, were co-coaches of the U.S. Olympic teams.

Tacoma native Gretchen Kunigk Fraser (who was married to 1936 Olympian Don Fraser) was the "unexpected heroine" of the games, winning a gold medal in the slalom and a silver in the Alpine combined, narrowly losing to Trude Beiser of Austria by 37/100 of a point in the combined. Fraser was the country's first athlete to win an Olympic medal in skiing.

Norway's Petter Hugsted won Olympic gold in jumping. Birger Ruud, the Norwegian team coach, decided to compete after arriving in St. Moritz and won the silver medal in jumping, to go with his gold medals in the 1932 and 1936 games. Birger said that the silver medal was his greatest achievement. U.S. jumper Gordon Wren kept up with Rudd's length but could not match his "impeccable style in the air" and finished fifth. Other U.S. jumpers finished twelfth (Sverre Fredheim), fifteenth (Joe Perrault) and forty-second (Walter Bietila). According to Anson, having three U.S. jumpers in the top fifteen during an Olympic competition was "an outstanding achievement.… The results…showed the Americans were definitely competitive on the world's jumping scene, although still behind the Scandinavians."[165]

In early March 1948, the national jumping championships were held at the Milwaukee Ski Bowl. The winner would receive the Torger Tokle Memorial Trophy, the "most coveted ski trophy in the nation," given by the Norway Ski Club of New York to the National Ski Association. The trophy was thirty-nine inches high, carved in sterling silver and valued at $1,200.

Right: Poster for 1948 National Ski Jumping Championships at the Milwaukee Ski Bowl. Olav's brother Arne Ulland, "a visiting Norwegian flyer, who makes ski jumping look so easy, topped one of the best fields of American skiing" to win the national championships. *Milwaukee Road Historical Society*.

Below: *From left to right*: Sun Valley's Alf Engen and Seattle's Olav Ulland, Gus Raaum and Kjell Stordalen fly off Sun Valley's forty-meter jump past the judge's tower, December 1948. *National Nordic Museum*.

Three 1948 U.S. Olympians competed: Ralph and Walter Bietila and Joe Perrault. Olav's brother Arne Ulland, "a visiting Norwegian flyer, who makes ski jumping look so easy, topped one of the best fields of American skiing" to win the national championships with jumps of 280 and 281 feet in "near perfect form," just missing Torger Tokle's hill record. Walter Bietila took second, Joe Perrault third and Gustav Raaum sixth.[166]

Arne Ulland won the Class A event in the Pacific Northwestern Association Class A, B and Senior Championships on Mount Hood after heavy snow caused the Class A event to be moved to the Class B hill. Ulland's exhibition jump of 148 feet set a new hill record. Gustav Raaum trailed Ulland but beat Kjell Stordalen and Reidar Ulland on form.[167]

In December 1948, Gustav Raaum, "one of the top skybusters in the Pacific Northwest," and his teammate Kjell Stordallen jumped in an exhibition at Sun Valley over the holidays, where the classic picture of Gus and Kjell going off the Ruud Mountain jump with Olav Ulland and Alf Engen was taken.[168]

1949: Competition Is Strong Between Norwegian Exchange Students, Local Norwegians and National Jumpers

The year 1949 was an exciting one for Norwest ski jumping. Norwegian exchange students attending Northwest schools competed against local jumpers and Norwegian and Finnish jumpers touring the country, including 1948 Olympian gold medalist Petter Hugsted and Finland's Matti Pietikainen and Leo Laako. Record snowfalls affected the winter's ski events.

According to Anson, "A strong contingent of jumpers from Norway and Finland toured the U.S. during 1949, delighting crowds wherever they went. Tournaments in the Northwest pitted Norwegian exchange students… against their visiting countrymen." The exchange students included Georg Thrane at Washington State College (one of Norway's top jumpers the prior winter; he had been replaced on the 1948 Norwegian Olympic team by Hugsted); Sverre Kongsgaard, attending the University of Idaho; and UW's Gustav Raaum and Kjell Stordalen. They competed against the visiting Europeans, national jumpers such as Arthur Tokle (Torger's brother), Sverre Engen (Alf's brother) from Salt Lake and local Norwegians such as Olav Ulland and Tom Mobraaten. The exchange students "won numerous awards in the U.S. and provided strong challenges to U.S. jumpers, Wren, Tokle and Devlin in West Coast meets."[169]

Gustav Raaum won the Mount Baker tournament in early January 1949, inaugurating a new ski jump and beating other "Norse skybusters" Svere Kongsgaard, Petter Hugsted (Olympic gold medalist) and Georg Thrane.[170]

In January 1949, the Milwaukee Road offered special trains to the PNSA's jumping tournament at the Milwaukee Ski Bowl, costing $2.67 for adults and $1.39 for children, including admission. Admission from the highway cost $1.40 for adults and $0.75 for children.

Sverre Kongsgaard, "the high-flying Norwegian ski ace" from the University of Idaho, soared to a new North American distance record of 290 feet on the Ski Bowl's Olympic Hill, beating Torger Tokle's 288-foot record set there in 1941 and his record of 289 feet set at Iron Mountain, Michigan, in 1942. Sverre was a cousin of Arnhold Kongsgaard, who had jumped 291 feet at the Ski Bowl two years before, although it did not count as a distance mark. However, the tournament was won on form points by Georg Thrane of Washington State College, despite his lack of practice that season. "Thrane spent three seconds with the angels." Petter Hugsted, the 1948 Olympic jumping champion, "was great…but try as he might, he couldn't match Thrane" and placed second. Kongsgaard finished third, Arthur Tokle fourth and Gustav Raaum sixth. The jumps made by Olav Ulland, the "daddy of the tournament, weren't enough to make him dangerous." Thrane had been a sensation in Norway in 1947, where he won "just about every meet in sight." He got his revenge at the Ski Bowl, since he was replaced at the last minute by Hugsted on the 1948 Norwegian Olympic team. Thrane had "a surprising technique…he simply took the most direct line from take-off to landing." He had built-up heels on his ski boots so rather than springing off the takeoff, he "simply bends into the breeze." Thrane "mastered the art of floating for great distances.…He seems motionless in the air until his skis slapped in the snow in a perfect telemark landing."[171]

The 1949 Leavenworth tournament in early February was also won by Georg Thrane. He looked even better than he did at the Milwaukee Ski Bowl, soaring 240 and 260 feet and displaying almost perfect form. Arthur Tokle finished second, Art Devlin third, Sverre Kongsgaard fourth and Gustav Raaum fifth.[172]

The Spokane Ski Club sponsored a jumping tournament on its new hill in mid-February 1949, featuring Class A, B and Senior events. Many of the best Washington jumpers, along with Georg Thrane, competed. Western

Competitors at the 1949 Leavenworth tournament. *Left to right, back row*: George Thrane, Art Tokle, Sverre Kongsgard and unidentified. *Left to right, front row*: Art Devlin, Gustav Raaum, Wilmer Hampton, Kjell Stordalen and Art Grandstrom. *Special Collections, Marriott Library, University of Utah.*

Washington skiers had to miss the tournament because the Cascade passes were closed by heavy snowfall.[173]

The National Ski Jumping Tournament at Salt Lake City the third week of February 1949 was called "the tourney of champions," featuring "the elite of the skiing world's aristocracy—American, Norwegian and Olympic champions." Competing were Arthur Tokle, who won the tournament at Brattleboro, Vermont, the prior weekend; Gordon Wren of Steamboat Springs, who made the longest jump in the 1948 Olympics by an American; Petter Hugsted, 1948 Olympic Gold medal winner; and Norwegian students from the Northwest. Petter Hugsted, representing the Norge Ski Club of Chicago, nosed out Art Devlin to win the tournament "in an amazing demonstration of poise" in front of a record 7,500 spectators. Georg Thrane and Sverre Kongsgaard were the next two finishers. Arthur Tokle was fifth and Gustav Raaum eighth, followed by Alf Engen. "Hugsted Adds U.S. Ski Title to Collection," the *Seattle Times* headline read.[174]

The Northwest Ski Jumping Tournament sponsored by the Cascade Ski Club at Mount Hood was won by Georg Thrane in late February 1949, beating Gustav Raaum. Olav Ulland, "showing his best form of the season," was third. Senior Class honors went to Helge Sather of Spokane.[175]

The 1949 tournament on the Pine Mountain jump at Iron Mountain, Michigan ("the ski jumping capital of North America"), featured an amazing exhibition of jumping talent. The existing distance record of 290 feet set at the Milwaukee Ski Bowl was exceeded five times. U.S. Olympian Joe Perrault, "the flying Frenchman" from Ishpeming, Michigan, jumped 293 feet in the first round, setting a new American and hill record. In the second round, Finland's Matti Pietikainen jumped 294 feet, breaking Perrault's record. Finland's Leo Laako and Norway's Petter Hugsted then jumped 293 and 292 feet, respectively. However, Perrault had the last jump, where he set another new American record of 297 feet and won the tournament.

The 1949 PNSA tournament featured the 1948 Olympic gold medal winner, U.S. Olympians and Norwegian students studying in the Northwest. *From the* Seattle Times, *March 9, 1949.*

Pietikainen was second, Hugsted third, Laasko fourth and Art Tokle fifth. "It was the first time an American had bested both a Norwegian Champion and an Olympic Champion."[176]

The Seattle Ski Club's Invitational meet at the Milwaukee Ski Bowl was scheduled for mid-March 1949. Joe Perrault's new American distance record of 297 feet was expected to be challenged, as the field included Perrault, Sverre Kongsgaard and Petter Hugsted. "That's why the patrons of Pine Mountain will have jumping dreams or maybe a nightmare Sunday night." Petter Hugsted edged out Georg Thrane for the title, continuing the battle between the two Norwegian stars. Hugsted was forced to "give one of the best displays of bad-weather jumping in Milwaukee Ski Bowl history." Art Devlin was third; Joe Perrault, the new North American distance record-holder, was fourth; and Gustav Raaum was fifth.[177]

MILWAUKEE SKI BOWL BURNS DOWN IN DECEMBER 1949, ENDING AN ERA

The Milwaukee Road spent $25,000 to $30,000 improving the Ski Bowl for the 1950 ski season. However, on December 2, 1949, the Milwaukee Ski Bowl Lodge caught fire and burned to the ground. "Fire Razes Ski Bowl Lodge; Loss $180,000; Two Story Structure Burns Fast," the *Seattle Times* headline read.[178]

The lodge was being readied for the ski season when a fire started in the recreation room "of the large rambling, Alpine-style frame structure" at 1:45 a.m., spreading rapidly. Calls for firefighting equipment went out to North Bend, Ellensburg, Cle Elum, Yakima and Seattle, but the structure was a roaring inferno when they arrived. All that remained the next day were chimneys of the lodge's kitchen, the main lobby fireplace and the heating plant. Milwaukee Road crews used dynamite to destroy the chimneys and half of the four-hundred-foot passenger-loading platform as a safety precaution.[179]

The May 1950 *Milwaukee Magazine* said that the fire was the railroad's largest fire loss of the year, totaling $190,000. The fire burned the lodge, snow shed, a Diesel switch engine ($23,000), seven older-type passenger cars ($15,800) and $10,000 of freight cars.

The Milwaukee Ski Bowl operated in the winter of 1950. A temporary building housed restrooms, first aid and the ski patrol, and train cars were

Published Daily and Sunday and Entered as Second Class Matter at Seattle, Washington, Vol. 73, No. 336.   SEATTLE, WASHINGTON, FRIDAY, DECEMBER 2, 1949.   46 PAGES   Price 5c

FIRE RAZES SKI BOWL LODGE; LOSS $180,000

FLAMES IN THE NIGHT: Doomed to destruction, the Milwaukee Road's Alpine-style ski lodge in the Milwaukee Ski Bowl near Snoqualmie Pass burned furiously early today. The blaze was at its height when this photograph was taken. The porch on the 'side of the lodge facing the ski jump and racing courses can be seen clearly, as well as the lodge's two stairways, down which the fire spread swiftly. The fire started about 1:45 o'clock and soon was out of control.

Two-Story Structure Burns Fast

The lodge at the Milwaukee Road Ski Bowl near Snoqualmie Pass was destroyed by fire early this morning.

The loss was estimated at $180,000 by L. K. Sorensen, general manager here for the Milwaukee Road.

The fire started about 1:45 o'clock, apparently originating in the recreation room of the large, rambling, Alpine-style frame structure.

Sorensen said two painters, who had been redecorating the lodge, reported everything was all right when they left the building about 9 o'clock last night. The painters were keeping the lodge's steam-heating plant in operation.

Flames Spread Rapidly

Calls for fire-fighting equipment were sent to North Bend, Cle Elum, Ellensburg, Yakima and Seattle. In a short time the flames were beyond control and the wooden structure was a roaring inferno.

Two Milwaukee Road trains, the westbound Hiawatha and the westbound Columbian, were halted several minutes by the fire. When it was determined that the blaze did not endanger poles which carry power for the trains, they proceeded. The Hyak station is about a quarter of a mile from the lodge.

The two-story lodge was being readied for the opening of the ski season January 7. The eighth annual Seattle Times Ski School is scheduled to open in the Ski Bowl on that date.

Other Facilities Sought

Sorensen was to confer by telephone with Milwaukee Road officials in Chicago today to determine what facilities could be made ready for the ski school, which annually enrolls up to 3,000 young Seattle skiers.

The blaze was discovered by John F. Olson, section foreman at Hyak.

Olson said he used dynamite to save approximately half of the Milwaukee Road's 400-foot passenger-loading platform.

All that remained standing this forenoon were chimneys of the lodge's kitchen, main lobby fireplace and heating plant, which section crews dynamited as a safety precaution.

It was snowing hard at the Bowl today.

The Ski Bowl is on the eastern slope of the Cascade Mountains, 62 rail miles from Seattle. The lodge, built in 1937, contained a cafeteria, large recreation room, rest rooms, skiing equipment shop, Ski Patrol office, first-aid station, ski instructors' quarters and other facilities.

H. A. Seering Named King County Judge

Harold A. Seering, Seattle attorney, was appointed by Gov. Arthur B. Langlie today to succeed the late James T. Lawler as a judge of the King County Superior Court. Seering, 47 years old, has practiced law in Seattle 19 years. He is a member of the firm of Maxwell, Seering, Jones & Merritt. He received his law degree from the University of Minnesota in 1929.

Seering is a specialist in labor law, and recently was appointed to the University of Washington Law School faculty to teach labor law.

During the Second World War Seering was vice chairman of the Northwest Regional War Labor Board and cochairman of the War Labor Board in Honolulu. He also was attorney for the area rent-control division of the Office of Price Administration.

For several years Seering has been active in labor arbitration, and is a member of the National Academy of Arbitrators.

Seering's appointment is effective next Monday.

Before receiving his law degree, Seering taught public speaking at Oregon State College and the University of Minnesota.

Chiang nearly captured by Reds in Chungking. Page 8.

Horse-race results and entries. Page 29.

HAROLD A. SEERING

TODAY

LONE SURVIVOR: This fireplace, in front of which thousands of young ski enthusiasts once warmed themselves at the Milwaukee Road Ski Bowl, virtually was all that remained of the big, two-story lodge this forenoon after an early-morning fire.—Times staff photo by Howard J. Vallentyne, Jr. (See Page 20 for other photographs.)

Demos Hear Barkley Rap 'Welfare' Foes

By Associated Press.

NEW YORK, Dec. 2.—Vice President Barkley tonight challenged all "tree-sitters and hitching-post devotees" who fear the "welfare state."

And he forecast Democratic victories for years to come, over the forces who see "Uncle Sam as a complacent old gentleman sitting astride the dome of the Capitol drawing his salary and doing nothing."

The 72-year-old vice president interrupted his Georgia honeymoon to speak at a $100-a-plate fund-raising dinner of the Democratic National Committee.

Mrs. Barkley accompanied him. Many members of President Truman's cabinet and other prominent Democrats were in the audience of 2,500 at the Waldorf-Astoria Hotel.

Barkley predicted in his prepared speech that the Democrats would increase their Senate and House majorities next year "in order that the democratic process may harmoniously continue in behalf of the American people."

Under Democratic reforms demanded by "the people themselves," he declared, Americans have become "more prosperous, more content and more universally employed than at any other period in history."

("Veep's Bride Wisecracks 'Em." Page 38.)

Old and New Friends Aid Christmas Fund

(For picture and today's list of contributors, see Page 25)

By ROBERT HEILMAN

Like the brilliant flames from a Yule log, contributions to The Times Christmas Fund for Needy Children flickered higher today and reached a total of $2,697.49.

Without solicitation — because no one asks for gifts to this Fund

Commies sought data on every longshoreman during strike. Bridges-trial witness testifies. Page 8.

Hiring halls in four Coast ports operate in violation of Taft-Hartley Law, says N. L. R. B. trial examiner. Page 37.

Andrew R. Hilen, lawyer, dies. Page 26.

membership drive paused to help

The Milwaukee Ski Bowl Lodge burned down in December 1949 and the area closed, ending an era in Washington skiing. *From the* Seattle Times, *December 1949.*

used for a kitchen and warming hut. The *Seattle Times* continued to provide free ski lessons to Seattle high school students (extending a practice that began in 1938) and jumping competitions took place.

In September 1950, the Milwaukee Road announced that it would not rebuild the lodge and was getting out of the ski business. "To replace [the lodge and trainshed] would cost about $125,000....It may come as a surprise to many people that the Milwaukee Road has been taking substantial financial losses in running the Ski Bowl. As much as we would like to keep the Ski Bowl in operation, we cannot afford to do so."[180] The area remained unused until 1959, when the Hyak Ski Area opened nearby.

The Milwaukee Ski Bowl jumping hill was only used for six years but was one of the country's most important sites, attracting the world's best competitors and hosting nationally important tournaments: the National Four-Way Championships (1940), the National Ski-Jumping Championships twice (1941 and 1949) and the 1947 tournament to select the U.S. 1948 Olympic team. New national distance records were set there by Torger Tokle in 1941 and Sverre Kongsgaard in 1949. Its loss was a major blow to skiing in Washington and to ski jumping nationally.

Chapter 9

Leavenworth Is the Center of Washington Ski Jumping After 1950

he loss of the Milwaukee Ski Bowl and its Olympic-caliber jumps was a serious blow to Washington skiing, made worse by the difficulty the Seattle Ski Club was having keeping its jumping program going. Competitive ski jumping continued at Leavenworth, Snoqualmie Pass, Spokane and elsewhere. Leavenworth became the center of Washington ski jumping and one of the most important sites nationally. Many of the world's best jumpers competed at Leavenworth; it hosted national championship tournaments and Olympic team tryouts and new national distance records were set on its slopes. Norwegian exchange students dominated the competition for many years. The Kongsberger Ski Club was formed in 1954 to carry on the tradition of ski jumping. Competition for the longest-distance mark continued.

Four Washington-based ski jumpers made the national stage. Ragnar Ulland, son of Olav's brother Reidar, moved to Seattle in 1951, became a high school jumping sensation and was a member of the 1956 U.S. Olympic team at the Cortina, Italy games. Torbjörn Yggeseth, an exchange student at the University of Washington and member of the 1960 Norwegian Olympic team, dominated tournaments in the early 1960s. Jim Brennan, a Leavenworth native, narrowly missed making the 1960 Olympic team, won the national championship (equaling the national distance record) and was on the 1962 U.S. team at the World Ski-Jumping Championships in Poland. Jim Steele, a Leavenworth native, was on the 1972 Olympic team at the Sapporo, Japan games and a star of the University of Utah ski team.

In 1950, the FIS World Ski Championships were held in this country for the first time, bringing the world's best skiers to compete. The Nordic World Championships were held in Lake Placid, New York, January 3–February 5, 1950, featuring competitions in jumping and cross-country. The men's and women's Slalom and Downhill World Championships were held in Aspen, Colorado, February 13–18, 1950.

Norwegian Hans Bjornstad won the World Nordic Championships, and Sweden's Thure Lindgren was second, followed by Norway's Arnfinn Bergman, Christian Mohn and Torbjörn Falkanger. U.S. competitors Art Devlin finished sixth, Merrill (Mezzie) Barber thirteenth and Art Tokle fourteenth. "Having three Americans finish in the top 15 was seen as a victory," according to Anson. The Norwegian winners (Bjornstad Bergman, Mohn and Falkanger) and U.S. winners (Devlin and Tokle) later competed at Leavenworth, showing the quality of the area's tournaments.[181]

The Spokane Ski Club built Class A, B and C ski jumps in 1948, near its lodge on Mount Spokane, at a cost of $5,000, removing sixteen thousand cubic yards of dirt. They were named after Helge Sather, the club's president. Sather was born in Trondheim, Norway, moved to the United States in 1924, became one of the country's top ten jumpers and was a longtime supporter of the Leavenworth Winter Sports Club and later the Spokane Ski Club. The club hosted Esmeralda Jumping Tournaments beginning in 1948. In 1949, the jump was lengthened to allow three-hundred-foot jumps. Jumpers from Switzerland, Austria, Yugoslavia and Norway entered the tournament, where Vermont's Kristian Mohen won the Class A event and Helge Sather won the senior event.

At the 1951 Pacific Northwestern Ski Association Jumping Championships on Mount Spokane, "[t]ransplanted Norwegians collected top honors." The Class A title was won by Washington State College's Torbjörn Falkanger (who was fifth in the 1950 Nordic World Championships). UW's Asborn Lunteigen was second, and Helge Sather won the open title. Gustav Raaum and UW's Per Peterson had the longest jumps, and Raaum finished second. The Spokane Ski Club's 1952 Esmeralda tournament was won by Ted Nelson from Payette Lakes, Idaho. The ski club hosted a tournament at Wandermere in 1954. Its last tournament was held on Mount Spokane in 1955, won by Ragnar Ulland of the Kongsberger Ski Club with a jump of 235 feet.[182]

During the 1950s, a new research-supported aerodynamic jumping style was developed that eventually replaced the historic Kongsberg technique, according to Anson. It reduced aerodynamic drag, eliminated the break at jumpers' waists and resulted in more graceful and longer jumps. Upon leaving the takeoff, jumpers thrust their bodies forward, with their heads near the ski tips and their arms extended behind them. This flight position was held until approaching the landing, where they became more upright to accommodate the force of landing. The new technique was first adopted by Finnish jumpers and spread to other countries. A more pronounced "V" position of the skis was adopted later.[183]

Leavenworth Ski Club, 1950–53; Visiting Norwegians Dominate Tournaments

For the 1950 tournament, Hermod Bakke "undertook a massive project [for the ninety-meter jump] on Leavenworth Hill, making 300-foot jumps possible. This involved cutting away dirt and rock, much of it done personally, and all of it under his direct supervision," redesigning the jumping hill to conform to the new FIS standards adopted by the National Ski Association, to be able to host FIS-sanctioned competitions. The changes made "Leavenworth Hill one of the best in North America."[184]

The 1950 Leavenworth tournament featured "top Norwegian jumping stars," including Birger Ruud, Norway's all-time great, and Torbjörn Falkanger, "one of the greatest Norwegian ski jumpers of all time…who won the 1949 Norwegian championships and the famed Holmenkollen meet" and finished fifth in the 1950 Nordic World Championships. Falkanger's chief rival was Switzerland's Fritz Tschannen, holder of the world ski jump record of 393.7 feet, set in Yugoslavia in 1948. They would compete against "just about every top-flight skybuster in the Pacific Northwest and Western Canada," seeking to break the hill record of 273 feet set by Torger Tokle in 1941. Torbjörn Falkanger won in a "record shattering 274-foot jump off the towering Leavenworth Winter Sports Club hill," which set a new hill record, to the delight of 3,500 spectators. The jump surprised Torbjörn, as he and Birger thought that jumps of more than 240 feet would not be possible since heavy snow slowed the hill. Torbjörn said, "It was a great thrill to watch 39-year old Birger Ruud soar out 250 feet and 242 feet" to take second. Fritz Tschannen was third, and Sverre Kongsgaard from the University of Idaho (who set the country's distance record of 294 feet at the Milwaukee Ski Bowl in 1949) was fourth.[185]

The 1950 U.S. National Championship tournament at Duluth, Minnesota, was won by Finland's Olavi Kuronen, followed by U.S. skiers Art Devlin, Art Tokle, Keith Wegeman and Ralph Bietila.[186]

Torbjörn Falkanger, "one of the greatest Norwegian ski jumpers of all time" and winner of the famed Holmenkollen meet in 1949, jumped 274 feet at the 1950 Leavenworth tournament to set a new hill record. *Joseph Scaylea photo, from the* Seattle Times.

In February 1950, "American ski-jumping records toppled like tenpins" at Steamboat Springs, Colorado, where the hill had been modified to make longer jumps possible by setting the takeoff back 20 feet and raising its height by 6 feet. New Class A, B and C marks were set, all exceeding Alf Engen's 1946 hill record of 250 feet. In the Class A event, Art Devlin jumped 307 feet, beating the national distance record of 297 feet set by Joe Perault in 1949. Art Tokle jumped 311 feet but fell. Gorden Wren said, "Art Devlin's jump…is one all present will never forget. It is one of their rare jumps which have power and perfect form." A new Class B record of 286 feet was set by Duluth's Fred Murphy, and a Class C record of 290 feet was set by Marvin Crawford of Steamboat Springs. The following week, Austria's Willi Gantschnigg set a new world jumping record of 406 feet at Oberstdorf, Germany, on a hill built for attempts on the world mark.[187]

The Seattle Ski Club's International Open Jumping Championship Tournament in early March 1950 was the last major event to be held at the Milwaukee Ski Bowl. The tournament was won by Gustav Raaum, "the stocky Norse exchange student at the University of Washington," with jumps of 255 and 266 feet, "despite a raging blizzard which slowed the inrun and cut jumpers' visibility to virtually zero." UW's Gunnar Sunde was second and Kjell Stordalen of the Seattle Ski Club third. A special Milwaukee Road ski train took spectators to the meet—round trip, including admission, was $2.43.[188]

Leavenworth's 1951 Northwest Intercollegiate Ski Association Classic-Combined Championships featured a battle between three competitors from the 1950 World Nordic Championships: Arnfinn Bergmann, "one of the outstanding Norwegian ski jumpers of all time," who placed third; Chris Moen, fourth; and Torbjörn Falkanger, fifth. Bergmann was the only jumper to beat Falkanger in Norway in 1949 and placed higher than Falkanger at the Worlds. However, Falkanger got his revenge and won his second straight Leavenworth tournament, leading Washington State College to victory. Chris Moen was second, Bergmann third, Gunnar Sunde fourth and Sverre Kongsgaard fifth.[189]

In February 1951, Ansten Samuelstuen, a Norwegian air force mechanic, jumped 316 feet at Steamboat Springs, setting a new North American distance record and breaking Art Devlin's record of 307 feet. His new record would stand for twelve years. Samuelstuen moved to the United States in 1954, became a citizen three years later and was a successful competitor for many years. He won the national championship tournaments in 1957, 1961 and 1962; was the North American champion in 1954, 1955, 1957 and 1964; competed on two U.S. Olympic teams (1960 and 1964); and represented the United States in a number of international competitions. Ansten was inducted into the U.S. Ski and Snowboard Hall of Fame in 1969.[190]

The 1952 Leavenworth tournament featured Norwegian students studying at local schools. Washington State College jumpers Svein Huse and Neils Hegvold placed first and second. Ted Nelson, the "fast improving Idaho flyer," was third. Hermod Bakke won the Senior Class crown. Fourteen-year-old Ragnar Ulland finished third in the B-1 event and would be heard from again, according to the *Seattle Times*.

During 1953, Norwegian Arne Hoel was a guest of Portland's Cascade Ski Club, where he helped train Northwest jumpers on the club's seventy-meter jump on Mount Hood. Hoel placed in the top ten jumpers in Holmenkollen tournaments seven times, finishing first five times. He competed for the Cascade Ski Club in 1953, winning the PNSA tournament on Mount Hood, setting a hill record of 259 feet at Ishpeming, Michigan, and winning the Portland Rose Festival in June on a scaffold built over a football field, beating Gustav Raaum.[191]

A shortage of snow plagued the 1953 Leavenworth tournament, so seventy-five "residents armed themselves with shovel, sleds and buckets and carried enough snow to cover the slide, landing slope and outrun." Leavenworth was extremely busy, as the Northwest Intercollegiate Ski Association's annual Nordic-Combined event and the Pacific Northwestern Ski Association junior championships were held the same weekend. The tournament featured a battle between Arne Hoel, two-time Norwegian Champion representing the Cascade Ski Club, and Hans Bjornstad, 1950 world champion. Hoel jumped 284 feet, setting a new Leavenworth hill record, exceeding Torbjörn Falkanger's record set in 1950. After hitting the takeoff, "he had a great deal of speed on the inrun, and he hit the take-off with tremendous power. The high-flying Norwegian rider floated for what seemed minutes before his triple-grooved skis smacked the snow way down the landing slope, where the hill begins to curve into the dip.…Then came the word from the hill captain, Two hundred and eighty-four feet! A new Leavenworth record." "Hoel Beats World Champ in Setting Leavenworth Record," the *Seattle Times* headline read after Bjornstad finished second. Olav Ulland finished fourteenth. Everett's Art Grandstrom won the Senior Class, fifteen-year-old Ragnar Ulland won the B-1 event and Leavenworth's Kjell Bakke, competing for the University of Washington, was second. Leavenworth's Duane Brown won the Pacific Northwestern Ski Association Junior Championship, followed by Wenatchee's Ben Day and Leavenworth's Knute Bakke. Brown also won the cross-country meet and the Nordic-Combined title. Bakke was second.[192]

1954–56: Ragnar Ulland Becomes a National Contender; Kongsberger Ski Club Forms

In 1953, Ragnar Ulland collected five first-place finishes competing in the B-1 Class, and in 1954, he began jumping in Class A events at age sixteen, unusual for a person his age. Ragnar benefited from participating in a two-week training camp at Steamboat Springs under Coach Gordon Wren, who had been one of the country's top competitors.[193]

In January 1954, the Ulland family competed at the Wenatchee Ski Club Ski Meet at Mount Squilchuck. Ragnar won the Class A division with a long jump of 130 feet, out-jumping his uncle Olav, who flew 122 feet. Ragnar's father, Reidar, won the senior-class event, and Kjell Ulland won the Class B-1 event. In February, at the National Junior National Ski-Jumping Championships in Duluth, Minnesota, Ragnar had the longest jump but was edged out for the title by Jerry Lewis from Duluth, who won on form points.[194]

The big news of the 1954 Leavenworth tournament was the emergence sixteen-year-old Ragnar Ulland. Ragnar, the most promising young snowflyer in the Pacific Northwest, "turned in nearly flawless jumps on the 75-meter Leavenworth hill, soaring 231 and 241 feet in his two efforts. The boy hit the snow-packed take-off like a steel spring uncoiling. His expert jumping form won the prolonged applause from the fans gathered at the dip of the hill and along the outrun." In spite of his "top-flight jumping," Ragnar lost to Olav Stavik, an exchange student at Idaho. Kjell Bakke, Magnus's son, who competed for the UW, won the Class B-1 event. Hermod Bakke won the senior event. Earl Little, longtime Leavenworth Winter Sports Club official, was leaving for the International Ski Federation Championships at Falun, Sweden, to be a judge at the World Championships.[195]

In 1954, Spokane Ski Club's president, Helge Sather, decided at the last minute to hold a tournament on Wandermere Hill, last used as a jumping site in 1938, to commemorate the fiftieth anniversary of the National Ski Association. In 1933, horses were used to prepare the hill, but in 1954, bulldozers were used. A field of forty-five jumpers from the Pacific Northwest and Canada competed in front of a crowd of five to seven thousand, making it one of Spokane's most successful outdoor sports events. Traffic congestion to the hill was "terrific." Olav Ulland won the tournament with jumps of 169 and 171 feet. Leavenworth's Wilmer Hampton was second, and Ted Nelson of Payette Lake and Jan Kaier of the Seattle Ski Club tied for third. Asbjorn Lundteigen had the longest jump of the day at 180 feet. Ragnar Ulland flew 172 and 178 feet but fell on his second jump.[196]

Hermod Bakke, a longtime supporter of Leavenworth Winter Sports Club who won the Senior Class crown at Leavenworth in 1952, jumps in front a crowd of excited spectators. *National Nordic Museum.*

In 1954, "a hardy group of Norwegian ski jumpers" left the Seattle Ski Club after it lost interest in the sport and formed the Kongsberger Ski Club to promote ski jumping and develop a center for the sport. The club was named after Kongsberg, the Norwegian town that produced the country's best ski jumpers. Its founders included Asgeir Bjerke, Ken Christensen, Jan Kaier, Gustav Raaum, John Ring, Leif Torkelsen, Ole Tverdal, Kjell Ulland, Olav Ulland, Ragnar Ulland and Reidar Ulland. Dues were three dollars per year. Olav Ulland's description of the club's formation was included in Gus Raaum's unpublished paper, "Scandinavian Influence in the History of Ski Jumping":

> *From the 1930s to the beginning of the 1950s ski jumping was one of the big sports here in the northwest....All major areas like Seattle, Portland and Spokane had organized ski jumping competitions with large participation of ski jumpers and spectators....Seattle Ski Club was the most important ski*

*jumping club in this area, and in cooperation with Milwaukee Railroad…
organized annual international and national competitions at the Milwaukee
Ski Bowl, Hyak. The world's best ski jumpers competed and spectators
came by the thousands.*

Ulland continued, noting that after the Milwaukee Ski Bowl lodge
burned down in December 1949, the railroad "turned sour on running ski
trains" and shut down the area, and the Seattle Ski Club tried to organize
competitions at Beaver Lake above Snoqualmie Pass. "But the crowds would
not hike the hills anymore…the support of these arrangements was limited,
and the majority of the club members lost interest in ski jumping." The
Seattle Ski Club turned into a family club, and ski jumping was ushered into
the background since it did not furnish revenue:

*We were in a minority and could not do much about it.…An era of ski
jumping promotion was coming to an end. Those members in the club who
were still interested in ski jumping thought something should be done to
preserve this sport. They withdrew from Seattle Ski Club and established
a new club…the first lines in the club's by-laws state: "this club is formed
for the protection of ski jumping only."*[197]

Ulland noted the club built a ski jump and an eight-foot-square warming
hut at Cabin Creek off the Sunset Highway (later I-90), eleven miles east
of Snoqualmie Pass, on Forest Service property. The area was covered
with heavy timber, but there were "many good lumberjacks among the
founding fathers." The club logged the area and sold the timber "for quite
a nice profit." Ole Tverdal and John Ring "were the engineers" of the ski
jump's scaffold. The Rustic Inn off the highway at Cabin Creek was used
to house jumpers.

The Kongbergers co-hosted a jumping competition with the Seattle Ski
Club on February 28, 1955, at Beaver Lake. Since lifts had been installed
at the ski area, spectators could "ride the chair lift at Snoqualmie Summit
virtually to the jumping hill, thus eliminating the one-mile hike of past
years," according to Ulland. The Kongsbergers organized the jumping
portion of the Seattle Winter Carnival in November 1955 in Seattle's civic
arena and built a jump with the scaffold outside and the landing inside.
Twenty-four jumpers competed, and Leavenworth's Kjell Bakke and Olav
Ulland did a somersault off the platform. The club's new jump at Cabin
Creek was tested in late 1955, when Ragnar Ulland had the longest jump of

150 feet. The Kongsbergers hosted a PNSA event at its club in January 1956 and the PNSA championship in April 1956, with Olav Ulland serving as the meet chairman and Gustav Raaum, Peter Hostmark and Magnus Bakke as judges. Club members taught jumping classes to high school students at their club and for the Seattle PI Ski School at Beaver Lake.

The 1955 Leavenworth tournament was a two-day affair. Seventeen-year-old Ragnar Ulland, from Seattle's Roosevelt High School, jumped 252 and 256 feet, becoming the national Junior Class champion. His 296-foot jump in practice did not count as the official hill record but was celebrated as the unofficial hill record. On Sunday, Ragnar competed in the open portion of the National Class A Championships against the best jumpers in the country: Art Devlin of Lake Placid (member of two U.S. Olympic teams); Roy Sherwood of Southbury, Connecticut (defending champion); Art Tokle from Chicago; and Ansten Samuelstuen ("the spring-legged Norse flyer" from Steamboat Springs who held the U.S. distance mark of 316 feet).

Ragnar stunned the crowd of five thousand by winning the open event. He tied the Leavenworth hill's distance record with a

> *tremendous flight of 284 feet made in a swirl of falling snow.... Ulland's 284-footer, made with tremendous spring from the towering take-off platform in Leavenworth with a perfect telemark landing, tied the hill record set by Arne Hoel of Norway in 1953. The youngster's jump was all the more impressive because of adverse weather conditions which plagued the jumpers all day. Falling snow cut their visibility and resulted in jumps far short of the efforts turned in last week in practice.*

Rudy Maki won the Class A event, beating Art Tokle and Ansten Samuelstuen.

Ragnar showed that "he is ready for Olympic Games Competition in 1956" to two men responsible for selecting the 1956 Olympic team: Gustav Raaum and Chicago's Guttorm Paulsen. Tournament judges Allan Granstrom and Peter Hostmark noted that "Ragnar Ulland is the best ski-jumper in the United States today off his performance in Leavenworth.... You can't keep him off the 1956 Olympic Games team." "Olympic Berth Looms for Ulland," a headline read.[198]

In late February 1955, Ragnar Ulland was named to the six-man U.S. jumping team for the 1956 Olympic Games in Cortina, Italy ("Ulland Youngest Ever on U.S. Ski Team"). Ragnar was called "the best this country ever has mustered to try to dent the monopoly of the Scandinavians." Teenagers "broke the hold of the veterans" by winning three of the six berths

Above: The Leavenworth Ski Area and its Class A and B hills as they looked in 1955. *J. Boyd Ellis postcard, Greater Leavenworth Museum.*

Left: Ragnar Ulland is shown jumping at the 1955 Leavenworth tournament. *Wicken, California Ski Library.*

Above: Seventeen-year-old Ragnar Ulland became national Junior Class champion at Leavenworth in 1955, setting a hill record and making the 1956 Olympic team. *National Nordic Museum.*

Right: Reidar Ulland, Ragnar's father, competing at the 1955 Leavenworth tournament in the Senior category. *Wicken, California Ski Library.*

on the team: Ulland, age seventeen; Rudy Maik, nineteen, from Ispheming, Michigan; and Dick Rahol, nineteen, from Iron Mountain, Michigan. Other members included Roy Sherwood, twenty-two, from Salisbury, Connecticut, and Bill Olson, twenty-five, from the University of Denver, a member of the 1952 Olympic team. Art Devlin, thirty-two, from Lake Placid, was the team veteran, competing in his third Olympics.[199]

An article in the *Seattle Times* on November 27, 1955, discussed the "Ski-Jumping Ulland Family," who were shown in an accompanying picture. The Ulland family from Kongsberg, Norway, learned to ski-jump soon after they learned to walk and "gained recognition in Norway as among the best flyers in the land." The brothers were Thore, forty-eight; Sigurd, forty-six; Olav, forty-four; Reidar, forty-two; Hallvard, forty; Arne, thirty-five; and Ole, who died in Norway after World War II. Five family members lived in the United States—Reidar, Olav and Sigurd, Mrs. Asgeir Bjerke of Seattle and Mrs. Thorleif Thowson of Chicago. The rest lived in Norway.

Arne and Olav had the family's best records, according to the article. Arne (manager of a Kongsberg ski factory) placed second the junior Holmenkollen event, regarded as the "World Series" of ski jumping, and won the 1948 National Jumping Championships at the Milwaukee Ski Bowl. Olav had set a world distance mark of 339 feet in 1935, becoming the first to break the one-hundred-meter distance mark. The article did not mention Sigurd Ulland, who was national jumping champion in 1938 and won the 1938 and 1939 Leavenworth tournaments (where he set a new national record that was surpassed by Alf Engen the same day) and many other tournaments.

Olav was the only Ulland to be on an Olympic team—the 1932 Norwegian Olympic team—but a leg injury kept him out of competition. Twenty-four years later, eighteen-year-old Ragnar had the potential to represent the family in international competition. Olav was coach of the 1956 U.S. Olympic jumping team "on the basis of his years of work in the Pacific Northwest to develop ski-jumping, his competitive record and his ability to coach the snow-flyers," according to the *Seattle Times*.

Olav was quoted as saying that Ragnar "hit his stride" the prior year when he trained on the "big hill" in Steamboat Springs during Christmas vacation. Ragnar won the attention of the skiing world when he set a hill record at Leavenworth of 296 feet and won the national junior championship:

> *He possesses every quality necessary to be an outstanding jumper for the*
> *next 20 years or more. He has all the heart it takes to fly into space from*

a towering ski jump and he has no tendency to "back-pedal" in flight as he nears a landing. Many jumpers…tend to pull back in mid-flight because they fear they are out-jumping the hill.…He has the ability to get a tremendous amount of float out of his jumps, and he has the legs to stand up under the terrific impact of landing in the dip of a hill.…We'll have to work on his take-off and his form when he reaches the peak of his flight.… He needs to lean forward even more than he does to get the maximum distance possible and to display the best ski-jumping form.

Ragnar Ulland went to the 1956 Olympic Games in Cortina d'Ampezzo, Italy, the youngest member of the team. Unfortunately, Ragnar fell during practice, suffered a concussion, hurt his back and could not compete in the games. Finland's ski jumpers won gold and bronze medals in the 1956 Olympics, German jumpers won third and fourth and the highest Norwegian finished eleventh. U.S. jumpers finished twenty-first (Art Devlin), thirty-sixth (Roy Sherwood), forty-third (Willis Olson) and fifty-first (Dick Rahoi). This was Art Devlin's last appearance at an international event. He became the ski jumping commentator on *ABC's Wide World of Sports* from 1962 to 1983, introducing the sport to the American audience. American jumpers did not fare well in 1956, according to Anson:

The United States jumpers had difficulty earning top-twenty finishes, placing none of its jumpers in the top twenty, and only one in the first thirty-five places.…It was a far cry from the excellent team strength exhibited in 1952, when all four jumpers were in the top twenty-five.[200]

Ragnar's back injury limited his jumping the following year, but he continued to try out for the national team. In 1958, Ragnar failed to make the six-man team (coached by Olav Ulland) that competed in the FIS World Ski Championships in Finland, finishing seventeenth in the tryouts at Isheming, Michigan, but qualified as an alternate. Ragnar tried out for the 1960 Olympic team but finished fourteenth in the national championships at Leavenworth. He was a trial jumper at the 1960 Olympics at Squaw Valley, testing hill conditions before the competition started.

Ragnar and his father, Reidar, often competed in the same tournaments. Ragnar won the 1957 Kongsberger Ski Club tournament, and Reidar won the Veterans Division. In 1958, Ragnar set a new hill record of 224 feet on Mount Hood to win the Western Open Jumping Meet. Reidar won the senior division. Ragnar won the Kongsberger tournament in 1958, and Reidar won the Class B Nordic-Combined Championship. In 1960, a *Seattle Times* headline noted, "Ullands Pace Ski Jumpers in Kongsberger Tournament."[201]

Leavenworth's silver anniversary (twenty-fifth) tournament was held in February 1956, in conjunction with the Wenatchee Junior College Intercollegiate tourney. Collegiate athletes jumped with the junior and Class B competitors. The notable contests over its twenty-five-year history were remembered in the tournament program:

> *Sigurd Hansen won the first meet, jumping 65 feet on a small hill. New hills were built on the present site in 1930, and the slides there have been enlarged and improved many times since. The late Torger Tokle set a hill record in 1941, when he soared 273 feet. That mark stood for nine years, with Torbjörn Falkanger, the great Norse rider, jumping 274 feet in 1950. Arne Hoel of Norway boosted that mark ten feet in 1953, and that 284-foot record still stands. However, Ragnar Ulland of Seattle flew 296 feet on a practice jump last year, proof that greater distances than the 284-feet mark can be registered on the Leavenworth Class A slide.*

Forty jumpers entered the 1956 meet, including Norwegian exchange students at University of Idaho, Washington State College, Denver University and Wenatchee Junior College. Einar Helgestad of the Blue Mountain Ski Club of Walla Walla won the Class A event. Paced by two Norwegian exchange students, the University of Idaho edged the University of Washington to win the tournament, based on the cross-country and ski jumping events.[202]

1957–59: LEAVENWORTH SKI JUMP IS REBUILT; TORBJÖRN YGGESETH ARRIVES; OLYMPIC TRYOUTS ARE HELD AT LEAVENWORTH; JIM BRENNAN MOVES INTO NATIONAL CONTENTION

By 1956, Leavenworth's Class A trestle had to be rebuilt and brought up to new national standards after it deteriorated and a heavy snowfall caused it to collapse. The replacement trestle was built within the original footprint and was used in 1957. This opened the door to hosting national championships in 1959, 1967, 1974 and 1978:

Elevated from the natural hill surface, the trestle and decking provided an artificially steep and smooth descent as well as an abrupt plateau from which skiers could take flight....

Below the jump, the natural slope has been enhanced with terracing and cleared of trees. At the top of the hill, the jump begins with a section of engineered earthwork which is at grade and transitions smoothly into the elevated trestle and decking portion. The earthwork features a wooden framework in-filled with dirt, forming a laterally even jump surface which is also the same width as the decking portion. The wood sidewalls of the earthwork are reinforced with concrete piers.[203]

More than sixty jumpers participated in the Twenty-Sixth Annual Leavenworth Tournament in 1957, led by Ansten Samuelstuen, who set the American distance record of 316 feet in 1951. Samuelstuen won the Class A event, followed by Per Windju of the University of Idaho, Tore Asberg of Washington State College, Harold Hauge of Seattle and Ragnar Ulland.

The 1958 Leavenworth tournament attracted "an impressive entry list from the Pacific Northwest, Western Canada and Norway," according to the *Seattle Times*. Three outstanding Norwegian jumpers flew in for the tournament: Odd Westgaard, Arfinn Karlstad and Arne Larsen (Norwegian junior champion). Westgaard finished first, displaying "nearly perfect jumping form to win the meet handily," and Karlstad finished second on the "steeply pitched ski slide at Leavenworth" that reminded them of home. The competitors jumped in fog and rain, which limited the event to two thousand spectators, who "braved the disappointing weather." Ragnar Ulland "pushed the visitors to all-out efforts with his best jumping display since he clinched an Olympic Winter Games team berth in 1955." His longest jump, 283 feet, was 1 foot short of the hill record he shared with Arne Hoel, and he finished third on form points. Tournament judge Peter Hostmark said, "This jumping...is the kind you dream about."[204]

Leavenworth native Jim Brennan made his mark at his hometown tournament in 1958, winning the Junior Expert title. Brennan won the Canadian Ski-Jumping Championships in late February 1958. In March, Brennan was named to the Pacific Northwest Ski Association Nordic-Combined team for the National Junior Championships in Winter Park, Colorado. Later, he competed at the Western States American Legion Tournament in Sun Valley, Idaho, where he finished ninth in the jumping event and fifteenth in the Nordic-combined.

Leavenworth's Class A trestle was rebuilt and brought up to new national standards for 1957 after it had deteriorated and collapsed. *Walt Doan and Bill Doan.*

1957 LHS SKI TEAM

1957—Back: Larry Southwick, Coach Lincoln MacPherson, Mearl Bergren, Jim Brennan. Front: Jack Brennan, Sam Pedleton

Above: Ansten Samuelstuen, three-time U.S. national champion and holder of the national distance record, competed at Leavenworth several times, as seen here in 1957. *Greater Leavenworth Museum.*

Left: Jim Brennan was featured in the 1957 Leavenworth High School yearbook. He was the 1960 national jumping champion and co-holder of the national distance record, and he was on the U.S. team that went to the World Championships in Poland.

1956 Jim Brennen did well in local ski jumping but traveled to NH where he won 1ˢᵗ in Jr. Nationals.

1957 Jim traveled to Reno and placed 2nd slalom and 14ᵗʰ in jumping.

Torbjörn Yggeseth represented Norway in the 1960 Olympics and dominated Leavenworth tournaments in the early 1960s as a University of Washington exchange student. His Norwegian coach called Torbjörn "the Mickey Mantle of the crags." *Greater Leavenworth Museum.*

In the fall of 1958, a Norwegian exchange student arrived in the Northwest who would dominate competition for several years. Torbjörn Yggeseth joined the Norwegian air force after high school, where he flew Sabrejets, retired at age twenty-five and came to the United States to study aeronautical engineering. "Regarded as the No. 1 rider in Norway last season," Yggeseth enrolled at Wenatchee Junior College and later transferred to the University of Washington. In December 1958, Yggeseth jumped 302 feet in practice at Leavenworth, exceeding the hill mark by 18 feet and jumped 290 feet in January. Neither counted since they were not done in competition, but they showed what could be expected from him.[205]

The Yakima Valley Ski Club built a 140-foot jumping hill at White Pass, Washington, for the National Junior title meet in March 1959. In February 1959, the Kongsberger Ski club hosted the hill's inaugural tournament. Ragnar Ulland "demonstrated the form which won the stocky flier a berth on the 1956 Olympic jumping squad," with jumps of 120 and 122 feet, according to Kirby Gilbert.

In February 1959, the Leavenworth Winter Sports Club hosted two events on the same weekend: the National Ski-Jumping Championships and the Olympic tryouts, where a new jumping star emerged. The Class A hill had

American Gene Kotlarek (no. 91), Norwegian Oyvin Floystad (no. 95) and American Jon St. Andre (no. 96) climb up a steep hill to reach Leavenworth's Class A jump in 1961. The judge's tower and the takeoff are in the picture's center, while the WPA-built warming hut in the background. These days, jumpers ride elevators to the top. *Leavenworth Ski Heritage Foundation.*

been rebuilt "to provide the spectators with an even more exciting view of the ski-jumpers," according to the *Seattle Times*. The dip on the main hill was dug out and widened to accommodate Class B jumpers on the same slide, using a different takeoff and a shorter run.

In Saturday's national championships, Gene Kotlarek, an eighteen-year-old from Duluth, Minnesota, competed in Junior Class events. Kotlarek jumped 299 feet, the longest of the tournament, in front of six thousand spectators, exceeding the national junior record of 290 feet and setting a new Leavenworth hill record. Willie Erickson from Iron Mountain, Michigan, won the Class A event with jumps of 273 and 268 feet; Rudi Maki from Ishpeming, Michigan, was second; Leavenworth's Jim Brennan seventh; and Ragnar Ulland a disappointing fourteenth.

Sunday's Olympic tryouts were also won by Gene Kotlarek, who "demonstrated convincingly that he is ready for international competition by winning a special round of flights for qualification for the 1960 Olympic games." He leaped 296 feet, "far outjumping the Class A flyers." "Kotlarek's tremendous spring from the take-off, his satin-smooth flights and his steady landings reminded fans of some great Norwegian skiers who have tested the Leavenworth hill in past years—Birger Ruud, Arne Hoel and Torbjörn Falkanger." Willie Erickson was second and Rudi Maki third. Jim Brennan finished tenth and Ragnar Ulland nineteenth. In Kotlarek, the "United States had developed a jumper who can hold his own against the best that Norway, Finland and Russia can offer....Another highlight of the tourney was the promising showing of James Brennan, Jr."[206]

At the North American Nordic Ski Championships at Squaw Valley in March 1959, the eighty-meter special jumping event was won by Finland's Kalevi Karkinen, "in Finnish-developed flying-V jumping style." Gene Kotlarek was a close second. Ragnar Ulland was eleventh and Jim Brennan twentieth. The Finns said that Kotlarek was the first American to master their jumping style. Olav Ulland, the U.S. Olympic Committee's jumping advisor, noted that "in Kotlarek, America finally has a real threat for next year's Olympics."[207]

The 1959 Pacific Northwestern Ski Association Championship meet was held on the "towering slide" at the Kongsberger Ski Club. Jim Brennan, "in quest of a berth on the Olympic Winter Games ski-training squad," won the event. Ragnar Ulland was third. Brennan's "impressive showing in the Olympic tryout meets this season and in the P.N.S.A. title tourney may well have earned him a Games-squad berth." Sixteen jumpers would be chosen for the squad and train in Westby, Wisconsin, after Christmas.[208]

In May 1959, Ragnar Ulland and Jim Brennan were named to the U.S. Olympic ski jump training squad. Herbert Thomas of Wenatchee was named to the Olympic Nordic ski squad.[209]

Chapter 10

1960–1970

Exciting Years for Leavenworth; National Championships Hosted and Distance Records Set

The 1960s were significant times for the Leavenworth Winter Sports Club. Jim Brennan, a Leavenworth native, attending high school in Edmonds but skiing for the LWSC, became a national competitor. Brennan started jumping at age eight and was reared on the Leavenworth hill. His mother remembered the many cold hours she spent watching Jimmy fly: "When he was naughty, we'd take away his jumping skis."[210]

1960: SQUAW VALLEY OLYMPIC GAMES

The eight-man U.S. Olympic jumping team for the 1960 games at Squaw Valley was selected after a tournament in Ishpeming, Michigan, on January 24 and 25, 1960. Each contestant had six jumps the first day and three the second; their best six jumps determined their point totals. On the first day, Gene Kotlarek and Bob ("Butch") Wedin had the longest jumps, but Jim Brennan gave "impressive performances, despite shorter distances."

The Olympic team selected was the youngest in U.S. history, led by two nineteen-year-olds just reaching their peak: Gene Kotlerek of the University of Minnesota and Butch Wedin, "fresh out of an Iron Mountain, Michigan high school." Others included Jon St. Andre, Ansten Samuelstuen, Dick Rahoi, Willie Erickson, Art Tokle and Rudy Maki. Coach Lloyd Steverud said, "This is the best team the United States ever has had."[211]

Jim Brennan finished ninth and "just missed making the team," a decision that was criticized later. Brennan won the National Ski Jumping Championships the next week at Iron Mountain, Michigan, tying the North American distance record of 316 feet set by Ansen Samuelstuen in 1951 and beating two Olympic team members—Samuelstuen, who finished third, and Butch Wedin. On February 1, 1960, Samuelstuen won the International Ski Jumping Tournament at Iron Mountain, Michigan; Jim Brennan took second (although he had the longest jump); and a Norwegian exchange student at the UW, Torbjörn Yggeseth, took third.[212]

Norway's jumping coach, Thorleif Schjelderup, said that if he were running the U.S. team, "Jimmy Brennan would jump in the Winter Olympics at Squaw Valley." Brennan, Gene Kotlarek and Butch Wedin were the best American jumpers. Schjelderup called his prize pupil, Torbjörn Yggeseth, "the Mickey Mantle of the crags." His description of the intense training jumpers receive in Norway, where "ski-jumping is no week-end frolic," appeared in the *Seattle Times* on February 7, 1960:

> *It's a combination of athletics and aerodynamics....We consult with aerodynamic engineers. We hang a ski-jumper over a bar in a wind tunnel and simulate a speed of 60 to 65 miles an hour. That's about how fast a skier is going when he leaves a 350-foot hill. We observe the best angles for the head, the hips and the skis. The skis ought to be about 25 degrees off the curve of the hill. The body should be as close as possible—about the same angle. We also put our skiers through courses in diving off a springboard, gymnastics and walking a tightrope. We're trying to get relaxed balance.*

The 1960 Leavenworth tournament was held just before the Olympic Games at Squaw Valley. Leavenworth's "Big Hill" had been lengthened to ninety meters, the top distance for an accredited hill, and the slope was in first-rate condition. Olav Ulland, chief of jumping at the games, convinced the U.S. and Austrian Olympic teams to compete at Leavenworth. Great Northern ran a special train to the tournament for eight hundred people and added a second when tickets sold out.

The tournament was a "star-spattered Olympic preview," featuring thirty-three Class A jumpers. Hopes were high that the North American record of 316 feet would be broken, since entrants included Ansten Samuelstuen and Jim Brennan, who shared the record. Torbjörn Yggeseth, "Norway's Top Skier" and UW ski team member, was in Squaw Valley, getting a refresher course from the Norwegian coach.

Gene Kotlarek won the 1960 Leavenworth tournament with a jump of 311 feet on a fog-shrouded hill covered with wet snow that was described as "eerie." His jump set a new Leavenworth hill record, breaking his own record from the year before, but fell short of the North American record by 5 feet and was 9 feet short of the world record. Bob Wedin was second and Art Tokle third. Ragnar Ulland finished fourth, jumping farther than Tokle but losing on points. Jim Brennan finished eighth. Reidar Ulland won the uncontested Veterans Class championship.[213]

"Leavenworth Champ Heads for Olympics," noted the *Seattle Times* of February 15, 1960. No American had ever won a medal in Olympic ski jumping, but the American team looked "pretty good" practicing against the Europeans in Squaw Valley the prior week. "We might surprise a few people," said Kotlarek in the article, crediting his jumping prowess to his father, George, who was the 1936 national champion. He envisioned "even a brighter future when he and a few of his young Olympic teammates—Bob Wedin, 19; Jon St. Andre—20; and Willie Erickson—21, reach their peaks. He's counting on Edmonds' favorite 20-year old, Jim Brennan, too."

The Love family from Bellevue, Washington, watched the 1960 Leavenworth tournament—Trinda, age twelve; Terry, age ten; mother, Pamela; and father, Melvin, who attended Leavenworth High School and jumped on the hill. Melvin took pictures of his family watching the tournament and of competitors on the hill.

Trinda and Terry interviewed Willie Erickson and Gene Kotlarek for a school report that summarized what they learned from the jumpers and included their observations about the event. Kotlarek started jumping at age four and later jumped 311 feet at Leavenworth in a blinding snowstorm. "Seeing Gene set a new hill record was breath-taking.…When he finished his christie-stop, on the outrun, he bowed to the hill to acknowledge the ovation of the crowd. This was the most unusual gesture at a ski tournament, but it was appropriate in view of the accomplishments." Kotlarek said "this hill is pretty good," and his jump that day was "the greatest thrill of his life." Erickson said that "a boy should start ski jumping as early as possible." His longest jump was 390 feet, and he said that every jump scares you, although he showed no fear that day. The Finns were the favorites at the upcoming Olympics. Trinda and Terry concluded by saying, "Ski jumping is thrilling to both jumper and spectators, but we were doubly thrilled to have the autographs of Ragnar Ulland, Jim Brennan and Gene Kotlarek."

Washingtonians played significant roles in the 1960 games. Olav Ulland was chief of ski jumping, assisted by Gustav Raaum and Leavenworth's

Pamela, Terry (ten) and Trinda (twelve) Love watch the 1960 Leavenworth tournament, a "star-spattered Olympic preview." *Terry Love*.

Ansten Samuelsteun jumping on a fog-shrouded hill at the 1960 Leavenworth tournament, which was won by Gene Kotlarek, who set a new hill record of 311 feet. *Terry Love*.

Terry and Trinda Love interviewed Willie Erickson (*shown here*) and Gene Kotlarek at the 1960 Leavenworth tournament for a school report. *Terry Love.*

Earle Little. Others helping in the jumping competition included Jan Kaier, Ole Lie, Reidar Ulland, Jim Brennen Sr., Ole Tverdal, Rolf Helle and Ragnar Ulland.[214]

Ski jumping would be the "grand finale" of the games, noted the *Seattle Times* of January 20, 1960:

> *It is the glamour spectacle of the frigid frolics. More kibitzers will throng Squaw Valley to watch it than any other event in the 11-day Games.... Like Icarus of the myth, we all want to fly. The jumper nearly makes it. Each strives to soar farther in perfection than the other. Yet jumpers themselves scoff at mere distance as the measure of a skier's performance.*

The official world distance record was 320 feet, set in 1949 by Sepp Weiler in Austria, and the unofficial record was 456 feet, set by the "Flying Finn" Tauno Lairo in Germany in 1951. However, Seattle's Gus Raaum, who helped design Squaw Valley's eighty-meter jumping hill, told the newspaper that jumpers shrug at such figures:

[The 456-foot jump] *was not ski-jumping…that was ski flying—really another sport. Ski hills are engineered purposely to keep a jumper from going too far. Weiller's jump was from an accredited hill, like the 80-meter hill here. The Finn's jump was from a hill with all controls and safety precautions waived. Nobody ever will do much better than 320 feet off an 80-meter or 90-meter hill, because the laws of physics won't let him.*[215]

An eighty-meter hill indicates the distance from the jumper's takeoff to a "critical point" near the foot of the hill's downward slope that controls how far a skier may leap with "reasonable assurance that he won't break his fool neck." Forerunners test the hill before the competition. If they consistently jump more than 8 percent beyond the critical point, officials shorten the length of the inrun by directing the competitors to start from a lower level, cutting speed at their takeoff. Raaum said that the Olympic jumps should be "very good," as the critical point was nearer to ninety-meters, so jumpers could go for good distance.[216]

The results of the ski jumping competition held on February 28, the last day of the games, were reported in the *Seattle Times* on February 29. The event featured forty-five competitors from fifteen nations, watched by twenty-eight thousand spectators. Germany's Helmut Recknagel won the gold medal with a best jump of 307 feet, Finland's Niilo Halonen won silver and Austria's Otto Leodolter won bronze. Torbjörn Yggeseth finished fifth. Ansten Samuelstuen was the highest U.S. competitor, finishing seventh, Jon St. Andre twenty-eighth, Butch Wedin thirty-second and Gene Kotlarek forty-second. "Looking on wistfully at the foot of the hill was Jimmy Brennan," who was one of a dozen trial jumpers who "laid the track" for the Olympic competitors, although "his jumps appeared to compare with most of the day's best."

The *Seattle Times* headline read "Husky Jumper Misses Medal by 3.3 Points." Torbjörn Yggeseth was "distressed" by his fifth-place finish, since officials shortened the takeoff run by 10 feet after Helmut Recknagel sailed 306 feet—too far for safety for the hill. Recknagel's victory was a blow to the Scandinavians, who popularized the "folded wings" style. Yggeseth felt that his two years at UW set back his ski jumping, as skiing was so far away compared to Norway. After the games, he left to compete in Europe for two months before reentering UW.[217]

Jim Brennan left in March 1960 for Europe, where spent a lot of time in 1960 and 1961 traveling around and competing in jumping events. He first jumped in Finland and then in Norway's famous Holmenkollen tournament. Brennan has a picture showing him floating through the air in front of sixty thousand cheering spectators, and he had dinner with Norway's King Olav.

1961–64: TORBJÖRN YGGESETH DOMINATES TOURNAMENTS; 1964 OLYMPIC GAMES IN INNSBRUCK, AUSTRIA

Between the 1960 and 1964 Olympic Games, the American jumping team was led by Gene Kotlarek, John Balfanz and Asten Samuelston, all of whom competed at Leavenworth.

At the 1961 National Ski-Jumping Championships at Brattleboro, Vermont, Ansten Samuelstuen won his second national championship, followed by Gene Kotlarek and Bill Wedin. Jim Brennan, 1960 national champion, missed the takeoff on his first jump and placed eighth.

The Thirtieth Annual Leavenworth Tournament in 1961 was a close contest full of "sheer drama—opiate of the thrill-hungry fans of ski-jumping," as the Northwest's two best jumpers battled each other, challenged by a flying Finn and several members of the U.S. Olympic team. Changing weather conditions added drama and danger to the meet.

"Yggeseth Barely Beats Brennan," read the *Seattle Times* headline. Torbjörn Yggeseth won, but he had to "share the honors" with young Jimmy Brennan, the hometown favorite, and Finland's Aarne Volkama, an exchange student at Michigan who had recently jumped 454 feet in Europe. Yggeseth's long jump of 305 feet edged Brennan for first place. Norway's Oyvind Floystad (a Denver University student) was third and Ragnar Ulland fourth. Gene Kotlarek, "the ace of the 1960 U.S. Jumping team," finished eighth, and another Olympian, Jon St. Andre, finished thirteenth. American jumpers took a third jump that counted in the race for positions on the U.S. team to compete in the World Championships in Poland later in the year. Jack Brennan, Jim's younger brother, won the B-1 event, showing his potential. Reidar Ulland won the Veterans event.

Frequent weather changes at Leavenworth caused the speed of the inrun to change quickly, so jumpers had to make dramatic adjustments. Volkama, the "flying Finn, shot high and long off the ramp…far beyond the bounds of safety," soaring 323 feet, 7 feet farther than the American distance record. He "over-reached" in his search for distance, jumping more than a football field and almost reaching the hill's flat before he fell down and "almost broke his neck." He was not seriously hurt, but he broke his skis and could not jump again. A competitor said that Volkama was going high and fast enough to jump 350 feet. Volkama said that in Europe, you never jump too far— you start low on the inrun and then work up to safety. In the United States, jumpers start high and work down. After Volkama's near-disastrous jump,

75 feet were cut off the length of the inrun to reduce jumpers' speeds and distance. Kotlarek and St. Andre were too cautious, staying too far from the hill's danger point.[218]

In February 1961, Torbjörn Yggeseth won his fifth title in a row at the Kongsberger tournament, setting a new hill record of 185 feet. Ragnar Ulland was second. Yggeseth took second in the Eighth Annual National Collegiate Athletic Association Ski Championships at Middlebury, Vermont, in March. Denver University won the tournament, followed by Middlebury and Dartmouth. Washington placed seventh.

In late February 1961, Jim Brennan competed in the annual Princes Ski Meet at Hokkaido, Japan, against top Norwegian and Japanese ski jumpers, the first American jumper to compete there since World War II. In July, Ragnar Ulland and Jim Brennan were selected by the National Ski Association for the twelve-man training squad for the World Nordic Championships at Zakopane, Poland, in late February. In January 1962, three tournaments were held to select the U.S. team.

At Steamboat Springs in early January 1962, John Balfanz of Ishpeming, Michigan, led "a star-studded field…in a tryout test of the United States ski-jumping team that will compete in the world championships." Willie Erickson of Iron Mountain, Michigan, was second; Jim Brennan was eighth; and Samuelstuen finished sixteenth, after falling.[219]

On January 15, 1962, John Balfanz soared to a new North American distance record of 317 feet at Westby, Wisconsin, and would lead the four-man U.S. team to the World Championships. Robert Keck from Wisconsin was second, Steve Reischl of Colorado third and Jim Brennan fourth. The U.S. team would receive federal aid for the first time to help pay for their trip to Poland. The U.S. team has "shown we can ski as well as the best in the world—and sometimes a little better." Brennan earned his place on the team in spite of a "spill that left spectators gasping." On his last jump, Brennan hit hard, lost his skis and rolled head over heel down the landing hill. His mother said that Jim was fine—he's "pretty tough"—and planned on competing the following weekend in the national championships. Jim jumped too soon, "then the tips of his skis were in his face, and still he leaned out for distance. He lost a ski on the landing—then blacked out." His mother said he jumps that way—"leaning so far out that he tips right over in the air," going for distance. Brennan said he was "rarin' to go for the world championships in Poland." In 1964, there might have been two Brennans competing for Olympic berths, as nineteen-year-old Jack was "one of the Pacific Northwest's finest Class B jumpers."[220]

Ansten Samuelstuen won his third national title at the 1962 national championships at Fox River Grove, Illinois, but was not selected for the team going to the World Championships in Poland. Steve Rieschl was second, Gene Kotlarek third and Willie Erickson fourth. John Balfanz, the new American record holder, finished fifth. Jim Brennan did not make the top twenty.

Expectations were high at the 1962 Leavenworth tournament for a "record-breaking performance." Three jumpers who might break the 317-foot barrier were Chris Selback, a "22 year old Norwegian by way of Canada," and Finland's Aarne Valkama and Oyvind Floystad. Missing were members of the U.S. team in Poland at the World Championships, including Jim Brennan and John Balfanz.

Norwegian exchange students at UW, who used different strategies, finished first and second: Torbjörn Yggeseth, who sacrificed distance for form, and Tom Nord (Norway's 1960 national champion and number one jumper on its Olympic team), who reached for every inch on the big hill. Yggeseth won his second consecutive Leavenworth tournament, sharing "honors and plaudits" with Tom Nord, who received the "oohs and aahs of 5,500 sun-drenched spectators." Nord's first jump of 316 feet was twelve inches short of the new American record, but he took a header and scooted backside across the outrun. Denver University jumpers took the next three places: Chris Selbeck, who also broke the "300-foot barrier," finishing second; Erik Jansen, third; and Oyvind Floystad, fourth. Ansten Samuelstuen finished fifth and Ragnar Ulland tenth.[221]

Jim Brennan was on the U.S. team that competed at the World Nordic Championships in Zakopane, Poland, in late February 1962. The seventy-meter jumping title was won by Norwegian Toralf Engan. East Germany's Helmuth Recknagel was second. William Erikson from Michigan was the highest finishing U.S. jumper, but he failed to place.

Brennan said that when he was in Poland, he was still struggling from his injury at Westby, Wisconsin, and was sent home after a week. "I wasn't able to ski. All I did for the next couple of months was sleep and eat. I couldn't work because I'd get numb and sleepy....It was more psychological than anything else, but I never recovered from it." He enlisted in the air force and spent six months on active duty, returning in late 1962 and hoping to compete at Leavenworth in January to try out for the 1964 Olympic team, although he had not jumped in a year since his fall, after which he was unconscious for three hours. The 1963 Leavenworth tournament was canceled because of a lack of snow, and Brennan did not compete at the national level again.[222]

Torbjörn Yggeseth graduated from the University of Washington in 1962 and returned to Norway. Tom Nord was Torbjörn's successor. At the 1962 Leavenworth tournament, Nord jumped 316 feet (twelve inches short of the North American distance record) but fell so his jump did not count. The other "Jumpin' Husky Nordskies" included Per Wegge, Edvin Ronnestad from Kongsberg and Per Valbo, Norwegian Olympic training team member. "Jumpers, as the home-run hitters in baseball, are the glamor boys of skiing. But in collegiate competition, it's a four-way route to championships—jumping, slalom, downhill and cross-country."[223]

In 1963, the Leavenworth Winter Sports Club was scheduled to host one segment of the Olympic ski jumping tryouts for the 1964 Olympic Games at Innsbruck, Austria. However, the tournament was canceled because of lack of snow in a winter "unprecedented in Leavenworth history." President Ralph Steele said, "We wouldn't try to put on a tournament unless we can put on a good one."[224]

Gene Kotlarek set a new national distance record of 322 feet at the Olympic tryouts in Steamboat Springs in mid-February 1963. Ansten Samuelstuen "flashed flawless style," sailing to first place. Jon Elliot was second and Kotlarek tenth. In the final Olympic tryouts at Ishpeming, Michigan, John Balfanz and Gene Kotlarek were the top two selections, followed by Ansten Samuelstuen and a surprise choice, eighteen-year-old David Hicks. Jim Brennan did not compete. "The 23-year old Edmonds jumper, injured seriously in a fall in Westby last year, has not had sufficient time to get himself in shape." Gustav Raaum was chairman of the Olympic Committee and a judge at Ishpeming.[225]

The U.S. Olympic team competed in March 1963 in Norway's Holmenkollen tournament, which featured an enlarged hill. Gene Kotlarek jumped 82.5 meters (269.8 feet) to set a new hill record, the only American ever to hold the record, only to lose it to the last jumper of the day, ex-UW skier Torbjörn Yggesth (then living in Norway and serving in its air force). Yggeseth won the tournament after battling John Balfanz, who was leading in points until Torbjörn's final jump. Yggesth made a tremendous leap of 276.5 feet to exceed Kotlarek's jump and set yet another new hill record. Balfanz finished second, the highest of any American ever. Yggesth had high praise for the U.S. team. "I was less surprised than anyone by the fine showing by Balanz and…Gene Kotlarek.…I competed with these boys in the United States. I know that they are good."[226]

The 1964 Olympic Games in Innsbruck, Austria, had two jumping events: the seventy-meter Normal Hill and a ninety-meter Large Hill. The U.S.

team held its own in the Normal Hill, finishing with three top twenty-five finishes. John Balfanz finished tenth, Gene Kotlarek fourteenth and Dave Hicks forty-first. However, the United States only had one top twenty-five finisher in the Large Hill event—Kotlarek was twenty-fourth, Hicks twenty-ninth, Samuelstuen thirty-third and Balfanz forty-first.

The 1964 Leavenworth tournament began with a disappointment, as "two top-notch leapers" withdrew at the last minute: Frithjof Prydz, a Norwegian exchange student at Utah, and Arne Volkama, a Finn at Denver U. In 1962, Volkama jumped 323 feet at Leavenworth but fell, so the hill record held by Gene Kotlarek remained. Prydz tied for fifth place on Norway's Olympic team but was left off "by the flip of a coin." Gus Raaum was irritated by their last-minute withdrawal, saying that they "don't seem to realize what Leavenworth has done for North European skiers." The tournament was won by UW's Per Valbo. Doug Dion of the University of Wyoming was second and UW's Karl Blom third. The tournament was watched by four thousand spectators.[227]

After the 1964 Olympic Games, Kotlarek, Balfanz and Samuelstuen continued to be the country's leading jumpers. Samuelstuen did not compete after 1965. Gene Kotlarek won national championships numbers two and three, competing until his career was ended by an injury in 1967. He served as coach of the U.S. team from 1968 to 1970 and was inducted into the U.S Ski and Snowboard Hall of Fame in 1982. John Balfanz won a number of tournaments in 1966 and 1967 and was a member of the 1968 U.S. Olympic team. After his jumping career was over, he experienced financial problems and committed suicide in the 1980s.[228]

1965–70: Three Distance Records Are Set at Leavenworth

The late 1960s were an exciting time for Leavenworth. Between 1965 and 1970, three new American jumping records were set by jumpers who traveled to this small town in Washington to compete.

A young Leavenworth native, Ron Steele, began to make his mark in a town where skiing was a family affair for him. Ron's father, Ralph, was the longtime president of the Leavenworth Winter Sports Club. His mother assisted with tournaments. Sister Dorothy was a princess in the court that reigned at tournaments. Sister Barbara was a downhill and slalom skier.

Both Ron and his elder brother Jim learned to jump on Leavenworth's hills, and Jim was on the University of Washington ski team in the mid-1960s. Ronnie was known as the "jumpingest fool" on Leavenworth's slopes. He had been raised on skis. He first skied when he was eighteen months old, made his first jump at five and won his first ski trophy at eight, in slalom. When Ron was twelve, he won six competitions, including the National Jaycee Ski Tournament. When he was thirteen, he competed at the Junior Nordic Championships in Duluth, Minnesota. At fourteen, Ron entered Junior Class competition jumping, competing against eighteen- and nineteen-year-olds.[229]

Leavenworth hosted its thirty-third tournament in 1965. There were predictions that Gene Kotlarek's hill record of 311 feet, and perhaps his national distance record of 322 feet, would be broken, as "the classiest field of international jumpers in many years will point skis down dead aim" at the records, noted the *Seattle Times*. Twenty-one international stars competed on a hill that had been lengthened 12 feet.

Toralf Engan, "the diminutive Norwegian who won the 1964 World Championships" and the gold medal in the ninety-meter event at the 1964 Olympics, set a new hill and North American record of 324 feet in front of 6,200 spectators. Engan said that "it is a good hill....It compares with the Vikersund hill [a hill in Norway where the record jump was 362 feet], although that's bigger." Engan never jumps for distance. "I aim for the perfect jump, style-wise...distance follows automatically." He used a short-cut technique, using power off the lip of the jump that jets him "on a hill-hugging trajectory." Japan's Yukio Kasaya was second, Jay Martin from the University of Wyoming was third and UW's Per Valbo was fourth.[230]

The Fourth Annual Nordic Festival on August 22, 1965, at the Seattle Center, featured a ski jumping exhibition to demonstrate "what this sport is all about." The ski jump, designed by Jan Kaier, a Seattle architect, ran from the top of the Coliseum, down the roof and onto the ground between the Flag Plaza and the International Fountain. It was built using pipe and clamps, plywood decking, chickenwire, hay and forty to fifty tons of crushed ice, topped by a two-to-one mixture of ammonium chloride and salt to create a consistency like corn snow. Boy jumpers under fourteen were featured, including Gustav Raaum's sons Dave (thirteen) and Chris (eleven). The youngest jumper was Pete Arcese, age eight, who said that he was not scared, showing the calm temperament of those of Norwegian heritage.[231]

In 1967, the Leavenworth Winter Sports Club gave Hermod and Magnus Bakke a fifty-four-inch Bakke Hills Trophy to honor them for their work to

Norway's Toralf Engan, 1964 Olympic gold medal winner, set a new national distance record of 324 feet at Leavenworth in 1965. *From the* Seattle Times, *February 8, 1965.*

The Fourth Annual Nordic Festival in 1965, at Seattle's Center, featured a ski jumping exhibition with boys under fourteen performing. *National Nordic Museum.*

develop and improve the tournament since the early 1930s. A replica would be given to the top jumper in the Junior Expert Class.

The 1967 Leavenworth tournament featured two separate jumping competitions: international championships and national championships. The pre-match favorite was Björn Wirkola from Trondheim, Norway, who set the world ski flying record of 479 feet in 1966. Wirkola was a legend in Norway and an outstanding athlete in four sports: ski jumping, cross-country, biathlon and soccer. He won the 1966 World Championship in the seventy- and ninety-meter jumps and the German/Austrian Four Hill's tour four times. Wirkola was touring the United States, where he set four new hill records and missed a fifth by 2 feet. Warm weather and a chinook wind melted the snow, requiring emergency action. According to the *Seattle Times*, tons of snow from outside of town were hauled by county and city trucks to the jumping hill. There, "virtually everyone in town, including many of the visiting jumpers," hauled the snow to the hill's takeoff using pulleys, cables and sleds or placed it into apple boxes;

Magnus and Hermod received the Bakke trophy in 1967 to honor their lifetime of work with the Leavenworth Winter Sports Club, presented by Olav Ulland. *Bakke-Gehring Collection.*

volunteers packed the entire hill from the inrun to the outrun with snow, rescuing the tournament.

Björn Wirkola won the International Ski Jumping Championships, beating Japan's Takashi Fujisawa and Norway's Chris Selbekk, the 1967 Holenkollen winner. Wirkola set the second North American jumping record at Leavenworth in two years, performing a "super leap" of 335 feet in front of 7,500 spectators, which was more than two and a half times the distance that Orville Wright flew his airplane in Kitty Hawk. "Wirkola Seemed to Soar Forever," the headline read. He exceeded the American record by 10 feet and erased the Bakke Hill record of 324 feet set two years before by

Left: The 1967 Leavenworth tournament included both the U.S. National Championships and International Championships, where Norwegian Björn Wirkola set a new national distance record of 335 feet. *Wicken, California Ski Library.*

Right: The program for 1967 U.S. National Championships and international tournament gave the hill's history. *Wicken, California Ski Library.*

Toralf Engan. "No one, on this continent, ever had traveled farther on two slim strips of plywood." Gene Kotlarek won his third national championship, beating John Balfanz (whose North American record was beaten by Wikola) and Dave Hicks, 1965 national champion.[232]

Wirkola's picture shows how jumping techniques had changed from the historic Kongsberg style, based on aerodynamic research designed to reduce drag and wind resistance. Leaving the takeoff, jumpers thrust their bodies forward with their heads near the ski tips and their arms extended behind them, maintaining the position until the landing is approached, according to Anson in *Jumping Through Time*.

In 1968, Ron Steele won Leavenworth's Class A tournament, which was moved from the ninety-meter hill to the forty-meter hill because of problems caused by gusty winds. Leavenworth's Wade De Tillman was second. Marc Buchanan set a record to win the junior-expert class, and his brother Dave won the Junior-Novice Class.

THAT'S

Tire

By HY ZIM!
Jimmy McLei
est goalie in
Hockey Leagu
his tired Toter
in the dressin
night and prot
pride:
"This Seattle
most spirited c
played with."
That spirit ju:
some fatigued f
playing their f
six nights, Bill l
weary warriors
some last - oun
master the l
Blades, 5-2, beft
in the Coliseum

THE EFFOR'
tive and the
spread. Earl Hi
two goals. Ch

—Times photo by Josef Scaylea.
BJORN WIRKOLA, ALMOST PARALLEL TO SKIS, SHOWED PERFECT FORM ON RECORD JUMP
Norwegian ace shattered North American record with leap of 335 feet at Leavenworth

Wirkola Seemed to Soar Forever

Norwegian Björn Wirkola, 1966 world champion, set the second new national distance record in two years at Leavenworth in 1967 (335 feet), which was more than two and a half times the distance that Orville Wright flew in his airplane at Kitty Hawk. Wirkola used a modern style (different from the historic Kongsberg technique), which was developed using aerodynamic research designed to reduce drag and wind resistance. *From the* Seattle Times, *February 6, 1967.*

In 1969, heavy rain washed out the Leavenworth hill, which had been named Bakke Hill as a tribute to the two brothers. It was rebuilt for 1970 with proper drainage, and the judges' tower was enclosed to provide comfort to the men who had to stand in it all day, according to Anson.

In 1970, the third North American ski jumping distance record in five years was set at Leavenworth—340 feet, by "the diminutive" Greg Swor, an eighteen-year-old from Minnesota. Swor "towered over all rivals in the 38th Leavenworth snow spectacle," swept the two day meet and qualified for the U.S. jumping team for the World Nordic Championships in Czechoslovakia. Swor said that "the hill was very fast. It really scares a jumper to go that far." Others who made the team included Adrian Watt from Duluth; Bill Bakke and Dave Norby, both from Madison, Wisconsin; Jerry Martin from Minneapolis; and Ken Harkins from Duluth.[233]

Chapter 11

Leavenworth in the 1970s

Ron Steele Makes Olympic Team;
Interest in Ski Jumping Declines;
Last Tournament Held in 1978

*I*n 1971, Ron Steele, a seventeen-year-old senior at Leavenworth High School, made a push to be selected for the U.S. Olympic team for the 1972 games in Sapporo, Japan. In January, at the National Class A Jumping Championships in Durango, Colorado, Steele placed third in the junior competition. In February, at Iron Mountain, Michigan, he was given a "good star" rating in the junior competition. Steele won the Junior-Expert title at the Pacific Northwest Ski Association Nordic Championships in late February at the Kongsberger Ski Club. In March, he won the National Junior Ski-Jumping Championships at Boreal Ridge, California, where he "dominated a field of 57 Americans and Canadians."[234]

Hopes were high for the 1971 Leavenworth tournament, as three Norwegian and two Finnish jumpers were invited. The Norwegians were Frithjof Prydz, Harald Vindspol and Dag Holman Jensen, and the Finns were Zeppo Rosenburg and Raimo Ekholm. Five of the top ten finishers at the U.S. National Championships entered, headed by Jerry Martin (national title holder); Jay Rand (runner-up); Ulf Kvendbo of Ottawa, Ontario (fourth); and Maine's Jim Miller (eighth). The international athletes initially declined their invitations, but Olav Ulland contacted his friend Sigmund Rudd, a Norwegian Ski Association official. He got a quick response, the jumpers accepted and the competition was expected to be outstanding.

However, a sudden thaw "wiped out the 1971 annual Leavenworth ski-jumping tournament." Besides World War II, officials could only recall one year (1961) when Leavenworth had "absolutely no snow." The tournament also had a washout in 1967, the year of the "mud" tournament, when a thaw "hit late in the week after contestants had gotten in sufficient practice jumps. Snow was trucked in and cemented on the hill. But it had to be preserved only for a couple of days, not for a whole week."[235]

Leavenworth received better news later in 1971. In July, Ron Steele was named to the U.S. Nordic Ski Team for the 1971–72 season. He had just graduated from high school and was its youngest member. The Olympic team would be selected in 1972 at three meets: Iron Mountain, Michigan; Westby, Wisconsin; and Leavenworth. In November, the team trained in Banff, where it got its first on-snow training of the season. Ron, who advanced to Leavenworth's ninety-meter hill when he was fifteen, described his training regime to the *Seattle Times* on November 27, 1971. He had been bicycling and lifting weights for months to develop quickness and strong legs so he could get into his air position quickly to minimize the amount of wind he would break. When asked why he jumped, Ron said, "It's the sensation, the feeling of floating in the air, the idea of soaring like a bird....You're only up there about 5 seconds, but it seems like hours. People ask me how I ever overcame the fear. I never had any fear. I didn't know fear when I started."

In December 1971, three longtime Leavenworth Winter Sports Club supporters were inducted into the U.S. Ski and Snowboard Hall of Fame: Magnus and Hermod Bakke and Earle B. Little. The Bakkes were named in the skisport builder category. Magnus Bakke, seventy-two, had been active in the sport for thirty-nine years as a ski jumping and cross-country coach, as well as a certified judge for national and international jumping and cross-country events, including the 1960 Winter Olympics. Hermod Bakke, sixty-nine, an outstanding jumper, was the LWSC hill captain or tournament chairman from 1932 to 1969. The Bakke brothers were instrumental in the construction and promotion of Leavenworth's "world-famous 90-meter jumping hill." Little made many contributions to skiing, and his thirty-year participation in skiing activities led to his selection as a top skisport builder.[236]

On January 9, 1972, Ron Steele finished second at the Olympic team tryouts at Iron Mountain, Michigan. The event was won by Jerry Martin, national jumping champion, who was the team's most consistent jumper. He set the North American distance record of 345 feet at Iron Mountain in 1971, consistently made 300-foot jumps, and felt that he could jump 350 feet under ideal conditions. Adrian Watt from Duluth was third. On January 16, Steele fell on his first jump at Wesby, Wisconsin, and did not finish in the top ten. Jerry Martin dominated the meet in weather fourteen degrees below zero. Scott Berry from Deadwood, South Dakota, was second and Adrian Watt third. The team would be selected after the Leavenworth meet, where Steele had to jump well to be in contention.

On January 23, 1972, the Leavenworth Winter Sports Club hosted the last tryouts for the five-man U.S. Olympic jumping team for the Sapporo games. Before the tournament, Adrian Watt, a veteran of the 1968 Olympic team, withdrew because of rules imposed by the director of the U.S. Nordic Program, reflecting the generational conflict of the time. Watt said that jumpers were told they could not wear mustaches, their hair had to be neat and they had to wear team sweaters in competition. The director was "completely ruining the jumping team" trying to make everyone into little puppets. Team morale was so low that the athletes were unable to concentrate on jumping. The program director said, "We're trying to develop an athletic program and to do so we had to establish some discipline. We're not running a country club."[237]

The Leavenworth meet was won by Jerry Martin, who awed the crowd of two thousand with his graceful form and took the top spot on the ninety-meter Bakke Hill, demonstrating why he was the country's top hope for a medal. Ron Steele soared 285 feet, winning the afternoon round and clinching the number two spot on the Olympic team, becoming its youngest member. Steele turned the tournament "into a dream day for himself and his hometown." Others selected for the Olympic team included Scott Berry from South Dakota, Dana Zelenakas from Vermont and Greg Swor from Minnesota.[238]

For the 1972 Olympic Games, the government of Japan developed excellent winter sports programs, and its jumping team "earned international acclaim." The ski jumps at Sapporo were carefully designed and constructed, with a unique system to control snow depth. Previously, Japan had only won one Olympic medal, but Japanese ski jumpers swept the jumping medals at Sapporo, to the surprise of the international community. A Norwegian placed fourth. In the Large Hill competition, Ron Steele was the highest finishing American, placing twenty-fifth; Swor was thirtieth, Martin thirty-sixth and Berry forty-seventh. In the Normal Hill event, the highest U.S. jumper, Jerry Martin, finished thirty-fourth, and Ron Steele placed forty-first. According to Anson in *Jumping Through Time*, "[t]hree United States jumpers finishing in the top half of the field on the Large Hill was a credible performance."

Problems facing the Leavenworth Winter Sports Club became public in January 1973, as the club was unable to operate its ski area or put on a

Leavenworth's Ron Steele competed at the 1972 Olympic Games, Sapporo, Japan, and was the highest finishing American in the Large Hill competition, finishing twenty-fifth. *Ron Steele.*

A happy Ron Steele is shown at the 1972 Winter Olympic Games in Sapporo, Japan. *Ron Steele.*

tournament because of the lack of snow. The club was facing a "financial cloud darkening its future, and filed an appeal to the Forest Service for a reprieve on its annual rent of $1,487....Our business is the ski business. No snow, no money." There was hope that year's rent would be rescinded, but in the long run, the club's hope for saving its ski area hinged on Congressional action to turn the area's land over to Leavenworth.[239]

In January 1974, the U.S. National Jumping Championships were the opening event of the Leavenworth Winter Sports Club's fortieth annual jumping tournament on Saturday. The club's annual tournament was held on Sunday. This was a special year, as Ron Steele, who learned to jump on Bakke Hill, as he won the national championship title in front of "a slim crowd of 1,500," as described by the *Seattle Times*:

> *Steele, 20, making a triumphant return to Bakke Hill, displayed championship form on leaps of 315 and 302 feet yesterday to win the United States ski-jumping title. Steele, a 1971 graduate of Leavenworth High School, just beat a fellow-United States ski-team jumper, Tom Dargay, 20, of Minneapolis who soared 322 feet, the day's longest effort....."I'm pleased. It's the best I've ever skied here," Steele said, "but I wanted to go farther on my last jump. I'm amazed how good the skiing was, considering the bad weather in midweek."*[240]

This was the second straight victory for Steele, who won the tournament at Eau Claire, Wisconsin, the prior weekend, upsetting Jerry Martin, Leavenworth's defending champion. It was Steele's second win at Bakke Hill, as he won the final round of the 1972 Olympic trials. Steele's performance "vaulted him into first place in the Sampsonite Nordic series," although he had only jumped in three events. Tom Dargay of Minneapolis finished second in the national championships and Jay Rand third. Jerry Martin, defending champion, had an off day and finished sixth.

Sunday's annual Leavenworth tournament was won by Jay Rand, who at age twenty-three was the oldest member of the U.S. team. Rand was a two-time national junior jumping champion, 1968 Olympian and 1970 National Collegiate Athletic Association title winner. Rand, who finished third in the national championships on Saturday, edged out Ron Steele with jumps of 315 and 302 feet.[241]

INTEREST IN SKI JUMPING DECLINES; LEAVENWORTH TOURNAMENTS END

Interest in ski jumping in North America began to flag in the 1960s and fell off significantly in the 1970s, affecting areas with long traditions of hosting ski jumping tournaments.

The last ski jumping event at Multopor Hill on Mount Hood was held in March 1971.

Ski jumping got an early start in British Columbia. Tournaments had been held at Revelstoke, British Columbia, since 1890, and beginning in 1915, the Revelstoke Ski Club held annual carnivals that attracted some the world's best jumpers. "However, throughout the 1960s, interest in ski jumping was declining, resulting in lower attendance." Its hill required a lot of volunteer work to maintain and run, and it became increasingly difficult to recruit new ski jumpers in the 1960s. The last Revelstoke tournament was held in 1974, and "the venue has since fallen into disrepair."[242]

The last Kongsberger Ski Club jumping tournament was held in 1974, the year the club celebrated its twentieth anniversary. The club still had seventy-four members, but it could not keep its ski jumping programs going. Olav Ulland said that the club drew good jumping fields in the beginning but it could not draw large crowds. It faced a number of other problems as well. The club's scaffold had fallen down, and the state highway department built part of the Interstate 90 highway across the club's property and would not allow members to park on the overpass. The Kongsberger Ski Club continued, however, as a cross-country ski club with an empahsis on racing and touring. Olav said that he was not unhappy to see the change, since more people could enjoy the pleasure of skiing. A fifty-year anniversary celebration for the club was held in 2004, attended by fifty members, including seven founders—Ralph Federspiel, Jan Kaier, Gustav Raaum, Phil Sharpe, Leif Thorkildsen, Kjell Ulland and Ragnar Ulland.[243]

The Leavenworth Winter Sports Club canceled its 1975 Leavenworth Jumping Classic when conflicts with other tournaments resulted in a lack of competitors. The *Seattle Times* of January 23, 1975, noted that it was a "Sad Day for Leavenworth." Only five American and two Canadian Class A jumpers had entered the tournament:

> *We're terribly disappointed, but we'd rather call it off than not do it right. The Leavenworth tournament, a highlight of the Pacific Northwest ski season since the 1930s, twice has been cancelled because of a lack of snow, but never before because of a shortage of jumpers.*

Six U.S. team members, including Ron Steele, were in Europe competing. There was an "age-old problem of getting Mid-west and Eastern jumpers to come out for one meet." Colleges in the Rocky Mountains had big meets scheduled the next three weeks. The U.S. ski team's money problems, leading to a reduction of its budget by $65,000, hit the Nordic program the hardest. U.S. Ski Association officials noted, "Let the people know we're not hurting, we're almost dead." There were only four ninety-meter jumps in the nation:

> *Now they scrub one of them....From a design standpoint, Leavenworth has the best hill in the United States. It comes closest to meeting the new international design specifications. This is very disappointing. I'd hate to see ski jumping die at Leavenworth. This certainly is not going to help keep it going.*[244]

In January 1976, Leavenworth canceled the North American Ski Jumping Championships scheduled for its hill because of lack of snow. In 1977, the LWSC announced, "There will be no ski jumping on Leavenworth's 90-meter

Mike Devecka of Bend, Ore., turned in a jump of 310 feet (94.5 meters) Saturday on his way to winning the national ski-jumping championship on Bakke Hill in Leavenworth. Yesterday, however, Devecka fell on his first leap and finished in a tie for eighth in the Bavarian Classic competition. — A.P. wirephoto.

Bassette wins ski-jumping title despite fog, mist, rain

John Bassette and Mike Devecka won the 1978 National Junior and Open Championships at Leavenworth, respectively, the last major tournament held there, *From the* Seattle Times, *February 6, 1972.*

Bakke hill again this winter....The traditional Leavenworth event—it dates back to 1929—now has been called off three straight years because of a lack of snow, unavailability of competitors or both."[245]

The year 1978 was the swan song for Leavenworth ski jumping tournaments, but it ended by hosting a national championship event that took place in the fog, mist and rain. Mike Devecka, thirty, of Bend, Oregon, jumped 310 feet on Saturday to win the national championships. John Bassette, eighteen, of Hartford, Vermont, won the National Junior A Championships on Saturday and outshined his more experienced rivals to win the Bavarian Ski Jumping Classic on Sunday, when juniors and seniors jumped together. Deveka fell and ended up tied for eighth place. Reed Zuehlke, seventeenth, from Eau Claire, Wisconsin, finished second in both events.

Kip Sundgaard, of St. Paul, Minnesota, who jumped 313 feet in practice, finished third. Ron Steele finished twelfth. Bassette said, "I've never jumped in the rain before, but I'm having a great time. I like this state."[246]

In 1979, the Leavenworth Winter Sports Club announced that "no ski-jumping tournament is scheduled at Leavenworth this year." The club "found it harder and harder to attract a quality field. Club members were especially upset last year, when the United States Ski Team sent four of its top jumpers home to rest the week of the Leavenworth jump."[247]

Declining interest in ski jumping in the United States in the 1970s led to the end of major tournaments at Leavenworth and elsewhere. Newer and larger ski jumps in locations such as Steamboat Springs, Colorado, and Iron Mountain, Michigan, caused historic jumping venues to close, as their facilities could not compete with the new ones, according to Anson in *Jumping Through Time*:

> *Bakke Hill, lacking the funds to be re-contoured to meet the revised USSA requirements, shut down after hosting the US Nationals in the 1978 season....Greg Swor's hill record jump of 340 feet, set in 1970, was still intact at shutdown. Leavenworth's closing marked the end of Untied States' West Coast major jumping competitions.*

Concern over potential financial liability from ski jumping injuries led to the discontinuance of all U.S. college jumping programs by 1981, "a severe blow to the sport." High schools followed their lead. Few formal jumping programs remained in this country, and ski clubs organized around jumping closed or focused on other winter sports such as cross-country skiing.[248]

In 1982, the *New York Times* published an article, "Ski Jumping Faces a Long Decline," in which it noted:

> *[I]n the United States, ski jumpers, sheathed in their distinctive skin-tight synthetic finery, appear to be heading for the endangered species of sports, going the way of gladiators and jousting knights. While the popularity of cross-country skiing has soared in the last decade, interest in the other Nordic skiing sport, jumping, has nosedived, and now it's struggling to hold its own....Last year, the National Collegiate Athletic Association dropped ski jumping as a national championship sport and as a sport that counted toward team standings in the national championships.*

Ski jumping was a Scandinavian sport brought to this country by immigrants who dominated the competition for decades. From the 1920s through the 1940s, ski jumping captured the attention of much of the country, as the "crazy Norwegians" battled one another to set new distance records. While some of the next generation embraced the sport, (such as Reidar Gjolme's sons Reidar Jr. and Tass, Magnus Bakke's son Kjell and Alf Engen's son Alan), most did not share their fathers' passion for ski jumping. In 1947, Olav Ulland said that jumpers from Norway were growing old and Seattle Ski Club's junior members avoided doing the work necessary to keep the sport going. "The boys like to jump, but they do not want to waste half the Sunday preparing the hills." Ironically, Olav's son Hans did not jump because his mother thought the sport was too dangerous. Exchange students coming to the United States after World War II reenergized the sport, and along with visiting jumpers from Europe, they dominated the competition for several decades. While some, like Gus Raaum, stayed and made significant contributions to ski jumping, many returned home after completing their education, rather than staying and continuing the traditions of the sport. Members of the Kongsberger Ski Club worked to keep the sport alive, but as Olav Ulland noted in 1974, "[i]nterest in ski jumping has faded…and the original dream of the founders did not materialize. Due to the change of times we were probably trying to do something that could not be accomplished." Leavenworth, with an easily accessible ski hill, kept ski jumping thriving until the 1970s, bringing several generations of young athletes into the sport. However, a wider range of winter sports and the growth of Alpine skiing attracted more and more native-born young athletes, and ski jumping remains a distant memory these days for most Americans.[249]

WORKING TO RESTORE LEAVENWORTH'S TRADITIONS

Between 1986 and 1988, efforts were made at Leavenworth to rekindle interest in ski jumping by constructing two new jumping hills, but they were not successful.

In 1993, Magnus Bakke's son Kjell moved back to Leavenworth after retiring from the forest service and worked to continue the town's legacy. Kjell began skiing on Leavenworth's hills at age three and competed nationally in downhill, cross-country and ski jumping, earning a skiing scholarship to the University of Washington. In 1955, he won the indoor

Kjell Bakke, Magnus's son, shown here in 2008, worked to restore ski jumping at Leavenworth after retiring and returning to town in 1993. *Lowell Skoog.*

jumping tournament at the Seattle Winter Carnival, beating Reidar Ullevaalseter, a Norwegian exchange student at the University of Idaho. In late 1955, Kjell participated in the National Ski Association's training camp for jumpers at Steamboat Springs, Colorado, and trained with the 1955 Olympic team but was not selected.

In the 1990s, Kjell started the Leavenworth Ski Hill Heritage Foundation and secured funding for and oversaw the construction of fifteen- and twenty-seven-meter jumps for the area's training hill. After a rope tow funded by philanthropist Harriet Bullitt was installed, these jumps provided training for juniors after 1997. The annual Bakke Cup, a Nordic-Combined Ski Tournament, was started in his honor. In 1999, Bakke investigated the possibility of rebuilding Leavenworth's ninety-meter jump to current standards but learned that it would cost $5 million to make it a year-round facility with snow-making to compete with other ski jumping facilities in the West.

The scaffolding of the famous Class A jump on Bakke Hill still stands at the top of the Leavenworth Ski Area but is in a state of disrepair. *Terry Love.*

The author's granddaughter Maren Lundin had her first day on skis at the Leavenworth Ski Area in 2020. *Author's photo.*

From 2002 to 2004, Leavenworth residents invested $100,000 and a lot of sweat equity into refurbishing the area's D-Hill, creating a twenty-seven-meter training jump, regrading the landing area, installing a rope tow and cutting trees that were used to build a thirty-five-foot launching tower at the top. The result was a lighted lift-served ski jump of around ninety-eight feet used by area skiers, "ranging from local old timers to brand-new recruits from the Puget Sound area—commuter jumpers." A tubing run was added in 2005 that was extremely popular. Since 2015, Bakke Cup competitions have been held to foster competition among the Leavenworth youth in alpine skiing, cross-country and ski jumping. Kjell Bakke was inducted into the Northwest Ski Hall of Fame along with his father, Magnus, and uncle Hermod. He passed away on May

The Leavenworth Ski Area still operates with two rope tows, a tubing area, a warming hut built by the CCC and 16 miles of cross-country trails. *Author's photo.*

28, 2020. The Class A scaffold on Bakke Hill still stands, but it is nearly in ruins.[250]

The Leavenworth Winter Sports Club still operates the Leavenworth Ski Hill, with two rope tows and a tubing area, as well as the historic 1936 warming hut built by the CCC. The club maintains twenty-six kilometers of cross-country ski areas in multiple locations.

Chapter 12

Washingtonians Earn
National Recognition

*H*ermod Bakke jumped competitively until age fifty-eight. Olav Ulland won his last senior jumping championship at age fifty-two and continued to compete until he was sixty. A teammate noted that "ski jumping was in his blood, that was his life." For decades, Olav was a mainstay of Northwest ski jumping, to which the Ulland family contributed. His brother Arne Ulland was the 1948 national champion; Reidar dominated senior division events in the 1950s and 1960s; and Reidar's son, Ragnar, was on the 1956 U.S. Olympic team. Sigurd Ulland was 1938 national champion, competed often in Washington and set a national distance record at Leavenworth. However, he battled mental health issues after his career ended. In 1958, he killed his wife with a rifle while living in Oakland, was found to be insane and was committed to a mental health facility.[251]

Washingtonians made major contributions to jumping events at Olympic Games and international events. In 1956, Olav Ulland was coach of the Olympic jumping team in Cortina, Italy, where his nephew Ragnar Ulland was a member. In 1958, Olav was coach of the U.S. team at the World Championships in Finland, and Gustav Raaum was team manager. In 1960, the Kongsberger Ski Club ran the jumping events at the Squaw Valley Olympic Games. Key officials included Olav Ulland (chief of competition), Gustav Raaum (assistant chief of competition), Corey Gustaffsson (chief of hill), Magnus Bakke (measurer), Hermod Bakke, John Berg and John Ring.

At the 1980 winter Olympics at Lake Placid, New York, more than two dozen individuals from the Pacific Northwest Ski Association worked as volunteers. Gustav Raaum was chief of competition, overseeing a staff of three hundred, and Olav Ulland and Magnus Bakke were measurers. Paul Hampton was a jumping steward. Claire, Chris and Lisbeth Raaum served on the ski jumping staff. Two of the games' paid officials were alpine event chiefs of course: Nelson Bennett, women's slalom, and Ed Link, women's giant slalom. Graham Anderson was in charge of alpine juries, and Betsy Withington directed preparations for daily team captain meetings.[252]

The Ken Comfort Award, for "outstanding service to the Pacific Northwest Ski Association and the sport of skiing," was awarded to Corey Gustaffson and Gustav Raaum. The U.S. Ski Association's Julius Blegen Award, its highest honor awarded to a member who contributed outstanding service to skiing, was awarded to Olav Ulland and Gustav Raaum.

The following Northwesterners were inducted into the U.S. Ski and Snowboard Hall of Fame for their contributions to ski jumping.

- Hjalmar Hvam (Portland, 1967)—one of the outstanding four-way skiers in U.S. ski history, winner of more than 150 trophies, longtime member of Portland's Cascade Ski Club and inventor of one of the first release bindings
- John Elvrum (Portland and Los Angeles, 1968)—outstanding ski jumper, holder of distance records in U.S. and Western Canada, member of Portland's Cascade Ski Club and developer of Snow Valley Ski Area in Southern California
- Hermod Bakke (Leavenworth, 1972)—excellent cross-country and jumper, designer of jumping hills at Leavenworth and Mount Hood and longtime supporter of Leavenworth Winter Sports Club (was hill captain or tournament chair from 1932 to 1969)
- Magnus Bakke (Leavenworth, 1972)—cross-country and ski jumping competitor, designer of ski hills at Leavenworth and Mission Ridge and tournament official and judge
- Earle Little (Leavenworth, 1972)—one of the outstanding skisport builders in North America, ski official for thirty years and longtime supporter of Leavenworth Winter Sports Club
- Olav Ulland (Seattle, 1981)—international record-setting ski jumper, coach, tournament organizer, longtime tournament official and judge and sporting goods retailer
- Gustav Raaum (Seattle, 1981)—ski jumping competitor, longtime tournament official and judge and professionally

involved in ski area management (Jackson Hole, Wyoming, and Big Sky, Montana)

The Northwesterners who were inducted into the Northwest Ski Hall of Fame for their contributions to ski jumping include:

- Hermod Bakke
- Kjell Bakke (2012)
- Magnus Bakke
- Hjalmar Hvam
- Gustav Raaum
- Olav Ulland

When Leavenworth native Jim Brennan was inducted into the American Ski Jumping Hall of Fame in 2009, he reflected on his early days in Leavenworth. The town of nine hundred had two hundred jumpers. "My dad put me on skis when I could walk. I can't remember not being on skis. We had a ski jump off the barn in our front yard." There were ski jumps all over the Northwest when he was growing up, but liability issues and insurance claims became problems. There were three ski jumps in Central Oregon in the 1960s and 1970s: Pilot Butte in Bend, at what is now Skyliner Sno-Park west of Bend and at McKenzie Pass near Sisters. At one time, there were more than ten thousand ski jumpers in the United States. Then alpine skiing became more popular because it is easier and a lot safer. After his competitive career ended, Brennan attended Western State College in Gunnison, Colorado, and after college, he ran the alpine skiing program at the Steamboat Springs Winter Sports Club. He started a ski program at Central Oregon Community College in Bend and later worked in real estate in Bend. Brennan suffered at least four concussions in his jumping career, but he "will never forget his days of flying through the mountain air as far as he could, most times sticking a perfect landing....Ski jumping was natural for us in those days....It was part of living." When jumping, Brennan would reach speeds of up to sixty miles per hour on the takeoff and fly 250 to 300 feet. He tied the American distance record of 316 feet in 1960: "Nowadays, ski jumpers go slower on takeoff, with more sophisticated technique and facilities that allow for better control and longer distance. The skis are also longer, about 280 centimeters today as opposed to 250 centimeters when [he] competed."[253]

Ron Steele had a distinguished ski jumping and business career. He was a member of the U.S. Ski Jumping Team from 1972 to 1977 and the 1974 World Championship team in Falun, Sweden. He attended the University of Utah from 1974 to 1978, where he was NCAA ski jumping champion in 1977; made all-American three consecutive years; and in 1974 won the Senior National Jumping Championships. Ron won many awards: the Alf Engen Sportsmanship Award in 1975 and 1976; the NCAA Individual Championship in ski jumping, 1977; and the team's David Novelle Outstanding Skier Award, 1978. He became president of Group Rossignol North America in 2012 and was inducted into the Utah Ski Hall of Fame in 2016.

Appendix

Highlights of Ski Jumping in Washington

MAJOR SKI JUMPING TOURNAMENTS IN WASHINGTON

1931   Beaver Lake on Snoqualmie Pass, regional tryouts in ski jumping and cross-country for the 1932 Olympic Games, Lake Placid, New York.

1935   Leavenworth, sectional tryouts in ski jumping and cross-country for the 1936 Olympic Games in Garmisch-Partenkirchen, Germany. Five Northwest jumpers compete in Salt Lake for team spots, unsuccessfully: Leavenworth's Helge Sather and Hermod Bakke, Spokane's Arnt Ofstadt and John Ring and Portland's Hjalmar Hvam.

1938   Beaver Lake on Snoqualmie Pass, famous Norwegian ski jumpers Birger and Sigmund Ruud compete at the Seattle Ski Club's tournament as part of their national tour.

1940   Milwaukee Ski Bowl, the jumping event for the National Four-Way Championships.

1941   Milwaukee Ski Bowl, National Ski Jumping Championships.

1947   Milwaukee Ski Bowl, U.S. Olympic ski jumping team final tryouts.

1948   Milwaukee Ski Bowl, National Ski Jumping Championships.

1955   Leavenworth, National Open and Junior Ski Jumping Championships.

1959   Leavenworth, National Ski Jumping Championships and U.S. Olympic team final tryouts for the 1960 Squaw Valley Olympic Games.

1963   Leavenworth, U.S. Olympic ski jumping team tryouts for the 1964 Olympic Games at Innsbruck, Austria; canceled because of lack of snow.

1967 Leavenworth, International and National Ski Jumping Championships.

1972 Leavenworth, U.S. Olympic ski jumping team final tryouts for the 1972 Olympic Games at Sapporo, Japan.

1974 Leavenworth, National Ski Jumping Championships.

1976 Leavenworth, North American Ski Jumping Championships; canceled because of lack of snow.

1978 Leavenworth, National Open and Junior Ski Jumping Championships.

National Ski Jumping Distance Records Set in Washington

1939 Leavenworth, Sigurd Ulland, 249 feet (exceeded the same day by Alf Engen, who jumped 251 feet at Big Pines, California)

1941 Leavenworth, Norwegian Torger Tokle, 273 feet (exceeding Alf Engen's new record of 267 feet set two hours earlier at Iron Mountain, Michigan)
Milwaukee Ski Bowl, Norwegian Torger Tokle, 288 feet (his second record in three weeks)

1947 Milwaukee Ski Bowl, Norwegian Arnhold Kongsgaard, 294 feet in an exhibition jump, exceeding Torger Tokle's record by 6 feet, but it was not official since it was not made during a competition

1949 Milwaukee Ski Bowl, Norwegian Sverre Kongsgaard (exchange student at University of Idaho), 290 feet

1965 Leavenworth, Norwegian Toralf Engen (1964 Olympic gold medal and world champion), 322 feet, beating Gene Kotlarek, who held the prior record of 322 feet

1967 Leavenworth, Norwegian Björn Wirkola (1966 world champion), 335 feet

1970 Leavenworth, Greg Swan (1966 U.S. Team at World Nordic Championships), 340 feet

WASHINGTON OLYMPIANS OR OLYMPIC OFFICIALS, AMERICAN NATIONAL CHAMPIONS AND DISTANCE RECORD HOLDERS

1932   Hjalmar Hvam wins the National Cross-Country Championship and National Combined Championship

1934   John Elvrum sets a national amateur distance record of 242 feet at Big Pines, California, bettering the Olympic record by 8 feet and the American record by 16 feet

1935   John Elvrum wins the National Jumping Championship; Elvrum finished third and fifth in 1936 and 1937, respectively

1955   Ragnar Ulland wins the National Junior Jumping Championship

1956   Olav Ulland, Coach, U.S. Olympic jumping team, Cortina, Italy
Ragnar Ulland, U.S. Olympic jumping team, Cortina, Italy

1958   Olav Ulland, Coach, U.S. jumping team at World Championships in Finland; Gustav Raaum was the team manager

1960   Kongsberg Ski Club runs the jumping events at the Squaw Valley Olympic Games: Olav Ulland (chief of competition), Gustav Raaum (assistant chief of competition), Corey Gustaffsson (chief of hill), Magnus Bakke (measurer), Hermod Bakke, John Berg and John Ring

1960   Jim Brennan wins the National Ski Jumping Championship, tying the North American distance record of 316 feet set by Ansen Samuelstuen in 1951; member, U.S. ski team at 1962 World Nordic Championships in Zakopane, Poland

1972   Ron Steele, U.S. Olympic jumping team, Sapporo, Japan

1974   Ron Steele wins the National Ski Jumping Championship, at Leavenworth

1980   Lake Placid Winter Olympic Games: Gustav Raaum is chief of competition and Olav Ulland and Magnus Bakke are measurers; Gustav Raaum holds the position of international jumping chairman for sixteen years

OTHER HONORS FOR NORTHWEST SKI JUMPERS

- Jim Brennan (Leavenworth) was inducted into the American Ski Jumping Hall of Fame in 2009.
- Corey Gustafsson and Gustav Raaum were recipients of the Ken Comfort Award for outstanding service to the Pacific Northwest Ski Association and the sport of skiing.

- Olav Ulland and Gustav Raaum were recipients of the Julius Blegen Award from the U.S. Ski Association for outstanding service to the sport of skiing.
- Ron Steele was a member of the U.S. Ski Jumping Team from 1972 to 1977 and the 1974 World Championship team in Falun, Sweden. At the University of Utah, he was NCAA ski jumping champion in 1977, made all-American three consecutive years and, in 1974, won the Senior National Jumping Championships. Ron won many awards: the Alf Engen Sportsmanship Award in 1975 and 1976; the NCAA Individual Championship in ski jumping in 1977; and the team's David Novelle Outstanding Skier Award in 1978. He was inducted into the Utah Ski Hall of Fame in 2016.

Notes

Introduction

1. Anson, *Jumping Through Time*, 17; *Olympic Review*, "Short History of Ski Jumping," 41, 42; Engen, *Skiing a Way of Life*, 4.
2. Anson, *Jumping Through Time*, 17–20; *Olympic Review*, "Short History of Ski Jumping," 41, 42.
3. Anson, *Jumping Through Time*, 20, 21; Skiforeningen, "Holmenkollen."
4. Lund, "Last Complete Ski Champion."
5. *Seattle Times*, February 22, 1939.
6. International Olympic Committee, "Petter Hugsted—Ski Jumping."
7. Anson, *Jumping Through Time*, 22–26; American Ski Jumping Hall of Fame and Museum.
8. Anson, *Jumping Through Time*, 26–33.
9. *Seattle Times*, February 5, 1937; February 19, 1946; Anson, *Jumping Through Time*, 15.
10. *Seattle Times*, January 20, 1960.
11. Wicken, *Fifty Years of Flight*, 9; Mikkelsen, "Ski Jumping and Cross Country."
12. Anson, *Jumping Through Time*, 22, 131.
13. Raaum, "Scandinavian Influence in the History of Ski Jumping"; Ski Jumping Hill Archive.

Chapter 1

14. Brown, *Wandermere*, 227–31; Currie, *Spokane's History of Skiing*, 3–5.
15. *Seattle Times*, February 7, 1916.

16. Ibid., February 5, 1917.
17. *Tacoma News Tribune*, July 11, 1917; *Seattle Times*, June 19, 1919.
18. *Tacoma News Tribune*, July 11 and 29, 1917; *Seattle Times*, June 23, 1918.
19. *Tacoma News Tribune*, July 8, 1918; *Seattle Times*, July 8, 1918.
20. *Seattle Times*, June 27, 29 and 30, 1919.
21. Ibid., June 29 and July 4, 1922.
22. Ibid., July 4, 1923.
23. Ibid., June 29, 1924.
24. Anson, *Jumping Through Time*, 120; Evan Bush, "Not Even Deep Losses Keep Lowell Skoog from Sanctuary in the Cascades," *Seattle Times*, November 9, 2017.

Chapter 2

25. Lundin, "Early Days of Skiing in the Northwest."
26. *Cle Elum Echo-Miner*, February 15, 1924.
27. Ibid., February 20, 1925.
28. Wormington, *Ski Race*, 319.
29. *Cle Elum Echo-Miner*, December 17, 1926.
30. *Seattle Times*, February 2, 1928; *Cle Elum Echo-Miner*, February 23, 1928.
31. Wikipedia, "Ski Jumping at the 1928 Olympics."
32. Wormington, *Ski Race*, 322–24; *Seattle Times*, February 18, 1929.
33. *Seattle Times*, January 5, 1930; Lundin, *Early Skiing on Snoqualmie Pass*, 32, 33, 41, 46–48, 119, 120, 188, 189, 203, 224.
34. *Wenatchee Daily World*, "The $20,000 Hill Cost Just $600," February 6, 1953; Anson, *Jumping Through Time*, 133; Roe, *Stevens Pass*, 128, 129.
35. *Leavenworth Echo*, February 22, 1929.
36. Ibid., October 4, 1929; National Register of Historic Places Form, Leavenworth Ski Hill Historic District. The district was added to the National Register of Historic Places in 2013.
37. Little interview.
38. U.S. Ski and Snowboard Hall of Fame, "Hermod Bakke"; Flynn, "Sochi Olympics Event May Stir Memories"; *Seattle Times*, "High Times in Leavenworth, Ski-Jump Revival Draws a New Generation," January 29, 2004.
39. Cascade Ski Club & Lodge.
40. Ibid.; *Seattle Times*, December 23, 1929; Henderson, *Lonely on the Mountain*, 98, 102, 103; Alpenglow Gallery, "Jack Grauer—Mount Hood."
41. Anson, *Jumping Through Time*, 131, 132; Brown, *Wandermere*, 231–44, 268; Currie, *Spokane's History of Skiing*, 6–9, 19–21; *Seattle Times*, January 13, 15 and 16, 1933.
42. Wormington, *Ski Race*, 330; *Ellensburg Capital*, December 27, 1935.

Chapter 3

43. *I-90 Skier*, 11.

44. *Cle Elum Echo-Miner*, February 21, 1930.

45. *Seattle Times*, January 31, 1931; Wicken, *Fifty Years of Flight*, 127–29.

46. *Seattle Times*, January 31, 1931.

47. Ibid., January 27, 1931; Litchfield, "When the World Came to Cle Elum; *Cle Elum Echo-Miner*, February 6, 1931.

48. *Cle Elum Echo-Miner*, February 20, 1931.

49. *Seattle Times*, February 18, 1931.

50. Ibid., February 26 and 27 and March 2 and 16, 1931.

51. Ibid., February 15 and October 15 and 18, 1931; January 14 and December 19, 1932.

52. Ibid., January 30, 1932.

53. Ibid., February 8, 1932.

54. Ibid., January 15 and 18, 1932.

55. Ibid., January 25 and 26, 1932.

56. Ibid., February 7 and 8, 1932.

57. Anson, *Jumping Through Time*, 71–74.

58. *Seattle Times*, February 1 and 11, 1932.

59. Material available in the Maybo Family Collection.

60. *Seattle Times*, February 14 and 15, 1932.

61. Ibid., February 27 and 28 and March 2, 1932; Wicken, *Fifty Years of Flight*, 58, 59, 66–68.

62. *Seattle Times*, March 6, 1932.

63. Ibid., March 7, 1932.

64. Ibid., March 14, 1932.

65. Ibid., April 21, 1932.

66. Anson, *Jumping Through Time*, 131, 132; Brown, *Wandermere*, 227–44; Currie, *Spokane's History of Skiing*, 3–21; *Seattle Times*, January 13, 15 and 16, 1933.

67. *Seattle Times*, January 23, 1933.

68. Ibid., January 22, 27 and 29, 1933.

69. U.S. Ski and Snowboard Hall of Fame, "Hermod Bakke"; *Seattle Times*, February 4 and 5, 1933.

70. *Seattle Times*, February 12, 1933.

71. Ibid., February 13 and 14, 1933.

72. Ibid., February 12 and 20, 1933.

73. Litchfield, *NKC Tribune*, February 16, 2012.

74. *Seattle Times*, January 1 and 23, 1933.

75. Ibid., "Girl Skiers Invited Here," January 15, 1933.

76. Ibid., March 13 and April 3, 1933.

Chapter 4

77. Ibid., January 22, 1934; Brown, *Wandermere*, 247–57.
78. *Seattle Times*, February 2, 1934.
79. Wicken, *Fifty Years of Flight*, 139; *Seattle Times*, February 5, 1934.
80. *Seattle Times*, February 12, 1934.
81. Ibid., September 9, 1934.
82. Ibid., September 20, 1934.
83. Ibid., February 2 and 4, 1935.
84. Clifford, "Tacoma Ski Queens."
85. *Seattle Times*, February 11 and 12, 1935.
86. Ibid., March 4, 1935.
87. Ibid., December 8, 1935; July 12, 1936; September 2, 1937.
88. Lundin, *Early Skiing on Snoqualmie Pass*, 92–95; Hildebrand, "American Skiers at the Olympics," 61.
89. *Seattle Times*, February 2, 7, 10 and 19, 1936.
90. Ibid., February 13, 1936; Anson, *Jumping Through Time*, 132; Brown, *Wandermere*, 257–59.
91. *Seattle Times*, February 23 and March 23, 1936.
92. Elkins, "Reviewing the 1936–37 Season," 144.
93. Anson, *Jumping Through Time*, 90.

Chapter 5

94. *Seattle Times*, January 25, 1937.
95. Ibid., January 12 and February 6 and 8, 1937.
96. Ibid., February 17 and 20, 1937.
97. Ibid., February 20 and 23, 1937; Binns, "Ecker Hill and Sun Valley"; Anson, *Jumping Through Time*, 217.
98. *Seattle Times*, August 12 and 15, 1937.
99. Ibid., March 26 and 28, 1937.
100. Ibid., March 29, 1937.
101. Helgrude, "Are Norwegian Americans 'Born on Skis'?"; Wicken, *Fifty Years of Flight*, 120–23.
102. Brown, *Wandermere*, 263–66; *Seattle Times*, January 24, 1938.
103. *Seattle Times*, February 11, 14 and 15, 1938.
104. Ibid., February 4 and 7, 1938.
105. Ibid., February 21, 1938; Anson, *Jumping Through Time*, 100.
106. Ibid., February 27 and March 5, 1938.
107. Ibid., March 7 and 8, 1938.
108. Ibid., March 28, 1938.

Chapter 6

109. Anson, *Jumping Through Time*, 86, 87.

110. *Seattle Times*, January 30, 1939.

111. Wicken, *Fifty Years of Flight*, 131–35.

112. *Seattle Times*, February 6, 1939; Anson, *Jumping Through Time*, 100.

113. Ibid., February 23, 1939.

114. Ibid., February 25, 1939.

115. Ibid., February 25 and March 3, 1939.

116. Ibid., March 6, 1939.

117. Ibid., April 10, 1939.

118. Lundin, "Norway's Crown Prince Olav."

119. *Seattle Times*, November 10 and 11, 1939.

120. Ibid., November 17, 1939; Milwaukee Ski Bowl, *Milwaukee Road Magazine*.

121. *Seattle Times*, February 5, 1940.

122. Ibid., March 18 and 20, 1940.

123. Lundin, "Sigurd Hall."

124. *Seattle Times*, November 14 and 17, 1940.

125. Ibid., January 5, 1941.

126. Ibid., February 5, 8, 9 and 10, 1941.

127. Ibid., February 21, 22, 23, 1941; Anson, *Jumping Through Time*, 216, 217.

128. *Seattle Times*, February 27 and March 3, 4 and 5, 1941.

129. *Sun Valley Ski Club Annual*, 1941.

130. Leavenworth, *Wenatchee Daily Record*.

131. *Seattle Times*, April 6, 9, 11 and 13, 1941.

Chapter 7

132. Ibid., January 11, 1942.

133. Ibid., January 22, 1942.

134. Ibid., January 25 and 28, 1942.

135. Ibid., January 21 and February 2, 1942.

136. Ibid., February 4, 1942.

137. Ibid., February 24 and March 2 and 19, 1942.

138. *Sun Valley Ski Club Annual*, 1942.

139. Lundin, "Skiing During World War II."

140. Moffett, "Brief History of Skiing in the Northwest."

141. *Seattle Times*, February 2 and 14, 1943.

142. Ibid., January 31, 1944.

143. Putnam, *Green Cognac*; *Polar Times*, "Dog Sleds Pass Army Tests."

144. *Seattle Times*, March 17, May 21 and September 16, 1945.

Chapter 8

145. Anson, *Jumping Through Time*, 148–50.
146. *Seattle Times*, February 11, 1946.
147. Ibid., February 15 and 17, 1946.
148. Ibid., February 18 and 28, 1946; Ulland, "Seattle Ski Club Jumping—Past and Present."
149. *Seattle Times*, February 21, 1946.
150. Ibid., March 18, 1946.
151. Ibid., August 1, September 23 and October 2, 1946.
152. Ibid., November 10, 1946; Bannick, "Revitalized Ski Bowl."
153. *Seattle Times*, March 18, 1947.
154. Bannick, "Revitalized Ski Bowl"; *Seattle Times*, January 19, 1947.
155. *Seattle Times*, January 13, 1947.
156. Ibid., January 19 and 26 and February 3, 1947.
157. Ibid., March 1, 1947.
158. Ibid., February 14 and 17, 1947.
159. *American Ski Annual*, 1948.
160. *Seattle Times*, March 18, 21 and 22, 1947.
161. Ibid., March 14, 18, 22 and 24, 1947.
162. Raaum, "Scandinavian Influence in the History of Ski Jumping."
163. *Seattle Times*, December 21 and 29, 1947.
164. Ibid., February 6 and 24, 1948.
165. Anson, *Jumping Through Time*, 151–53; International Olympic Committee, "Petter Hugsted—Ski Jumping"; International Olympic Committee, "Birger Ruud—Ski Jumping."
166. *Seattle Times*, March 8 and 9, 1948.
167. Ibid., February 16, 1948.
168. Ibid., December 22, 1948.
169. Anson, *Jumping Through Time*, 154.
170. *Seattle Times*, January 1, 1949.
171. Ibid., January 31, 1949.
172. Ibid., February 7, 1949.
173. Ibid., February 11, 1949.
174. Ibid., February 23, 1949.
175. Ibid., February 28, 1949.
176. Anson, *Jumping Through Time*, 154; *Seattle Times*, March 11, 1949.
177. *Seattle Times*, March 11 and 14, 1949.
178. Ibid., December 2, 1949.
179. Ibid., December 2 and 3, 1949.
180. Ibid., September 13, 1950.

Chapter 9

181. Anson, *Jumping Through Time*, 157, 158.

182. Currie, *Spokane's History of Skiing*, 69, 70, 79; *Seattle Times*, February 19, 1951.

183. Anson, *Jumping Through Time*, 209–12.

184. U.S. Ski and Snowboard Hall of Fame, "Hermod Bakke"; *Seattle Times*, February 13, 1950. The LWSC looked into a complete rebuilding of its ninety-meter hill, to include a warming hut, snow-making, a lounge/waxing room and related equipment, for a cost of $1,183,313. The cost to also rebuild the seventy-meter hill and build a lift (preferably a chairlift) was $1.854 million. "Cost Analysis of Rebuilding the Leavenworth Complex."

185. *Seattle Times*, February 9 and 13, 1950.

186. Anson, *Jumping Through Time*, 158.

187. Ibid., 158, 159; *Seattle Times*, February 26 and March 1, 1950.

188. *Seattle Times*, March 5 and 6, 1950.

189. Ibid., February 12, 1951.

190. U.S. Ski and Snowboard Hall of Fame, "Ansten Samuelstuen."

191. Anson, *Jumping Through Time*, 169, 170.

192. *Seattle Times*, February 1, 6 and 9, 1953.

193. Gilbert, "Ragnar Ulland Extended."

194. *Seattle Times*, February 1, 6 and 9, 1953.

195. Ibid., February 1, 1954.

196. Ibid., February 8, 1954; Brown, *Wandermere*, 268, 269.

197. In Raaum, "Scandinavian Influence in the History of Ski Jumping"; *Seattle Times*, January 31, 1954.

198. *Seattle Times*, February 6 and 7, 1955.

199. Ibid., February 28, 1955.

200. Ibid., January 24, 1956; Anson, *Jumping Through Time*, 170, 171.

201. Gilbert, "Ragnar Ulland Extended"; *Seattle Times*, March 21, 1960.

202. *Seattle Times*, February 16 and 20, 1955.

203. National Register of Historic Places Form, Leavenworth Ski Hill Historic District, 6, 7.

204. *Seattle Times*, February 8, 10 and 20, 1958.

205. Ibid., December 7 and 20, 1958; January 26, 1959.

206. Ibid., February 23, 1959.

207. Ibid., March 2, 1959.

208. Ibid., March 16, 1959.

209. Ibid., May 29, 1959.

Chapter 10

210. Ibid., January 15, 1962.

211. Ibid., January 24 and 25, 1960.

212. Ibid., January 30 and February 1, 1960.

213. Ibid., February 12, 14 and 15, 1960.

214. Ibid., February 14, 1960.

215. Ibid., February 17, 1960.

216. Ibid.

217. Wikipedia, "Ski Jumping at the 1960 Winter Olympics"; *Seattle Times*, February 29, 1960.

218. *Seattle Times*, January 30, 1961.

219. Ibid., January 8, 1962.

220. Ibid., January 15 and 19, 1962.

221. Ibid., January 29, 1962.

222. Ibid., December 14, 1962.

223. Ibid., December 21, 1962.

224. Ibid., January 6 and 21 and February 14, 1963.

225. Ibid., March 8, 1963.

226. Anson, *Jumping Through Time*, 232, 233; *Seattle Times*, March 18, 1963.

227. *Seattle Times*, February 13, 14 and 17, 1964.

228. Anson, *Jumping Through Time*, 180–85.

229. *Wenatchee Daily World*, "Skiing Is a Family Sport," April 29, 1959; *Leavenworth Echo*, "Ron Steele—A National Champion," March 1971.

230. *Seattle Times*, February 8, 1965.

231. Ibid., August 17, 1965.

232. Ibid., February 5 and 6, 1967.

233. Ibid., February 2, 1970; Anson, *Jumping Through Time*, 161, 209.

Chapter 11

234. *Seattle Times*, July 18, 1971.

235. Ibid., January 28 and February 4, 1971.

236. Ibid., November 27 and December 8, 1971.

237. Ibid., January 19, 1972.

238. Ibid., January 23, 1972.

239. Ibid., January 25, 1973.

240. Ibid., January 27 and 28, 1974.

241. Ibid.

242. Wikipedia, "Nels Nelsen Hill."

243. Raaum, "Scandinavian Influence in the History of Ski Jumping."

244. *Seattle Times*, January 13, 1977

245. Ibid.

246. Ibid., February 6, 1978.

247. Ibid., January 18, 1979.

248. Anson, *Jumping Through Time*, 195, 196, 236–38.

249. Ibid., 236, 237.

250. Flynn, "Sochi Olympics Event May Stir Memories"; *Seattle Times*, January 29, 2004; Kinney-Holck, *Leavenworth*, 84; *Seattle Times*, "Col. Kjell Magnus Bakke," June 7, 2020.

Chapter 12

251. Anson, *Jumping Through Time*, 195, 196; *Seattle Times*, May 16, 1958, and January 29, 2004; Kinney-Holck, *Leavenworth*, 84.

252. Raaum, "Scandinavian Influence in the History of Ski Jumping"; *Seattle Times*, January 31, 1980.

253. *The Bulletin*, "Winter Sports."

Bibliography

The Alpenglow Gallery. "Jack Grauer—Mount Hood: A Complete History." http://www.alpenglow.org/ski-history/notes/book/grauer-1975.html#grauer-1975-p49.

———. www.alpenglow.org.

American Ski Jumping Hall of Fame and Museum. http://www.americanskijumping.com.

Anson, Harold. *Jumping Through Time: A History of Ski Jumping in the United States and Southwest Canada.* Portland, OR: Port Hole Publications, 2010.

Bannick, Nancy Meredith. "Revitalized Ski Bowl." *Western Skiing,* March 1947.

Binns, Ken. "Ecker Hill and Sun Valley." *American Ski Annual,* 1937–38.

Brown, Ty. *Wandermere: Legacy on the Little Spokane River.* Spokane, WA: Gray Dog Press, 2019.

The Bulletin. "Winter Sports: A Big Jump." November 29, 2009. https://www.bendbulletin.com.

Cascade Ski Club & Lodge. https://www.cascadeskiclub.org.

Clifford, Howard. "The Tacoma Ski Queens." *American Ski Annual,* 1944.

"Cost Analysis of Rebuilding the Leavenworth Complex." Bakke-Gehring Collection, Leavenworth, Washington.

Currie, Chris M. *Spokane's History of Skiing, 1913 to 2018.* Spokane, WA: Gray Dog Press, 2018.

Elkins, Frank. "Reviewing the 1936–37 Season." *American Ski Annual, 1937–38.*

Engen, Sverre. *Skiing a Way of Life: Saga of the Engen Brothers, Alf, Sverre and Corey.* Sandy, Utah: Scotio Enterprise, 1976.

Flynn, Mike. "Sochi Olympics Event May Stir Memories of Leavenworth's Historic Ski-Jump Pre-Eminence." Flynn's Harp, 2018. https://www.emikeflynn.com.

Gilbert, Kirby, "Ragnar Ulland Extended a Great Kongsberger Jumping Tradition." *Ancient Skier* (Fall 2019).

Helgrude, Kristofer Moen. "Are Norwegian Americans 'Born on Skis'?: Exploring the Role of Skiing in North America Ethnic Identity in the 1930s through the Adventures of Sigmund and Birger Ruud." Master's thesis, University of Oslo, 2003. https://www.duo.uio.no/handle/10852/37086.

Heller, Ramon. *Mount Baker Ski Area: A Pictorial History*. Bellingham, WA: Mount Baker Recreation Company, 1980.

Henderson, George M. *Lonely on the Mountain: A Skier's Memoir*. Portland, OR: George M. Henderson, 2006.

Hennig, Andy. *Sun Valley Ski Guide*. Omaha, NE: Union Pacific Railroad, 1948.

Hildebrand, Joel H. "American Skiers at the Olympics—The Men." *American Ski Annual, 1936.*

The I-90 Skier, Alpental, Ski Acres, Snoqualmie. Advertising brochure published by Ski Lifts Inc., October 1967. Moffett Family Collection.

International Olympic Committee. "Birger Ruud—Ski Jumping." http://www.olympic.org.

———. "Lake Placid, 1932." https://www.olympic.org.

———. "Petter Hugsted—Ski Jumping." https://www.olympic.org.

International Skiing History Association. "Timeline of Important Ski History Dates." www.skiinghistory.org.

Kinney-Holck, Rose. *Leavenworth*. Images of America. Charleston, SC: Arcadia Publishing, 2011.

Litchfield, Sue. "When the World Came to Cle Elum." *NKC Tribune*, February 16, 2012.

Lund, Mort. "The Last Complete Ski Champion." *Skiing Heritage Journal*, January 2011.

Lundin, John W. "Early Days of Skiing in the Northwest: Organized Skiing Began in Cle Elum." Scholar Works, Central Washington University. https://digitalcommons.cwu.edu.

———. *Early Skiing on Snoqualmie Pass*. Charleston, SC: The History Press, 2017.

———. "Norway's Crown Prince Olav Skis at Mount Rainier on May 24, 1939." Free Online Encyclopedia of Washington State History, Essay 10974. http://historylink.org.

———. "Sigurd Hall—Ski Racer & Mountaineer Northwest Four-Way Ski Champion: A Life Tragically Ended Too Soon in the Silver Skis Race on Mt. Rainier in 1940." Scholar Works, Central Washington University. https://digitalcommons.cwu.edu.

———. "Skiing During World War II: Army Mountain Troops First Train on Mount Rainier, Military Personnel Learn to Ski on Snoqualmie Pass." Scholar Works, Central Washington University. https://digitalcommons.cwu.edu.

———. "Winter Sports at the University of Washington: 1934–1950." Scholar Works, Central Washington University. https://digitalcommons.cwu.edu.

Marquette 365. "Ishpeming Ski Club." https://www.marquette365.com.

Mikkelsen, Roy. "Ski Jumping and Cross Country." *American Ski Annual*, 1936.

Milwaukee Road Archives. "Milwaukee Ski Bowl." https://www.milwaukeeroadarchives.com.

Moffett, Webb. "A Brief History of Skiing in the Northwest." *Puget Soundings Magazine* (1978).

National Register of Historic Places Form, Leavenworth Ski Hill Historic District. Filed in 2013. Department of Archaeology and Historic Preservation. https://dahp.wa.gov.

Olympic Review: Official Publication of the Olympic Movement 315. "A Short History of Ski Jumping" (January 1994). https://library.olympic.org.

Polar Times. "Dog Sleds Pass Army Tests on Western Front." 1948.

Putnam, William Lowell. *Green Cognac: The Education of a Mountain Fighter.* New York: American Alpine Club, 1991.

Raaum, Gustav. "Scandinavian Influence on Northwest Skiing." Unpublished manuscript at the National Nordic Museum, Seattle Washington.

Roe, JoAn. *Stevens Pass: The Story of Railroading and Recreation in the North Cascades.* Caldwell ID: Caxton Press, 2002.

Scholar Works, Central Washington University. "Works by Local Authors: Winter Sports at the University of Washington: 1934–1950." https://digitalcommons.cwu.edu.

Seattle Star. "Big Jump Realized a Dream!" November 17, 1939. Via Milwaukee Road Archives. https://www.milwaukeeroadarchives.com.

Seattle Times historical archives.

Skiforeningen. "Holmenkollen: History." https://www.skiforeningen.no.

Skiing History Magazine. "Olav Ulland, Ski Jumper, Retailer" (September 2003).

Ski Jumping Hill Archive. http://www.skisprungschanzen.com.

Skoog, Lowell. "Leavenworth." Alpenglow. www.alpenglow.org.

Ulland, Olav. "Seattle Ski Club Jumping—Past and Present." *American Ski Journal*, 1947.

U.S. Ski and Snowboard Hall of Fame. "Ansten Samuelstuen." https://skihall.com.

———. "Hermod Bakke." https://skihall.com.

———. "Magnus Bakke." https://skihall.com.

Wicken, Ingrid P. *Fifty Years of Flight.* Rancho Cucamonga, CA: Worldwide Press, 2017.

Wikipedia. "Nels Nelsen Hill." http://en.wikipedia.org.

———. "Ski Jumping at the 1960 Winter Olympics." http://en.wikipedia.org.

———. "Ski Jumping at the 1928 Olympics." http://en.wikipedia.org.

Wormington, Sam. *The Ski Race.* Sandpoint, ID: Selkirk Press, 1980.

About the Author

ohn W. Lundin is an attorney, historian and author with homes in Seattle and Sun Valley, and he has written extensively about the ski history of Washington and Idaho. This book is a sequel to John's first book, *Early Skiing on Snoqualmie Pass*, which received an award as outstanding regional ski history book in 2018 from the International Ski History Association. John's two books about Sun Valley were published in 2020: *Sun Valley, Ketchum and the Wood River Valley* (Arcadia Publishing) and *Skiing Sun Valley: A History from Union Pacific to the Holdings* (The History Press).